ARE WE THERE YET?

ARE WE THERE YET?

PERFECT FAMILY VACATIONS

and

OTHER FANTASIES

SCOTT HAAS

A PLUME BOOK

PLUME
Published by the Penguin Group
Penguin Group (USA) Inc., 375 Hudson Street,
New York, New York 10014, U.S.A.
Penguin Books Ltd, 80 Strand, London WC2R 0RL, England
Penguin Books Australia Ltd, 250 Camberwell Road,
Camberwell, Victoria 3124, Australia
Penguin Books Canada Ltd, 10 Alcorn Avenue, Toronto, Ontario, Canada M4V 3B2
Penguin Books India (P) Ltd, 11 Community Centre,
Panchsheel Park, New Delhi - 110 017, India
Penguin Books (N.Z.) Ltd, Cnr Rosedale and Airborne Roads,
Albany, Auckland 1310, New Zealand
Penguin Books (South Africa) (Pty) Ltd, 24 Sturdee Avenue,
Rosebank, Johannesburg 2196, South Africa

Penguin Books Ltd, Registered Offices:
80 Strand, London WC2R 0RL, England

First published by Plume, a member of Penguin Group (USA) Inc.

First Printing, March 2004
10   9   8   7   6   5   4   3   2   1

Excerpt from "This Be The Verse" from *Collected Poems* by Philip Larkin.
Copyright © 1988, 1989 by the Estate of Philip Larkin.
Reprinted by permission of Farrar, Straus and Giroux, LLC.

Ⓟ REGISTERED TRADEMARK—MARCA REGISTRADA

LIBRARY OF CONGRESS CATALOGING-IN-PUBLICATION DATA
Haas, Scott.
Are we there yet? : perfect family vacations and other fantasies / Scott Haas.
p.   cm.
ISBN 0-452-28513-5 (trade pbk.)
1. Vacations—Humor. 2. Family life—Humor. I. Title.

PN6231.V2H27 2004
814'.6—dc22   2003060879

Printed in the United States of America
Set in Bembo with Mrs. Eaves
Designed by Daniel Lagin

*This book is dedicated
to the memory
of Evelyn Goldman.*

CONTENTS

To Say Before Going to Sleep

I would like to sing to someone
and sit beside and be with that person.
I would like to cradle you, sing to you softly,
and accompany you when you sleep and then wake.
I would like to be the sole person in the house
who knew: the night was cold.
And I would like to eavesdrop on you in and out,
in the world and in the woods.
The clocks are striking,
and one sees time as at the very beginning.
Down below yet another stranger goes by
and then an unknown dog barks.
Beyond that there will be silence.
I have gazed at you:
my eyes hold you tenderly and then let you go
when a thing stirs in the darkness.

—Rainer Maria Rilke
Translation Scott Haas, 2003

THE MOUNTAINS

Was Madeline a conehead? If so, I decided close to tears, I would love her more fiercely than had she been born normal like every other baby I had ever seen. She was not normal, but she was my little girl.

I pictured Madeline and me, hand in hand, walking on the sidewalk in front of our home in Cambridge. She tottered, I saw, because of her deformity and I stooped to reach her. The hunchback and her father. But I would die for my new sweetheart. She needed me to protect her, the poor thing, the poor, vulnerable little thing! And I would defend her, I would take a beating, I would . . . Who was that on the corner in front of the Armenian grocery store laughing? Hey! You have something to say, motherfucker?

"Laura?" I whispered. "Have you noticed?"

Laura stirred from what appeared to be slumber, but was in fact fatigue, the result of twenty-four hours of labor and drugs.

"Wha'? Wha' is it?"

"Madeline," I said. The first time I said her name. "Madeline. Madeline. Her head. It's . . . a . . . she's got a big point at the top."

I did not wish to upset my wife. I knew she would be disappointed by the pathetic results of pregnancy and birth. Having sex like fat people! Hours of nightmarish pain! For a conehead?

"Scott," she said. Painkillers made her speech sound slurred. "You insane?" Laura is a doctor who practices family medicine at Boston University and has knowledge instead of psychotic worries about health. "She fine. Her head. It has slope. It was pressed against my vagina. The walls of my vagina. When she came out. You know?" She craned her neck to look at our baby resting on her swollen belly and breasts. "She beautiful. I'n't she? Beautiful. To-morrow she look normal, too. OK?"

Laura and I had been together from the first contractions until the baby was born. The birth had taken place in one of eight modules that led out of a central operating theater. We were deep underground. I had imagined we were in a space shuttle like the one in *2001: A Space Odyssey*. The modules and the theater were made out of stainless steel, glass, plastic, and aluminum. Lights were recessed. The temperature was about seventy degrees Fahrenheit. The air was still. Everything had been sterilized. Ex-cept for screams, the only sounds were the hum and ping and murmur of technological equipment. I saw graphs, charts, and num-bers on little aquamarine-colored computer screens. Anyone not screaming spoke in whispers. The nurses moved with cool efficiency and while we were overwhelmed by the magnificence of what was happening, the audacity of bringing about life, they had been trying to extricate an alien that wanted to remain inside Laura.

We heard screams where other aliens also refused to leave hosts. Pale blue curtains, thin as bed sheets, functioned as doors to the modules. No one had the least bit of privacy. *"Aiyyyyyyyyyyyyy! Por Dios! Por Dios!"* "Omigod! Please! Please! I can't take the pain! Please help me!" Several women had lost the capacity of language to describe experience.

It didn't sound a bit like life being brought into the world. I've heard men at dinner parties—normal looking, honest men—say "when we had the baby," or "when my wife and I gave birth," or "when we were pregnant," and I do admire cunning, but on those occasions I've listened to all that New Age rubbish and managed not to call them liars.

After more than a dozen hours pushing, Laura convinced the

nurse, who should have worked with plants, to induce labor and give her an epidural. I was asked to leave. The doctor sensed that my mood, which could be fairly described as somewhere between clinical paranoia and a thief's desperation after the alarm has sounded, was not well suited for witnessing the procedure.

So after the long ordeal when Madeline came into the world, I hid my shock as best I could at seeing her head shaped like a turnip.

"That what you thought?" Laura asked. "That it's permanent?"

"Well, yes," I admitted.

I was too upset to laugh. I had spent the day imagining us as parents who would be utterly responsible until the day we died for all of the needs of a deformed child. I had tried to convince myself that we could take care of her no matter what. I kept saying: I can learn to live with that. But how? Why, through rage, of course! We'd been cheated, hadn't we? Nothing like rage to start the engine. I loved it. It meant I fit in at last. Have a nice day? Fuck you!

"Oh, Scott," my wife said. She began to laugh. "She's beautiful. She's a beautiful baby."

I was enormously relieved. Laura had cured me of my worries again. Remarkable how facts can get in the way of misery. I was now free to worry about anything I liked! I decided that being married is liberating.

Boston and its *rive gauche* Cambridge are not known for being friendly. A long time ago the mayors must have posted signs at its borders: "IF YOU'RE NOT FROM HEAH, GETOUTA HEAH!" Our neighborhood, for example, was home to families whose grandparents had been born in the same houses.

Our neighbor Jean, who worked as a monitor in an elementary school cafeteria, once asked me, "Where ahhh you from?"

I told her my wife and I had moved from Harvard Square to her street in Cambridgeport.

"NO, NO! I mean, where ahhh you *from*?"

"New Jersey."

"NO, NO, NO! Where ahhh your people from?"

"Oh," I said. "My father's from Germany and my mother grew up in Brooklyn."

"You're from fahhhh away," she said.

Nor does Boston have regard for *joie de vivre*. The French Library closes off Marlborough Street for its annual Bastille Day event and Julia Child lived here many years, but the *idea* of pleasure excites Bostonians more than the actual experience. Students and professors, the calculated ways of Brahmin, and a large emigrant population from Ireland have all had a hand in making the city dull. It is an extraordinarily dull place to live, which is part of the appeal.

Boston is not a place where people laugh wildly or kiss with abandon. It is a city of poor eye contact. Certainly not a place to celebrate the birth of a child.

But just after the baby was born, Laura and I discovered that while Bostonians and Cantabridgians *are* unfriendly, all along they had been responding to me and not me with a baby. Madeline was born "heah." The natives loved my daughter the moment they laid eyes on her. She was one of them.

Soon after bringing Laura and Madeline home from the hospital, I walked to Central Square with Madeline secured to my chest in a pinstriped Snugli. The uneven brick made strides difficult, but I showed pride. And then something odd took place. In the corner store, where the owner had not spoken to me in the two years I had been his customer, not even to say hello, good-bye, thank you, or you're welcome, I was greeted like a member of the family.

"Hey, howahya?" he said. "Howyadoin'? That your baby?"

Of course she's my baby, you idiot.

"Madeline," I said. "Three days old."

"Aww, she's adawable," he said. "In't she somet'in'? Hello! Hello dere! Hi! Hi dere, you cute little t'ing! Hello!"

Variations of this exchange, which I have abbreviated, took place at the food co-op, a newspaper stand, and a coffee shop. I was shown family photographs and given instructions. I realized I should have done this years ago. *I was a member of the club!* In their eyes I was no longer free to belittle anything. I was encumbered and my life no longer mattered as much as my child's. I had grown up.

But while there was some truth to the presumption I saw in the eyes of people who, until only seventy-two hours before, had treated me like an interloper, I was still the same unlikable person I had always been. Couldn't they see past my rosy glow? Solid reasons remained to be unfriendly toward me and I hoped they would never forget them. I hadn't really grown up. Not in the nine months of Laura's pregnancy, not since Madeline had been born.

Having the baby on my chest gave me an I.D. People granted me access to their hearts. But I was a spy rather than a true member of the club.

Why would I want to give up my isolation? That was the perspective I needed to observe others. Who would choose freely to participate in the holy family? Certainly not me.

Relatives had moved in. Sisters, brothers-in-law, grandparents, cousins, aunts and uncles were in our kitchen, living room, home office, and bedroom trying to engage Laura and me in normal conversation. They were all rather nice, I have to say—well meaning, well intentioned—and like all nice people they wanted to know how we felt and they wanted to tell us how they felt.

But what if we didn't want to talk about our feelings? What if the nine months of pregnancy, the process of birth, and the miracle that had forever transformed our connection to one another as husband and wife—to life, death, sexuality—were so complicated and overwhelming that it seemed impossible to try, let alone want to try, to tell anyone what it felt like? What if we didn't want to know what it felt like? What if feelings were not the right way to convey what we had gone through and were still thinking about? Why were feelings so important? What is it about this country? No civilization has ever been built on how people felt.

None of this mattered to our families. Their only concern was Madeline. If we did not wish to talk about our feelings, we could nap, take a walk, see a movie, or go to a restaurant.

My father photographed the baby's feet, head, arms, and hands as if making a documentary. My mother could not do enough to show she cared.

Although everyone made an effort to ensure our happiness, and despite the way Boston had turned into the Emerald City, I had believed in the early stages of Laura's pregnancy that after the baby was born we would need time away to figure out what had happened to us. Centuries of paintings show Mary, Mother of God, holding the infant Jesus. Every narrative has at its core the irredeemable contact between mothers, fathers, daughters, and sons. It's all we know, it's our only chance of happiness. But it's also an opportunity to make a complete wreck of things. I think often of Philip Larkin's poem "This Be The Verse" with the first lines of its opening stanza:

> They fuck you up, your mum and dad.
> They may not mean to, but they do
> They fill you with the faults they had
> And add some extra, just for you.

"We can go anywhere we want," I had said to Laura after she had passed the first trimester of the pregnancy. We were in the kitchen. Laura was looking through stacks of catalogs: baby furniture, baby equipment, baby clothes. "You have a maternity leave. I can get time off. Let's go to Europe. It will give us a chance to get to know one another as a family."

"Europe," she said. "Why, you must have read my mind. I was just thinking: Where can I travel with my new baby? Of course, Europe. It's got to be Europe."

"I knew you'd see it that way," I said.

"And where are we going in Europe, my dear?"

"Switzerland." Ursli, my best friend, is Swiss. "Ursli can find us a place. We'll stay in a beautiful village. It will be . . . it will be . . ."

"Yes?"

"Intimate."

"Intimate? Of course," she said. "Fantastic! What a great idea! We will travel three thousand miles in order to find intimacy. Scott, you are a genius."

"Exactly," I said. "We will have long dinners with wine. We will walk through forests. We will have a beautiful cottage in a romantic village. We will find out *by ourselves* what it means to be a family. Don't you think we need time to see how we've changed? Don't we need our privacy?"

"Certainly," she said. She dog-eared a page on which a crib made of mahogany was priced at three thousand dollars. "But, honey, we can do that here. Right here. In our own home. That's why we have a home."

"We're going to be invaded," I said. "Hundreds of family members will move in. They'll camp on the lawn. It will be a disaster."

"Oh, really?"

"You'll see," I said. "They won't leave us alone. And when you want to get away, it will be too late. We must plan now."

"I am planning now," she said. She looked up. I had never seen her so in love. The father of DNA said that happiness only comes when you are doing things that are good for you. Having a baby was the answer to my wife's most profound desires. I had not known. "Now I am planning to have a baby. And after the baby is born I may not want to leave home."

"Then we will stay home. But let's *plan* to go away. Plan A: We go to Europe. Plan B: We don't. Look, it's a great opportunity—you never get this much time away from work. We've always talked about living in Europe. When will we *ever* have this opportunity again?"

"When we have more babies?"

"Ha ha ha. More babies. Ha ha ha."

"Oh, I'd love to go to Europe," she said. "You know that. But is this really the best time? A newborn baby is a ton of work."

"We'll have to do that work no matter where we are."

"But we have help here," she said. "Our mothers will help us."

"Mmm," I said. "Mmm hmm."

"The thing is . . . you know, I like family, Scott. I like being around family."

"Like family?" I said. "I *love* family."

"And I'd like to see my mother and father and sisters after the baby is born. I'm not sure I want to travel so far away that I wouldn't be able to be with them. Don't you want *your* parents to see our baby?"

"Of course," I said.

"You don't even know what you're agreeing to," she said.

"I'm not suggesting we go right after the baby is born. We'll give it a few weeks. But you've got the time off. Why not use it to go to a beautiful place? Where we are now is not beautiful."

"That's true," she said.

It was February. Our house was freezing. Snow and ice filled the yards. Daily shouting and shoving matches took place between neighbors over parking reserved illegally by putting trash barrels into spaces that had been vacated. Bits of trash would not be removed until April when the city renewed street cleaning. Our views from the house were of dead trees, the stump of a pussy willow felled in a lightning storm, a three-story apartment building covered in aluminum siding, and a parking lot.

We lived in a two-family house. Next door was a myopic mother who screamed constantly at her three teenage sons. These boys went regularly from jail to mental hospitals. Two weeks ago, they had had a bloody fist fight on our front steps that had ended when four police officers in two police cars came down our dead-end court. The fight had taken place at 2 A.M.

"When would you want to go?"

"No," I said. "You tell me."

"I suppose we could go when the baby is about eight weeks old. That might be OK. Babies are pretty resilient."

"They are known for being tough," I said.

"When the baby gets past the first month or two I think we could be all right."

"Perfect," I said. "I will call Ursli and set it all up. You won't need to give it a thought. It will just happen."

"You understand I'm not committing myself."

"Don't be silly."

"If this becomes a distraction, forget it. I need your help."

"Absolutely!"

"We need to focus on the baby."

"Sure!"

"Where in Switzerland?"

"Babies are wonderful traveling companions," the doctor said.

We had gone to see Dr. Rappaport six months before Madeline was born in order to see whether or not he was the right pediatrician for us. Laura had asked him many questions about his medical practice. I had wanted to know if he approved of traveling with newborns. Dr. Rappaport is a big fellow with a head of hair inspired by Einstein whose outlook on life had been pounded into shape by decades of loving children.

"The best," he said. "Much easier than small children. You won't need a lot of equipment—pull out a drawer, line it with towels and sheets, and there you have it! A bed! They can't turn over! They're tiny!" He took a breath. His enthusiasm built up our confidence. We had never been completely responsible for a life before, but we were capable and the baby would be healthy. "You won't need formula or food—the baby will still be breastfeeding. You won't have to keep him or her amused: All they want to do is eat and sleep.

Boy, oh, boy! I wish more people would show babies the world! And if you break them in early, they'll be good travelers for life!"

A week after she was born, we took Madeline to be photographed for a passport. She weighed just over seven pounds. The photographer showed Laura how to hold her. Her right hand held the baby's head up. Her left hand cupped her bottom. With her blank look and lack of muscular ability, Madeline looked like a puppet. We were taking a puppet to Europe.

Few families were at the airport on September 25th. Instead we saw men and women preoccupied by business and adult affairs. This was before the age of the cell phone. People's expressions, movements, and voices were flat. But of course I was observing their flatness, the dreary human landscape, from the perspective of being part of a new family. We had beaten the odds. We were so happy to be taking our baby on the road. We wanted to show Madeline the world, but more crucial: We wanted to show the world Madeline.

The baby insulated us against fatigue, worrying, painful and stupid waiting on line for tickets and passports, and nearly endless inquiries. We grinned like idiots.

Until I boarded a plane with Madeline, flying to me contained all life's elements. I was bored, terrified, bored, terrified, bored, terrified—until at last we landed. We hit a pocket of air and dropped five feet and I would picture a longer, faster, fiery descent. The movie ended and before becoming distracted by terror or restlessness, I would read a few pages of a classic I had brought along convinced that seven hours from Boston to Zurich was the ideal time to settle in with a good book. Who in their right mind brings Proust aboard a plane? But I was never in my right mind when I flew before Madeline. I was too agitated to think clearly in anticipation of what my needs and abilities would be thirty-five thousand feet above the earth. Traveling with an eight-week-old baby shifted the focus to her needs.

She cried, she needed to be fed, she wanted her diaper changed, she needed to be held, she didn't know what she wanted, we had no idea what she needed or wanted. And the moods, desires, and needs kept shifting at rapid speed and then achingly slowly and then everything would be fine for awhile and then, for no reason we could identify, not fine at all.

It wasn't like this every minute we were in flight. Swissair at the time had little baskets screwed into the ceiling above passengers with infants and for up to an hour at a time the motion of the plane periodically lulled our baby to sleep.

But even when she dozed above us, concerns about ourselves gave way to love for her. We had started to see our lives through her eyes. She wasn't the only filter, just the most important one. And what a deep pleasure to have the filter of our child and not only, as had been true two months earlier, that of our parents. The trip over made her significance to us evident in new ways.

Ursli and his mother Erika met us at the airport in Zurich. Then they drove us to her home in Kusnacht, which is a nearby village.

When he is with us, Ursli speaks Swinglish. His vocabulary is technically correct. But his inflection of the words goes up and down in the rhythm of Swiss-German. His sentence structure isn't English either.

"The flight?" he said. "Not so bad was it?"

"No, not bad at all," I said.

"It was awful," said Laura. "I didn't get any sleep. I'm exhausted."

"This it's possible to imagine," he said.

"I need a nap," Laura said. "Right now."

"Sure," Ursli said. "At my mother's flat one can sleep a bit before a lunch she has prepared for us."

Ursli and his mother had no interest in the baby. His mother's horror at seeing the child was based squarely on her hatred of noise and filth. He was bothered by her helplessness.

But Madeline was so tiny! Her feet together fit into the palm of one of my hands. Her mouth and lips were like petals. Holding her—the warmth, the form she took while cradled—was botanical. She was returning us to the earth through being here. She was the link we had needed to feel at home in the world. We explained these and related matters to Ursli and Erika. They got the gist of what we were saying and then asked us to sit down and eat.

The cold flat Erika inhabited on the outskirts of the village was practical and austere and made of poured cement. The architect had laid down carpeting in a parking garage and then put furniture and wall hangings up.

We ate poached eggs.

"Now you can rest a bit," he told Laura.

Laura took Madeline down a flight of stairs to the guest room in the cellar. They slept together in a narrow bed. Then Ursli and I went for a walk in the hills above the village. We headed to his father's house where we had been invited for tea.

"Tell me about the house," I said to Ursli.

"I have seen a photograph," he said. "The house appears to be adequate."

Ah, adequate, I thought. Perfect for a month of love with a new-born. Before our arrival, all I'd wanted to know was what it would cost. No point in letting details get in the way.

We walked past a field where sheep grazed. Mid-afternoon, but mist was still visible above the grass. Then light rain fell. The Swiss prize silence. I did not wish to disturb my friend. I also had the habit of taking on the manner of my companions and their sur-roundings. Soon I was speaking Swinglish.

"Adequate is good," I said.

"Exactly," he said.

"No need for fuss with pretensions," I said.

"No, none at all."

And yet a few facts might be of use. Laura might at last ask about what was in store. She had trusted me up until now. Find the house, she had said, and find the village. The rent was one thousand Swiss francs, roughly equivalent to eight hundred dollars at the time. Two hundred dollars a week was fair, I thought. It was even less than staying at a youth hostel. I had done very well. But where were we going?

"Have you seen the home's interior?" I asked.

I was tentative and did not wish to pry. No, no! That would be rude. My friend was lost in his thoughts and his temper was legendary. If I said the wrong thing in the wrong tone, I might upset his weekend. No sense spoiling things.

"The interior?" he asked. He stopped mid-stride. "What are you saying?"

"Nothing," I said. "Just curious, I suppose."

"I am sure the interior is adequate," he said. Then he continued walking. "Certainly in Switzerland, with its infrastructure, a minimum has been established providing adequacy in all properties. This is not the States, Scott, where variability is so great and where one's income dictates the choice."

"Certainly not," I said.

I was intimidated, but needed to persist. Laura and Madeline depended on me. In less than twenty-four hours we would be in an adequate home.

"Yet, I suppose I have a bit of curiosity about the house."

"Oh, yes," he said. "As do I. I do wonder what it will be like. Tomorrow we shall see, no?"

"Yes, yes," I said. "Tomorrow." I hesitated. "And of course the village will be of interest, too, I suppose."

"Exactly," he said.

"On the map I saw it's not far from Lugano," I said.

"Nine kilometers north to be precise," he said. For the first time all afternoon, Ursli looked happy. Facts, statistics, numbers, lists, and categories livened him up. "Its name, Ponte Capriasca, means bridge of the valley of Capriasca. So at one time it has been a refuge for shepherds who took animals there in summer. Famous is its little church with a copy of Da Vinci's *L'Ultima Cena*, painted in 1495."

"I wonder: Do you suppose the village is primarily for tourists?"

"The owner of the house where you are to stay has said to me that the village is made up of year-round residents and holiday guests, most of whom possess newer flats encircling the center."

"I wonder: This owner," I said, "is he a friend of yours?"

"No," Ursli said. "He is the husband of a colleague I am familiar with from university. I have met him only once. He's a bit strange."

"Oh?"

"Yes," he said.

"Strange," I said.

"Yes, strange."

We had reached the foot of a stone staircase, which was slippery in the light rain. We maintained our balance by taking slow steps and gripping the metal handrail. I had learned next to nothing about what awaited us on our first holiday as a family. But I had not upset my friend, which I considered an achievement.

At the top of the staircase was a narrow road better suited for horses than cars.

"Strange in what way?" I asked.

"He's a bit unclean," he said.

I supposed the U.S. equivalent would be saying someone looked broke.

"What sort of work does he do?" I asked.

"In Europe we are not so concerned with one's work," he said. "You know for us the character of the person matters more."

"And yet: One wonders," I said. "Perhaps the profession this man has chosen reflects in some way characteristics of his personality."

"His work is not known to me," Ursli said.

"No, I see not."

"No," he said.

"The house has two bedrooms," I said. "And yet: I wonder. Do you suppose it has a large kitchen? A dining room? Do you suppose the beds are new or old?"

"We don't know as yet," he said.

"No," I said.

"You must learn to be patient."

We had reached his father's house.

The next morning Ursli drove us to the Ticino, which is the name of the region where the house was located. North of the Alps heavy clouds had threatened rain. Then we went through the St. Gotthard tunnel. When we rolled down the windows, sunlight warmed our skin. We saw brooks, waterfalls, pine forests, and pastures. The cows were practically dancing.

Enclosed by mountains, not exposed or open to new experience, Laura's mood improved. Then we talked about the baby and our families. Soon we were a bit like who we had been before becoming responsible parents.

By the time we left the high mountains, Ursli's silence was as powerful as our conversation. From its *Ruhewagons*—train cars where talking is forbidden—to its quiet cafes and streets, Switzerland keeps expression minimal. Coming from a country where everyone wanted to know how everyone else felt, it was a pleasure to be in a place where no one cared.

After lunch at a café beside a train station, Ursli drove us to hills above Bellinzona in order to view its castles: Il Castel Grande, Il Castello di Montebello, and Il Castello di Sasso Corbaro. We walked around Il Castel Grande.

Bellinzona had been at the crossroad between Italian and Swiss warlords in medieval times and what's left of the bloodshed are a few towers and some rather large gray stones. We made certain to show Ursli how much we appreciated the enterprise. Certainly a lot of effort went into building the fortresses. It would have been remiss not to mention it.

Ponte Capriasca is down the road from Bellinzona. Although he had never been, Ursli knew from studying maps precisely how to reach our house. We pulled off at Taverne. Then we made our way up a narrow road. On the outskirts of the village, rows of two-story holiday flats had been built into the hills. Their balconies were partially hidden by orange-striped awnings and trellises of vines. Then we drove into the oldest part of the village.

"It's lovely," said Laura.

The village had six lanes. Its houses were typical for the Ticino. Each one was a one-story or two-story gray structure made of cobbled-together stones. The charm of the place was rather obvious. We felt as if we had stepped back through time and were faced now with simpler predicaments than the ones we faced. The villagers were all over ninety years old except for a farming family dressed in bright colors. They were marching off to their vegetable garden when we arrived. I think they supplied the old people with food. Laura and I had no idea what anyone was saying. I am sure it had to do with the weather and who was sick or dying, which is depressing stuff.

Then we saw the church said to contain the da Vinci knockoff; a shop as big as an elevator; and a post office. That's all there was to see.

Ursli had arranged for us to meet Oswald, the owner of the house, at precisely 2 P.M. in front of the shop.

"Right," Oswald said. He was tiny and had the worst posture of anyone I had ever met. "You must be the Americans! Welcome to my little slice of heaven! You're gonna love it here. I do, anyway."

Oswald reveled in being filthy. Bits of black stuff were crammed beneath his fingernails. He had a beard in which bugs had nested. His teeth were the color of egg yolks. His long hair glistened. The clothing he had on was stained, tie-dyed, and baggy. He appeared to have been hallucinating since 1967.

"Oswald is originally from England," Ursli said.

"Right," said Oswald.

He grinned. He looked like a happy fellow. So he was unclean. This did not necessarily mean, I reasoned, that his home was unclean. His happiness surely depended on the same sorts of things clean people need to be happy. Clean people, I knew, being one of them, need clean homes. No doubt Oswald focused all his efforts on keeping the home clean rather than himself. He was probably so keen on keeping his home clean and orderly that he neglected his appearance.

"The place is a bit of a mess," Oswald said. We walked to the home a few feet away. "But I spent the week here tidying up and it's a lot better now than the past month. I let it to a family of Germans and they mucked it up."

"Germans," said Ursli. "Since when are Germans notorious for mucking things up?"

"Oh, you wouldn't know," said Oswald. He winked. "Brits and Yanks know about the Germans though, don't we?"

"Switzerland is quite familiar with German aggression," said Ursli. "We have a governmental policy of neutrality and our army was instrumental in preventing an invasion in the last war. But perhaps we are not as familiar with . . ."

Oswald pushed open the door.

"You can lock it if you like," he said, "but the village is perfectly safe."

He handed us the key.

We carried in enough heavy equipment to stay a year or two. Suitcases, backpacks, bags of diapers, a stroller, and a car seat.

The kitchen was long and narrow. We had to proceed single file. Beside a refrigerator that had been made at the beginning of the Industrial Age were a rickety table and four wooden chairs. A strip of plastic depicting sunflowers had been tacked to the top of the table. A sink of the sort found in a professional garage was bolted into place next to an antique, whitewashed fireplace.

"I love this place," said Oswald. "It's become more of a home than any place else. Fixed it up myself."

No one in our group was over six feet, but the ceilings were so low we had to stoop as we walked. This might have explained Oswald's posture. The living room had a few couches and a chair covered with drapes. Upstairs were two bedrooms and above that an attic Oswald warned us never to enter.

"Bees," he said. From his tone it was clear he envied their industry. "Can't get rid of them, but at present they are harmless, I believe. Dying off, late summer. A few creep into the house proper by way of a gap between the door and the floor, buzz around a bit 'slow-mo' as it were and then drop to the floor. Careful where you're walking if you're without shoes. I've stuffed the gap with newspaper and I don't anticipate much of a problem. Still, they might not like it if you disturb them in what I believe they consider to be their home. I personally don't mind sharing the place with them."

All of a sudden everyone was eager to be rid of us.

"You're not staying the night?" I asked Ursli.

"It is not possible," he said. "However, I should like to visit for a day or two at the end of your stay before bringing you back to the airport."

"I thought you were staying until tomorrow morning."

Rather suddenly Ursli looked miserable and enraged. Then he got as calm as a witness to a catastrophe. Whatever was troubling him had best be kept quiet.

We shook hands.

"You're OK?" I asked.

"Yes, fine," he said.

"Well, then," I said.

"Well," he said.

He got in the car and then stepped out.

"I almost forgot," Ursli said. He handed us a gift-wrapped package. A woolen hat and mittens his sister had made for Madeline. "In case of cold nights."

Laura and I saw him off. Then we went to the shop. After dinner we walked in the village. No one was out. There wasn't a sound. All the homes were dark. The baby slept in a Snugli attached to my chest. And then, like the bees, Laura and I settled in for the night.

Madeline slept in a drawer we had pulled out from the chest in our bedroom. We put the drawer on the floor and lined it with towels, a sheet, and a pillow. Then we covered her with a wool blanket. Flat out was how she saw the world. Her raspy breath calmed us as we lay in bed.

"I'm sorry about the place," I said.

"It's fine," said Laura. "Really. I'm very happy we came."

"You're not disappointed?"

"I didn't expect much for a thousand dollars a month," she said. "And it's not much. But it is romantic. And cozy. And we are alone. I think it's sweet that you wanted us to be alone."

"Well, I'm sorry," I said.

"We won't be inside much, anyway," she said. "We'll hike every day, explore, and spend time in Lugano."

That first night at Oswald's was as perfect a night as we'd spent together. One of those times when we had enough.

We didn't have a car. It would take forty-five minutes to walk to the train station in the valley. A bus to Lugano left several times each day from the post office. Trips to Bellinzona or Lugano cost about eight dollars per person round-trip by train or bus. Our budget was about fifteen hundred dollars for the month.

Ponte Capriasca didn't even have a café. It was surrounded by chestnut forests filled with shepherds' paths connecting the villages.

But the point was to get to know one another. It would be a month-long first date with a baby.

We started out the next morning by following signs that directed us to Taverne. The path was lovely and we met no one. It was idyllic walking hand in hand, Madeline strapped in, and notes of music sounded each time we stepped on husks of chestnuts. Each moment offered a glimpse of a new world. We were rather hopeful.

We reached the station, which was a concrete foundation between sets of tracks going north and south. The only other structure was a big store next to the road where it was possible to buy building supplies and garden equipment.

It wasn't Italy or France. No cafés or bistros for drinking and talking. I had always loved the Swiss for their refusal to be indolent, but now that seemed a failure to celebrate life's harvest. Even here, in the Italian-speaking region, where people were reputed to be more southern and relaxed in temperament, I saw no evidence to suggest they would take off the afternoon to drink wine and make love. Too busy building and gardening, I supposed.

We also found that sex and wine were not as important as they once had been. Our passions had been tempered by recent experience. Laura was breast-feeding. The baby was the cause of all our good fortune. We were starting to live with these changes.

We got on the train to Lugano. In town, we wondered what Madeline would think of people smoking in the restaurant. What would Madeline say about the paintings in Villa Favorita? What fruit would Madeline pick out in the shop?

We walked through Lugano from morning until late afternoon. Although the Swiss have managed to sanitize the city and place it so outside history that it resembles a theme park, the medieval quarter has many steep alleys we enjoyed walking up and down in an effort to create the sort of exhaustion we once associated with sex. The modern district is no more than a bunch of shops selling things normally found in duty-free shops at airports. These shops cater to the servants of the world's money launderers.

Walking with Madeline in a chic, foreign city made us ecstatic.

We couldn't think straight. Hardly a moment passed before one of us would say, "Oh, I'm so happy, I'm so, so happy." It was pathetic.

What had happened to our hard-earned, burnt-out grip on life? Where had all that anger gone? Had our revolutionary and artistic sensibilities been destroyed by a baby? Were we becoming nice? I shuddered to think of it.

But we were changing. There could no longer be a doubt. Our daughter was like sugar in coffee, syrup on pancakes, etc., etc. Being isolated with her in a beautiful city, unable to speak more than a few sentences in Italian, made the three of us more dependent on one another than we would have been had we stayed at home.

At least we weren't fooling ourselves. We knew we had been defeated. But I felt certain that our joy would make us vulnerable to all sorts of schemes.

That afternoon we took the train back to Taverne. Unless we took the bus we had to return before nightfall. The village could only be reached through the chestnut forest and we didn't want to walk in the dark.

Then life slowed down. In the quiet, bee-filled house, we began to recognize a new sort of romance. We made soup. Laura breast-fed Madeline. After reading we went to bed.

On our third morning in Ponte Capriasca, we heard the sound of a torrential downpour so loud and steady we actually had to raise our voices.

"Little mountain storm," I said to Laura.

"More like a hurricane," she said.

"No, don't be silly," I said. "Ursli said it never rains in the Ticino this time of year."

"Oh?" she said.

"It'll pass. It sounds bad because we're on the second floor. I'm sure outside it's a lot better."

Laura suggested I get out of bed and go to the store to buy

bread. I got dressed and went downstairs. A small leak appeared in the kitchen ceiling. I put a pot down to catch the rainwater.

Once outside I faced a mountain storm like nothing I'd ever seen before. Icy cold torrents poured down as thick as curtains. By the time I reached the shop I was soaked through and freezing.

"Little storm," said Laura when I returned. The bread was soggy.

"I'm sure it's all right," I said. "Probably will be gone by the afternoon."

"But I'd say we're stuck inside until then," she said.

"Oh, it's not bad," I said. "Not that bad."

"Mmm," she said.

We had lots of books. But we didn't feel like reading. We hadn't come this far to read. We could read at home.

"Let's read," I said.

We went in the dark living room and sat in chairs so soft we were almost on the level of the floor. The ceiling in the kitchen sprang more leaks. The baby cried. We felt a chill.

"I'll go turn up the heat," I said.

Then I discovered there didn't seem to be any heat.

"You had better call Oswald," Laura said. "Maybe the heat is regulated in the cellar."

"There doesn't seem to be a cellar."

Nor was there a phone. I walked to the post office and used the booth outside the entrance.

"What's that? I can't hear you! Speak up," I said to Oswald.

The rain pounding against the glass made normal conversation impossible.

"I said, 'There's no heat,' " said Oswald. "But it's cold, you say?"

"Right, cold," I said.

"That's strange," said Oswald. "It usually doesn't get cold this time of year. That's why I never bothered about the heat. We shut the place down over the winter."

"Well, what would you suggest?" I asked.

"I don't really know what to suggest," he said.

"Does the fireplace work?"

"Don't know. Never tried it. Ornamental, I suspect. Wouldn't chance it if I were you. Might explode."

After changing out of wet clothes for the second time in an hour, I told Laura the news. It was not yet 10 A.M.

The baby nursed on her breast. A standing lamp beside the chair cast a light on my family. Laura held a book open.

"It's fine," she said. "Sit down. Read. Have a cup of tea."

"Right," I said.

I got up after twenty minutes. We were in Europe. We should be out and about.

"Let's go to Lugano," I said.

"It's pouring," Laura said. "We were there yesterday."

"We could see the paintings at Villa Favorita again."

"I'm happy doing nothing."

"I'm not."

"Give it time," she said.

I read for an hour. Then I fell asleep.

"See?" she said. "You had a nap. Naps are nice."

"Now I won't be able to sleep tonight," I said.

"You worry too much," she said.

"What's enough worrying? How do you know when you've worried enough?"

I went to the kitchen. Five pots had collected enough water to fill up a ten-gallon tank. I dumped them into the sink and waited for the ceiling to cave in. It looked soft. Ceilings, I knew, are not supposed to look soft. A soft ceiling is a bad sign. But brown rings around each of the leaks suggested that the rain and the ceiling were old friends. They had been through this before. They were in a relationship.

I returned to Laura.

"I'm going to check out the bus schedule," I said.

"Oh, don't waste your time. We've been running around. Let's just relax."

"But I find running around relaxing."

"In the rain?"

"I'm sure it will stop soon," I said.

But it continued for three more days. We ventured out to breathe fresh air and returned soaked through. Being in the house was like being in a cave. We had to wash our clothes in the same sink where we did dishes and then hang them up on a jury-rigged line stretching to both ends of the kitchen. Water dripped from the ceiling into pots and from wet clothes onto the stone floor. Cold drafts seeped through cracks in the walls. After forty-eight hours, the clothes smelled from mold that grew with ambition I admired.

"My mother," Laura said, "lived through the Blitz in London. And she often told us when we were growing up that down in the underground it was a lot of fun. There were musicians and comedians there to cheer up the crowd. People told a lot of jokes. They sang together."

"What was fun about it?" I asked.

"They had a common enemy," she said.

When the rain finally stopped, we walked through the chestnut forest to the train station. The sky had not cleared. Every plant we brushed up against got us wet. The woods were misty. It appeared as if we were walking on a path through clouds.

Then we took a train to Lugano and ate at a café. By the time we were done, the rain had started up again. Rubbing the plate-glass window clean of condensation, we saw people run across the main square facing the lake. I had expected to hate the sight of everything and I did. All the banks, watch shops, jewelry stores, cafés, and restaurants were corrupt by any standard. The nonsensical way the Swiss pride themselves on establishing order over the Italian terrain had robbed the city of life. On previous visits to Lugano, I had felt sentimental and romantic, but in the café, Laura and the baby beside me, I was an expatriate with everything I needed by my side. Obviously, we were in the wrong book.

It was difficult to leave the café and get soaked again, but we had no choice. We walked through the rain, hugging the sides of buildings to avoid the downpour. Then we reached the funicular that took us to the upper part of town and the train station.

This was so long ago that Europe still looked like Europe. No fast-food outlets. Whacky hairstyles of the men made them look like paramilitary who had gotten cut and trimmed by army barbers. Old people who glared at all comers with patrician disregard suggestive in their arrogance that we knew nothing and would go through life knowing nothing. Even the style of walking was different than back home. People carried themselves erect, heads up and shoulders thrown back, with pride that has only been established by an unyielding routine of dull schooling and the belief that civic responsibility is paramount.

Back home the walls were as damp as paste. Our laundry, strung up everywhere, could not dry out. Snuggling under the covers warmed us up, but when bare parts of our bodies made contact with the air it was like being outside. We made plans to find a laundry the next day. Then we thought we'd look for a sauna.

We found neither.

It continued to rain.

A week later, Laura's parents arrived to stay with us for a week. They had flown from Zurich to Lugano and then without pausing taken a bus to Ponte Capriasca. We found them standing exhausted and cranky with nearly a dozen suitcases below the eaves of the post office in order to avoid getting soaked. They were an attraction. We had to step through a ring of umbrella-toting villagers looking them over.

"We're very tired and need to rest," Laura's mother managed to say. She was dressed as if ready for a night on the town. "Where do we find a cab?"

"We don't need a cab," said her husband.

"It's pouring, Max, and I'm not getting wet," she said. "You can walk in the rain if you like, but I'm taking a taxi and you're paying for it."

"I'm not paying for a taxi," he said. He had on a "#1 Grandpa" cap and a Philadelphia Phillies sweatshirt displayed through an open coat. "We can walk. It's healthy to walk. We've been sitting for hours."

"Don't argue, Max. Try to be pleasant."

"*Non ho capito*," said a villager. "*Questi americani o inglese?*"

"*Non lo so*," the fellow next to him said.

We had blended in, more or less, mimicking the posture of the locals and speaking German and a bit of Italian. We came to Europe to forget America. Max and Ev came to represent it.

"There are no taxis," I said. "We'll have to walk. But it's not far."

"The poor baby," said Ev. "The poor, poor baby." Madeline peeked at her from marsupial digs of the Snugli. "What were you thinking? Bringing her here. She'll catch cold and I don't want to think what could happen then."

"Wait 'til you see the house, Mom," Laura said.

"What's that?" I said. "What did you say? Something about the house?"

"It was a private conversation," Laura said. "None of your business."

She pointed to the luggage. A half dozen trips from the stop to the house and before nightfall we had settled them in.

Then Evelyn sat down in the living room and said, "Omigod. Omigod."

She kept shaking her head. She drank tea. Madeline was in her lap.

"I can't believe it," she said. "How can you stand it? You've been here two weeks? You must be going out of your mind."

A bee crept across the low table near her saucer.

"It's cozy," I said. "It's very romantic."

"What nonsense," said Evelyn. She made funny noises to attract the baby. "Look, why don't you come back home with us when we leave? I don't see the point of staying any longer."

"We're fine, Mom," said Laura. "It's actually OK. And Lugano is beautiful. We'll go tomorrow. You'll see."

"I suppose you can get used to anything," she said.

When Max woke from a nap, we crowded around the table in the kitchen for pasta and salad. The rain falling into pots at our feet made a contrapuntal noise to the sound of flatware tapping the bowls.

"Isn't this nice?" I said.

It was still raining the next day, but in Lugano the sun came out for nearly an hour. Then we strolled along the lake, through civic gardens, and toward the Villa Favorita. Evelyn walked beside me. She knew the names of trees and plants. Everything she saw that afternoon was from the point of view of being in love with Madeline. I had not known up until that moment how Evelyn's joy in being alive was based on observation of events around her. Her ability to show me how she was seeing was irresistible. I could imagine being blind, led by her through the gardens and beside the water. And I loved the sound of her voice, the Cockney pronunciation charmed me.

That night Max and Evelyn offered to take care of Madeline. Laura and I walked to a restaurant south of the village. I had read about food and wine, but this was the first time either of us had ever had porcini mushrooms and Barolo. Everything tasted so good and the setting was so ideal that we thought mistakenly that we were having a cultural experience. Very little is left of real European culture—its literature, artistic restlessness, belief in progress, its Jews. Enjoying the gastronomy is a way to recall the best of its past. How ridiculous to write about food and wine without describing what they evoke. Imagine if Proust's novel was all about a cookie.

Within a few days, the four of us got used to being together. Madeline calmed everyone down. The rain kept falling and quarters were cramped, but no one *seemed* to mind.

Then later that week we took a bus in the rain to Luino, just over the Italian border, to shop and eat pizza. No one wanted to go. But sitting in the house another day was more than any of us could bear. After we arrived, we separated and began to buy lots of unnecessary things the Italians had arranged artfully in store windows.

We met for lunch.

"We've been waiting an hour to be served," said Max. He was glum.

The restaurant was jammed with Swiss tourists. We were the only Americans. No one had any food. The wait staff went back and forth from the kitchen to the customers carrying trays of drinks.

We waited another thirty minutes before I insisted we leave. Standing up with Madeline strapped to my chest in the Snugli, I took strides to the cash register.

"We must go now," I told the manager. I spoke in German and pretended to be Swiss. My manner was authoritative and uncompromising. I rather liked being inflexible.

The manager was surprised, but she prepared the bill. We had been charged for three pizzas.

"I do not pay for food I have not eaten," I said.

I slapped down money for the drinks. The manager took the money and walked off. I turned to go.

Then the chef burst through the doors of the kitchen. He moved fast for a big man. In moments he was by my side. Two waitresses ran and held his arms back.

"Who thinks he's leaving without paying?" he screamed in Italian. "Is it you? I'll call the police!"

The Swiss, in addition to being self-righteous and unyielding, will do anything to avoid conflict. Decorum and civility define their culture. Although they are unhappy or worried most of the time, they do not show it. I do not as yet have sufficient information to support the opinion, but I believe that the Swiss government has ordered Prozac to be added to the water.

When the chef appeared, screaming and enraged, the restaurant began to empty. Not waiting for checks to arrive, the Swiss around us stood up, threw money on their tables, and hurried out.

"You go ahead and call the police," I said in German. "If you don't, I will."

"Calm down," said Ev. "Let's just go. He's crazy. Don't argue with him."

"What did you say?" the chef shouted. "You give me my money!"

"Why don't you go back in the kitchen where you belong?" I said.

He broke free from the waitresses and untied his apron.

"*La bambina!*" screamed a waitress. "*No! La bambina!*"

I began to remove the straps of the Snugli in order to hand Madeline over to Laura so that the chef and I could have a physical fight.

"Are you nuts?" shouted Max.

But the chef allowed himself to be restrained by the waitresses.

"I am calling the police!" he screamed in the empty restaurant as I made for the door. "I am having you arrested!"

Outside, in the rain, an elderly Swiss couple who had witnessed the incident asked sympathetically, "What happened?"

"*Sie haben Recht,*" they said after I explained. You are correct.

I was very proud of myself.

We were all going crazy. While the other adults were not picking fights with pizza makers or pretending to be Swiss, they were letting go of the conduct that defined them. Each day was a test. We struggled to adjust to being confined. Holidays create conditions that liberate you from routine. On this holiday, normalcy was becoming a thing of the past.

Laura and I knew if we got out and saw the countryside, everything would be fine. The mountains are filled with sanitariums and spas where for at least two centuries the wealthiest, most miserable, worried, and confused people in the world have come to look at snow-capped Alps and listen to doctors and therapists tell them everything will be fine. Everything will be just fine. I would have liked to hear a doctor say those words to me. But how could we get into the mountains? We couldn't even see them through the rain and the fog.

The morning after the border incident, we woke to silence. Water sluiced down gutters attached to the house and through grated drains in the streets, but the percussion of the downpour had ended. I walked outside. Blue skies and temperature suitable for walking. I hustled everyone out of bed. The big day was here at last! We would hike in the Alps! We would be happy again!

We took the train from Taverne a few miles north to Rivera. Then we rode a cable car to a place called Alpa Foppa. By the time we reached the top, clouds had rolled in and cold fog had replaced the visibility and warmth we had celebrated down below. We chose not to believe what we saw. Turning back meant another day indoors with a crying baby and cranky in-laws.

The path from Alpa Foppa was wide and graveled. We planned to take it to Monte Lema, in the south, and then walk back to Taverne. I had a map from the tourist office in Lugano that I had picked up when we first arrived. It was a cartoon map. The colors and lines made the mountains look like a theme park. There were no indications of distance, grade of climb, time necessary to complete the hike, directions, or specific turns to follow on the trail. We figured it would be a ridge hike with no incline, lasting about three hours. Why would we need a real map?

We heard gunshots at about one hundred yards from the cable car station. The Swiss army was practicing the use of rifles. Near the entrance of the firing range, I spoke to an officer.

"We won't get shot, will we?" I asked.

"You are secure," he said.

Which for the Swiss is the next best thing to being clean.

It was wonderful being in the mountains, at last, out of the rain, and away from the house. We all began laughing. Laura and her mother sang English music hall ballads. Even the military was a good thing. We were having a real adventure. How many tourists, I thought, get to this point? We were off the beaten track. We were Swiss.

About an hour into the hike, the trail narrowed to the width of a person's body. Then it became grassy and marked only by small alpine signs in red and white. Then it disappeared. I could see about ten feet ahead of us, but from there on it was as white as cotton.

"I think we should turn around," said Max.

But when we looked back the trail had vanished.

Evelyn wondered what we would do next. Under ordinary circumstances, this is a reasonable question. But at the time I regarded it as traitorous.

Both Evelyn and Max were suburban runners accustomed to jogging at a high school track or walking in the mall. Neither had hiked before. I had assured them the hike would be fine, nice and easy, a walk more than a hike really. I had told them the Swiss trails were well-marked, the best in the world, and that the infrastructure of the routes was designed for ordinary people to enjoy wandering. I had promised them a few hours outdoors with splendid views, a picnic of bread and cheese and fruit and wine. I had said the weather would be good. They looked at me as if I were a liar.

We knew we were still on the trail from looking at the little white and red rectangles painted on stones, but these markers were about ten feet apart and we could no longer see that far. We knew we were on a ridge. If we diverged from the trail, we could fall off the mountain.

The baby made a cry Laura and I associated with hunger.

Then it began to rain. There was no shelter. We were above the tree line. The path got slippery.

I handed Laura the baby. Everyone got very quiet. It was the sort of quiet heard during extreme turbulence on a plane.

"We're fine," I said. "This will pass and then we'll be on our way again."

"Oh, shut up," said Evelyn.

"We'll be fine," I said. "Everything will be just fine. We'll take little steps and before you know it we'll be off the mountain and in some woods. Or something."

"Let me see the map," said Laura.

"Where are you?" I asked.

"Over here," she said.

"Keep talking so I can find you," I said.

I reached her on hands and knees.

"This is a cartoon map," she said. "Is this all we've got?"

"Shhh," I said, "please don't alarm the others."

"Is this is how we're going to get off the mountain? Don't say it's going to be fine. We need a plan."

"We just need to keep walking," I said. "We'll go slowly."

"We have to go slowly," Laura said. "We can't see anything. But that's not a plan."

The plan was to stay close and hold hands in a single file while Laura and I alternated the lead. Then we crawled for awhile. If we got more than five feet without seeing a trail marker we stopped and took tentative steps in another direction. It was still early in the day, but we didn't want to get lost.

We got lost. We'd gone what seemed to be about half a mile without seeing any markers. But we decided it would be dangerous to turn around and try and find the point where we must have diverged.

"If we keep heading down the mountain, I think we'll be all right," said Laura.

Laura has a doctor's calm, which is especially soothing when panic is the obvious choice. Max and Evelyn were in too much pain to argue. Their knees were not holding up.

We had to rest a lot on the bare slope, in the rain, on the slippery path. Madeline fell asleep on my chest. We got lucky as no one wanted to be the first to express fear and outrage.

At last we saw trees. We knew then we had gotten below the ridge. Soon we found ourselves in a pine forest on a wide, well-maintained road. Between sections of the road, going through woods, there were handrails and wooden steps. The road was wide enough for a car. We had no idea where we were, but we knew we were safe.

The steps had been built at an incline of forty-five degrees. We wanted to try and get home before nightfall so we took the stairs. They got us down faster, but caused more pain in our knees. After descending hundreds of steps, we found ourselves in a cluster of homes just outside of Taverne. We climbed the hill through the chestnut forest to Ponte Capriasca and reached the house ten hours after we'd left.

The next day Max and Evelyn walked to a nearby village for lunch while Laura and I stayed in bed until noon. Laura was having back and neck spasms. My legs were so sore I walked like a mannequin. No one said a word about what we'd been through, nor did we mention the rain, which continued to fall, or the cold that got into our bones.

Within hours we all decided to go to Italy. Max and Evelyn took a train the following day. We left on the weekend. They had departed for the States by the time we reached Florence. It rained, but the weather was warm and there were few crowds. It was October and years before mass tourism ruined the city. We could get into the Uffizi without standing in line and crossing the Ponte Vecchio did not involve entering a swarm of people as it does nowadays.

Laura breast-fed Madeline beside the Pitti, on the steps of the

Duomo, at a café in the piazza facing the Palazzo Vecchio. Every-where we were greeted like regulars as the Italians fussed over her. In Switzerland, we had been acknowledged; here we were em-braced.

We loved walking along the Arno, hand in hand, the baby at-tached to one of us, surrounded by the smells of cooking. Then we talked about the paintings we had seen of the holy family. Life made sense in Italy, as it had not in Switzerland. Why we had traveled this far, why we had devoted ourselves to this journey, what we had in-tended. We had made a pilgrimage, trying to understand what it meant to be a family, devoted to becoming one, not knowing how to go about it.

Ursli showed up a week later for a few days before bringing us back to the airport for the flight home. He was in a better mood. We took him to places that were by now familiar. Old-fashioned wait-ers served us at our favorite restaurant with ceremony better suited to a church. We went to the market in the medieval quarter. We saw an exhibition of Impressionist art from the Soviet Union. We felt at home.

Night fell before 5 P.M. We were still in Lugano's main square.

"*Marrone! Marrone!*" yelled vendors in the dark. "*Marrone! Mar-rone!*"

We smelled burnt chestnut husks and their singed interiors and I thought of the forests we had walked through almost daily.

Then we heard the sound of umbrellas being opened.

After supper Laura went to bed. Ursli and I stayed up to talk about history. We still thought of ourselves as friends who had met at a youth hostel in Florence when we were both seventeen and then had spent the next fifteen years exchanging letters. Do you collect anything? What kind of question is *that*? But that night we exchanged facts about empires and wars. Then we talked about Vi-enna and Prague where we had traveled together as students. It was one more distinctively European night. I'd had hundreds before. I saw again how European civilization had been built: Nothing got in the way of facts. We spoke until 3 A.M.

Finally I said, "Good night. If we don't get to bed now, tomorrow will be ruined."

I stood up.

"Right," said Ursli.

He looked puzzled.

"I am gay," he said. He took a deep breath. Then he spoke without pausing. "I have found this out in Berlin. There I had an affair with a man from Turkey. It is not possible to lie any longer to myself."

Although I had been convinced for years that Ursli was gay, I looked surprised. I was certain this reaction would please him.

"I wanted to tell you before," he said. "I'm sorry. If you don't want to be my friend any longer, I'll understand."

"Do you really think so little of our friendship?"

"I told friends in Zurich," he said. "They have not called me since then."

"Look around," I said, gesturing to the wet clothes suspended on ropes stretching across the rooms, to the package of diapers by the kitchen door, to the Snugli and the stroller and the car seat, to the suitcases and boxes of books, to the bees mounted on the moist plaster walls, to muddy hiking boots on newspapers, to the junk on the staircase leading up to where my beloved slept with our daughter. "You think being straight is so easy?"

CÔTE D'AZUR

"No! No! NO! Don't go in the forest! There're wolves! Look out! Run! RUN! They'll chase you! They'll try to kill you! RUN FOR YOUR LIFE!"

Seven A.M. on a Tuesday morning and I'm in bed with Madeline and Nicholas. We are, for what must be the two hundredth time in two months, watching a video of *Beauty and the Beast*. Madeline attends kindergarten at Shady Hill, an exclusive and expensive school that is often closed. Nick, born three years ago, has not yet started school.

Laura is at work having left at six-thirty to attend a meeting at which her fellow doctors will criticize the impact on patient care of managed care. They talk for hours. Laura wants to come home, but can't.

Madeline has buried her face into my chest. Her brother is, at the age of two, drawn to the colors of the cartoon rather than moved by its plot. Primarily he points and makes sounds I have come to associate with pure love. More than expressing love of what he surveys, he is detecting that which is loveable in things and emitting identifying sounds. Sort of like baby radar.

"Is it over? I hate this part."

Madeline is referring to the terrifying scene in *Beauty and the Beast* when Belle's father is nearly torn to bits by wolves.

"I don't understand, Daddy," she says after it's over. "Why does he keep going into the woods when he knows the wolves are there?"

"He doesn't know the wolves are there," I explain again.

"Of course he does. He went in the same woods yesterday. He saw the wolves then. Does he just forget?"

"It's a cartoon, Madeline. He doesn't forget, but he doesn't remember either."

"I hate when he's chased by the wolves," she says mournfully. "It's so sad and scary."

"It is."

After the children watch the video a second time, while I fall back asleep, I get them washed and dressed so we can go to Chinatown and have a lunch of hot-and-sour soup, vegetarian spring rolls, and fried noodles with shredded chicken and bean sprouts. Then we drive to the Museum of Science where they will climb into a real space capsule, see a sheep's lungs, wallow in a basin filled with hundreds of colorful plastic balls, and play with a water wheel. We return home for a nap before I prepare dinner for the four of us. This is my routine on Monday, Tuesday, and Thursday—we vary it by dining on pizza in the North End or at a Japanese restaurant in Central Square. I write late at night, but most of the time I'm helping raise the babies.

Laura has arranged with the hospital to work three days a week. When she's home during the day, I leave to work as a clinical psychologist either seeing patients or interviewing mentally ill people at clinics, schools, and hospitals in order to determine their diagnoses so that doctors, teachers, and social workers can come up with treatment plans. We get together as a family in the evening and on weekends, usually over meals.

With no notion of investment, blinded by the pull of the children and demands of work, we forget to buy stocks in the early 1990s. I am so deranged that I tell myself it's wrong to profit from the labor of others. Laura is too busy to think about money markets, mutual funds, real estate, treasury strips, or certificate deposit accounts. Nowadays with friends whose early profits enable them to live like emperors, we turn to one another and wonder why it's them instead of us.

"We wanted to help people," Laura says. "We wanted to stay at home."

"Man, oh, man," I say, reaching for the gin. "What were we thinking?"

We didn't stay home. The first years after the babies were born, in addition to Switzerland, we rented in Italy, Hawaii, Normandy, and London. Once we arranged to house-sit for a friend's family in Tuscany. But when Madeline got older, we put her into private school and, as a result, had very little money left.

We argued about being short of cash. Laura wanted to save in order to buy a house in a nicer neighborhood while I was content to live like a graduate student: clothing strewn in the closet, money spent on CDs, books, eating out, and traveling.

The moment arrived on a cold autumn afternoon. We decided we had to choose. Madeline was keeping up with us as we walked through a deciduous forest in a state park on the south shore of Boston while Nicky was in a pack on my back. It was cold. Rain drizzled as we stepped up and down big rocks and roots in the dirt path.

"Do you really want to spend the rest of your life on Gillis Court?" asked Laura.

"I don't mind," I said. "It's a cool neighborhood."

"It's not a cool neighborhood. It's not even a friendly neighborhood. I find it depressing."

"Depressing? How can you say that?"

Madeline found a fern.

"Isn't this pretty?" she said.

Nick wanted to get down and touch the fern so I undid the straps, lowered the pack, and let him out. Moving tentatively so as not to trip, but still with focus and intention, he reached his sister and together they crouched and touched some moss growing beside the ferns.

"It *is* depressing," Laura said. "We go to these gorgeous places and after it's all over we return to that horrible house and our crazy neighbors."

"It's not that bad."

"No, it's worse. The streets are covered with garbage from December until the end of March, it's not safe to walk at night, none of our neighbors talk to us, and the house is too small for four people. I love traveling as much as you do, but if we spend all our money on these trips, how we will ever be able to afford to move?"

"It will work out," I said. "It always does."

"How? How will it work out? You infuriate me when you say things like that. We need a plan."

"What sort of plan?"

"Maybe we should go away for less time and stay closer to home. What would be so terrible about going to Vermont for two weeks?"

"Vermont?! How can you even suggest Vermont? I want to get out of this country! I want to practice speaking other languages! I want to be in a different culture! You know that Clash song? 'I'm so bored with the U.S.A.!' *That* is exactly how I feel."

"Oh, don't be ridiculous." Laura said. She knelt down. "Children, your father is being ridiculous."

"I am not ridiculous!" I shouted.

"Oh, but you are," Laura said. She sang the words more than spoke them.

"Daddy's silly," Madeline said.

Nick stuffed dirt in his pockets.

The terrain was familiar to all of us. We loved and fought like a family. My job was to adopt a position utterly removed from reality and stick to it. The task for everyone else was to bring me back down to earth. It was sort of a game which kept our attention.

"Nicky, please don't put dirt in your pockets," Laura said. "I just washed those pants this morning."

"But I need it," he said.

"Look," I said, "there's got to be a way for both of us to get what we want. I have an idea."

I reminded Laura that the housing office at Harvard kept listings of houses for rent in the area. Maybe we could list ours and use the money to rent a place in France or Italy.

"I don't know," Laura said. "I don't want strangers in my bed."

"We don't have to do it," I said. "But how about tomorrow morning I take a look and see how it's done?"

"I don't want people in my house when I'm not there," Laura said.

"I don't either," I said, "but I do want to look."

"I'm not agreeing to anything." Laura said.

"Of course not."

But the next morning, instead of listing our house, I came across a book at Harvard's office showing home owners, coming to Boston or Cambridge to teach or visit family, who offered to exchange their properties. This was a revelation.

Immediately, while the children climbed on chairs and knocked over office equipment, I saw a way out of our financial dilemma. We would live like the rich. The rich hate to spend money. They pick up the phone and call up friends and say: "Graham, is the flat in Paris free the first week in September?" I had met dozens of rather wealthy families at Madeline's school. They all sponged off friends. I had thought it was a closed system until that morning.

I had been appointed as an instructor at Harvard Medical School in exchange for three hours of unpaid supervision I provided to graduate students each week. The appointment provided me with useless benefits. I was granted access to the university's libraries and museums. I could tell people I taught at Harvard. The opportunity to use the housing office was the first good thing to come out of the appointment.

The book, which wasn't easy to read over the clamor made by

the children, contained a ton of duds. Lots of homes were listed in
Oxford or Cambridge (England) or Berkeley. Not places ideal for
summer holidays. But then I saw a notice that at first I thought was
some sort of joke: Two bedroom flat in historic section of Cannes
on the French Riviera available for four to eight weeks in summer
for comparable exchange in Cambridge.

The French Riviera?! Wow! Laura and I had never been to the
south of France. I knew Picasso had spent time in Antibes and I had
read Fitzgerald's accounts, but what I really thought of when I
thought about the Riviera were the Cannes film festival, St. Tropez,
topless beaches, and Brigitte Bardot! Brigitte Bardot!

It had been five years since we'd started having children—Laura
and I, not Brigitte and I. We were no longer having sex the way
we'd had sex before the babies. We'd been invaded and occupied.
Laura and I never locked doors and at any time we might find
Madeline or Nick in bed with us. Or, if not stopping by to visit, the
children were crying or running amuck. And even when they were
sound asleep, we felt so responsible for their pleasure and well-being
that it was difficult to think of ours. Sex had become another activity in our home like doing dishes or baking bread. It had become
functional. Robbed of spontaneity, exhausted from chores associated with breeding, sex relaxed us, but no longer stirred us up.

I was having these and other morbid thoughts when I noticed
the children were playing catch with a stapler and a box of paper
clips while letting out whoops of unbridled pleasure. Experience
told me it was only a matter of time before the office lay in ruins.
I called the local number of the woman who had placed the ad. Her
mother owned the flat. Summer on the Riviera. We would have sex
the way we had before having children.

I gathered the children and left before being thrown out.

The old lady's granddaughter Francoise fetched us at the airport in
Nice. Then she drove us to Cannes.

The building we were to live in for the month was magnificent. Holding only four flats, one per floor, it had huge windows, balconies big enough to hold a table and chairs for *petit dejeuner*, and a wide spiraling staircase with a brass banister.

All its inhabitants were French. Neither of us spoke much French. Why bother? I knew enough to order a meal, buy groceries, ask directions, read a newspaper headline, and avoid arrest, but why spoil the Gallic charm by knowing what they're saying?

The flat itself was cozy and old-fashioned. The old woman had filled it with pieces of heavy, wooden furniture, stenciled glassware, and antique lamps. The kitchen was the size of a broom closet.

The widow had lived with her husband in colonial French West Africa. Most of her stuff, like the building itself, was pre–World War II vintage. Wall hangings and black-and-white photographs of village life, a few masks, and a tall statue of a black warrior were souvenirs of their forty years abroad. After he retired from accounting, they had bought this flat. Then he died a few months later.

The bed was new. The granddaughter showed us how to make it go up and down by pushing a button. She found this extraordinary. With effort we managed to get her to stop playing with it.

Then she shook hands with us and left.

We showered and took naps.

Then we explored the town.

The French feel about pleasure the way Americans feel about work. They see it as an obligation. On boulevard de la Croisette, men and women strutted rather than walked. They thrust their pelvises forward and threw their shoulders back. Their hair was perfectly coiffed, their sunglasses were in place, and their tans were ideal.

The boulevard was between the beach and azure waters where yachts with helicopter pads lolled and the hotels resembled palaces. No wonder the world's most famous film festival takes place in Cannes. People behaved like movie stars, as if we should know who they are. They were beyond cool—they invented cool. It wasn't an act.

The jaguarlike movements started between their legs. What we witnessed was so utterly adult, so foreign to the way Americans interact with the environment, so unlike the way anyone other than the French regard their bodies that Laura and I felt as if we were back in junior high.

"It's a prolonged floor show," I said, "a display of base sexuality, a demonstration of erotic prowess and desire, an incontrovertible . . ."

"Daddy," said Nick, "I want to go swimming."

"What?"

"Swimming. I want to go swimming. Take me swimming."

"I want to swim, too," said Madeline. "If he gets to go swimming, I do, too."

Hand in hand, the four of us made our way to the beach.

It was late in the day, in the middle of the week, so not at all crowded. We found a good spot. Everyone around us was relaxed about nudity. The kids noticed of course, but didn't say a word and neither did we. Other families had spread out towels and opened blue-and-white-striped umbrellas. Laura and I took turns swimming to a platform with the children on our backs.

"This is heavenly," said Laura.

Returning to the flat we strolled through a little park of plane trees, past a fountain, a few benches, and a kiosk that sold fries and baguettes containing cheese or meat. On the rim of the park were half a dozen identical outdoor bistros. Late that night the tables would hold huge platters of seafood and bottles of chilled white wine. We came across an elderly woman, dressed as if en route to a wedding, who walked a miniature poodle Nick wanted to pet.

"May my son pet your dog?" Laura asked.

"May I pet your son?" she said.

Then she turned her head abruptly to the right and walked past us.

Early the next morning I took the children to Marche Forville. We were one block away. The market is housed beneath a roof and open on all sides. We saw Cavaillon melons, soft, young goat cheeses, fish shimmering on planks, squash blossoms, and baskets of *fraises du bois*. The vendors sang and shouted the names of their products with erotic passion. They caressed the vegetables. They held fruit up to their noses to demonstrate their perfume. They made suggestive movements with their eyes and tongues.

The sellers had lewd *relationships* with what they were selling. Everything looked delicious of course, but for a price. I could see it in their eyes, hear it in their voices, observe it in the way they stacked and assembled everything. The woman selling Cavaillon melons the size of grapefruits had arranged the pale golden fruit in two baskets before her. She couldn't have been happier had she been selling aphrodisiacs.

We left the market to go to the walking street in Cannes, which is called rue Meynadiers. We were looking for Ceneri, a cheese shop I had read about.

Inside a small room we saw shelves where dozens of cheeses were displayed next to pots of butter and cream. Staff dressed in robes attended to customers' needs in whispers. If they did away with the cheese, the two women working there could have been masseuses.

Back at the flat, we woke Laura up and served her breakfast in the dining room where doors led to the balcony. Then we dressed for the beach. We swam and lolled on the sand all day. I read a novel by Henry Miller and watched women undress.

"Enjoying yourself?" asked Laura.

"What?"

"You must be in heaven."

"I have no idea what you're talking about," I said. "I'm reading."

"How's the book?" she said.

"It's good."

"You're such a liar," she said.

"What are you talking about? Really," I said.

"*Oh, I say*," she said. "No idea what I'm talking about? I see you looking around. I see you eyeing the women."

"Enough about me," I said. "When are *you* going topless?"

"That's not happening."

"Oh, and why not? I think you have a beautiful body."

"Thanks, but forget it."

"You went topless when we were on our honeymoon."

"I don't know why this is so important to you."

"I never said it was."

"Well, keep it to yourself."

"But why not?"

"Because my breasts will get sunburned."

"*Her* breasts aren't sunburned," I said.

"Why don't you spend the afternoon with her then?"

"Hey, kids, don't you think Mommy should go topless?"

"Yeah, Mom," said Nicholas. "Why not?"

"I'm not choosing teams," said Madeline.

"Well, Laura, there you have it. Two of us think you should go topless."

"If you don't stop harassing me, I'm going to sit by myself."

Then we returned home to shower and nap. When we woke up, we drank pastis and ate cured meat and olives. Then we strolled on the boulevard. After a late supper in the flat, we put the children to bed. Then we went to our bedroom.

By the third morning, I had a regular table at a café. The waiter would bring me a coffee and say "*Bonjour, monsieur!*" before I asked for anything. Within a week, I was shaking hands with vendors in the market. One afternoon a tourist asked me for directions, which I considered an achievement. Were we strutting?

"We are no longer tourists," I told the children. "Now we're visitors."

"Why is that so important to you?" asked Laura.

"I prefer to fit in."

We had purchased colorful clothing, chic sandals, and sunglasses, all of which appeared to have made a difference if not to others than at least to us. I wouldn't say we were delusional, but we had no interest in distinguishing between our fantasies and what was real.

The routine hardly varied until we rented a car for a week to explore the region. One morning we drove to St. Tropez. Although it is less than thirty miles away, we spent five hours getting there. The road was filled with thousands of people in cars, vans, and mobile homes from every nation in Europe. All of them were looking for Brigitte Bardot.

One night we asked Francoise to stay with the children. Laura and I had reserved a table in a restaurant in the hills above Cannes called Le Moulin de Mougins. I had read about the chef, Roger Vergé. He was said to make sauces the way some people make love. For years, the restaurant had been a three-star Michelin. Now it was two stars. It would be our first time in a gastronomical temple.

At the table next to ours, a man was on a date with a prostitute. He wanted her to allow him to choose the menu, but she insisted on steak. She wouldn't stop giggling. Soon they were both drunk.

Across the room, a businessman from Damascus was playing host to eight sullen people, none of whom looked like they could afford more than a bag of nuts on the beach. One of his guests was a tall, thin man who sang all night in German-accented English. I assumed he had taken refuge in Syria after the war. When the dessert was brought to their table, he stood up and sang a toast.

"*Ach*, the wine is good, but it's never enough," he sang over and over again.

Then Vergé came out of the kitchen. He had on chef's whites, clean, starched, and pressed. He looked as if he had been reading about food rather than cooking it. He went to each table and asked the same question.

"*Ça va?*"

An American woman seated beside her English husband spoke up.

"Oh, chef," she said, "we are so sorry to hear you lost your third Michelin star and now have only two, but let me assure you that this meal was every bit as good as dinners we've enjoyed here when you had three stars!"

The restaurant had staged a party that appeared as if it would last forever.

The food inspired everyone to let go. We all gave in to desire. The flavors of what we put in our mouths dissolved our inhibitions.

I had never known before that food had that power. It's been over a decade since we went to Vergé, but I still savor what we ate that night: squash blossoms stuffed with black truffles, braised duck legs and breast. Eating *was* as pleasurable as sex.

One morning I varied the routine by sleeping late and going to the beach alone before shopping in the market. I sat by a young Parisian. She said she was a philosophy student. She got undressed as we spoke. Then she lay down on her towel. She handed me a book by Foucault called, *The History of Sexuality: An Introduction*.

"Have you heard of him?"

"Of course," I said.

"Most Americans have not," she said.

"I suppose not," I said.

"What are you doing here?"

The two of us acted as if we were two people engaged in the idea of flirting rather than the act itself. It was meta-flirting. It turned out I was a writer traveling alone through Europe. I had just finished my novel.

That evening I saw her again on the boulevard. This time I was with my family. She looked at me the same way the old woman had looked at Nicky when he had asked to pet her dog.

Although the children did not mention the fact that the world around them had gone erotic, they certainly sensed it. They gained confidence and looked to be liberated. Nick got rid of his diaper. Madeline swam in water above her head. They were made more secure surrounded by adults who were sleepy and consumed by desire.

One night Madeline came into our room while Laura and I were making love. I saw her before Laura did and we got untangled.

"Hi, there," I said. "What's up?"

"Hi, Maddy!" Laura said cheerfully.

"I can't sleep," she said.

"Uh-huh," I said.

"What are you doing?"

"Hugging and kissing," said Laura.

"Now go back to bed, sweetheart," I said.

"She can stay if she wants," said Laura.

"She can? Oh, of course she can! That's a splendid idea."

"That's OK," she said. "I'm tired now."

Then the next day Laura removed the top of her bathing suit while on the beach.

"There," she whispered, "satisfied?"

"You look great," I said.

Nicholas, who'd been playing with a bucket in the water saw her from the surf.

"HEY, MADDY," he shouted. "LOOK! MOMMY TOOK OFF HER BATHING SUIT!"

Dozens of French bathers looked over and laughed at us as Laura covered back up. Heh, heh, heh, the Americans, they will never acquire French sophistication, heh, heh, heh.

We amuse the French. The job of visitors to France is, in fact, to help the French, famously insecure about their place in history, to feel better about themselves. We perform a therapeutic function.

Every summer, since our first trip as a family six years before, Ursli had come to stay with us for a few days. We met him at the train station. He seemed more tense than usual. Then I wondered if I was right. Perhaps three weeks of abandoning ourselves to the erotic made him appear worse.

Laura took the children to the beach so that Ursli and I could have a beer together at a café. He seemed to want to talk in private. He didn't ask to talk alone. I never knew with Ursli. He is a lot like my father. He conveys his wishes wordlessly and others must guess.

"So," he said.

"So," I said.

"*Ja, ja,*" he said. He took a deep breath.

"You're dressed for the mountains," I said. "You must be un-comfortable."

"Yes, in Bern it was raining when I left," he said.

"Raining," I said.

"We have had quite a lot of rain this summer," he said.

"None here," I said.

He finished his beer in one long gulp and signaled the waiter.

"Let us both have another," he said.

Before long we'd had a few beers.

"A lot of attractive guys are here," he said.

"What would Rolf say?"

Rolf was Ursli's lover. They had been together five years.

"He sees other people," he said. "As do I. What about you?"

"I'm married," I said. "I have children."

"You are very practical," he said.

"But don't you mind?" I asked. "Doesn't it bother you to know Rolf sleeps with other men?"

"We have the rules," he said. "For one thing, we do not introduce our lovers to one another. Never. And most of the men I am becoming involved with, you know, it is temporary. 'No big deal,' as you would say."

"But what if you fall in love?"

"That won't happen, believe me. I meet them in parks or at the sauna. It's only sex. Nothing more."

"I see," I said.

"The thing is," Ursli said, "what I wanted to say it's not so easy. What I want to tell you is that Rolf has tested positive for HIV."

"Oh, no," I said.

"Yes, I am also quite upset about this news," he said.

"It's terrible news," I said.

"Well, we don't know quite what it means yet. I think I should maybe talk to Laura as she is a doctor. Maybe she has knowledge or statistics that would be useful to consider in this situation."

"What has Rolf's doctor told you? Or told him?"

"He has not said so much."

"But what *has* he said?"

"Not much."

He looked angrily at me.

"And you? You're OK?"

"My tests so far are negative," he said. "But I am worried about Rolf. And also, the thing is, I am worried about what this means for our relationship. Because I will not have sex with him. I don't think it's a good idea. Do you?"

"No," I said.

"We kiss and touch, but that's all. That's the limit."

"No wonder you have sex with other men," I said. "But what about Rolf? Aren't you concerned he's spreading the virus when he sleeps around?"

"He uses condoms," he said.

"But that's not enough, is it?"

"No, it probably is not," he said.

"What will you do?"

He hesitated a few moments before speaking.

"Let's buy some cheese," he said.

He paid the tab and we went to Ceneri. I pointed out the cheeses I had bought during our stay, but he ignored me and asked the clerks to recommend local varieties. Then mountain cheeses. Then young goat cheeses. Then a nice Roquefort. Then some sheep's milk cheeses from Corsica.

"We're never going to eat all this cheese," I said.

"Never mind," he said. "I love cheese. What we don't eat you can have later in the week with your family."

"I suppose," I said.

"It must be nice to have a family," he said.

We bought wine. Then a fishmonger sold us the jaw of a skate.

At the apartment, Laura was watering plants.

Ursli gave the children presents he had brought with him from Switzerland. Nicholas got a wooden toy that had wheels. Madeline got felt-tipped pens in bright colors.

The children played. We sat on the balcony. A police car roared by. It bleated. I have always associated the sound of a European police car with a Gestapo roundup. Ursli told Laura about Rolf. Then the two of them talked for over an hour about the disease.

Before dinner Ursli returned to his hotel. Laura and I went to bed in order to nap, but talked instead.

"He's lucky he's not infected," she said.

The children came in and we promised them we would go for a second swim even though it was late. We were leaving in a few days.

Ursli returned for dinner. He drank too much wine and ate too much cheese. Then he got sick.

"I didn't want to spoil our evening," he said by phone the next morning. "I hadn't meant to eat so quickly."

"You haven't ruined anything," I said.

He had his doubts. We agreed to meet later that day on the beach.

Ursli has never enjoyed life, but he is athletic and loves to swim. He took the children for rides on his back. Then we all took turns swimming to the platform, which was about a hundred yards out.

"This is invigorating," I said to Madeline and Nicholas when we got back.

"What's that mean?" asked Nick.

"It means it's fun," I said.

"So why not say it's fun?"

"I just did."

"No, you didn't," said Madeline. "You said it was invigorating."

"Same thing," I said.

"But it's not the same thing," said Nick.

"Yes, it is," I said.

"You just said it wasn't," he said.

"I'm not doing this," I said. I could feel myself getting irritated. "It's the same thing."

"It isn't," said Nick.

"Fine," I said. "Whatever you say."

"I'd like to have kids one day," said Ursli.

"You're a tourist," I said. "You don't know what it's like. We have no privacy and every day there's a silly argument about nothing."

"That would be nice for a change," he said.

After Ursli returned to Switzerland, we drove west along the coast to swim in coves formed by rocky cliffs. Francoise had told us the views were serene and there were no crowds. Along the way we passed by villas built on rocky parapets and surrounded by tropical gardens with luxurious pools and long staircases that led to the sea.

"Imagine what it's like to live there," Laura said. "I've never seen anything more beautiful."

We didn't see anyone lounging around these homes. Perhaps they only came in August.

"A king lives there," said Nicholas.

"Or a sheik," I said.

"What's a sheik?" he asked.

"He's like a king," I said.

"So why didn't you say a king lives there?"

The narrow road curved out and gave us the opportunity to see ahead. Each cove we eyed looked perfect. We kept going just to see more. Then the children had enough of sitting in the car so we pulled off to the side and parked. About a hundred steps led down.

The earth was a ruddy color. The air was dry and the soil looked parched. By the time we reached the bottom, we were covered in sweat. We had lots of stuff with us. A picnic cooler, plastic floats, and beach toys.

The beach was made up of shiny, quarter-sized black stones. Cliffs rose to our left and right. A few bathers put down towels beside us.

The ground in the water dropped several feet close to shore. The children could not go in without us. The water was clean and cool.

"I like the other beach better," said Madeline.

"Why's that?" Laura asked.

"Because of the sand."

"But this is pretty beautiful," said Laura. "You have to admit."

Laura took Nicholas for a ride on her back and I swam with Madeline. Then we traded children.

I decided to go for a long swim by myself. The water was soothing and still and before long, not having looked back in order to gauge the distance, I was about a half mile out. A boat full of tourists snapping pictures motored by only a few feet away. I had never been this far from shore. I began to tread water.

I am a strong swimmer so I wasn't worried yet. But then a new sensation swept over me. Looking up at the clear sky, embraced by the water, within view of the land and the beach where my family played, I thought it would be good to die there. The pleasure was overwhelming. I became convinced that I belonged in those depths. This must be how it feels to be French, I thought as I struggled to make it back to shore, seduced by sex and close to death.

A SWISS FARM

Each time we returned from holidays, we faced a run-down urban neighborhood. The ugliness of where we lived had great depth and integrity, similar to that of a political prisoner who won't wash in order to protest conditions in jail. The few trees and shrubs that managed to survive in lead-filled soil looked embarrassed. Cars were old, huge, dented American-made models. Neighbors characteristically appeared older than their actual ages as well as unhappy, effects of having suffered decades of grinding jobs or unemployment, diets noted for fat and frying, and sedentary lives in front of TVs.

Our own home had been built in the 1870s from a kit sent to its first owners from a department store in Chicago. While adequate in every way possible, the rooms had a blunt uniformity that would have depressed us more had our first child not been born within a year of purchase. As a result of Madeline's birth and then Nick's three years later, our home was filled with baby smells—an olfactory experience that our senses mistook for pleasure. The children filled us with joy, but not to the point where it was possible to forget our home was unpleasant.

Our appreciation for these facts was heightened by comparing where we were to where we had been. The rare beauty of distant places made home seem as if we had been thrown out of paradise and sent to purgatory or worse.

On holidays the four of us were completely devoted to being a

family, while back in Cambridge we had little pleasurable time together. Laura and I were fortunate enough to be able to organize
our lives based on the needs of the children. Our work was flexible
enough for that luxury. But rather than engaging in activities that
might increase our love and awareness of one another, we adhered
to tight schedules built on routine.

A great deal of driving was necessary. Nicholas's nursery school,
which he attended part-time, and Madeline's elementary school
were located in different parts of town and by the time I completed
the task of dropping them off and returning home it was less than
two hours until it was time to pick them up. Between drives I
would sit in front of my computer and pretend to write.

Other times I pretended to write were after lunch and before
preparing dinner for the family as well as after the children had
been bathed, had books read to them, and been put to bed. Laura's
job took place in its entirety in an office while most of my time was
spent at home. As a result, little progress was made on my work during this period of time, although I did manage to complete a book
and have it published.

But the arrival of Madeline and Nicholas was beneficial in every
way imaginable. Anxiety, with which I had been on intimate terms
for as long as I could remember, appeared more ridiculous each
moment I spent with them. Sadness lost a great deal of its appeal. I
suppose now that these changes are what love brought about. But
back then no time was available or even necessary to think about
or analyze why our lives had changed due to our efforts to become
a family. The *what* matters more than the *why* when you're in love.

Our parents, living out of state, arrived more frequently than
ever before. We all crowded together in our small home. My office
became a bedroom for my parents or in-laws. The grandparents
photographed and recorded our children with the zeal of anthro-
pologists. They were in love, too. We were, to quote the Ramones,
a happy family.

Sisters, sisters-in-law, brothers-in-law, nieces, and a nephew, thrilled by the promise of free food, chose our home to celebrate births, anniversaries, and most of the important national and religious holidays. These occasions were accompanied by an outpouring of emotions. Our families had boundless energy for explaining how they felt about us and would insist on knowing how we felt about them. I thought it would have been obvious by now. How often can you tell someone you love them? Not often enough. Knowing that this was a deficiency in my character rather than theirs—my not wanting to emote—was of no importance to others. I acquired a reputation for wanting to be left alone.

I wanted to be with Laura, Madeline, and Nicholas. Back then I thought a lot about Ezra Pound's poem: "And the days are not full enough, and the nights are not full enough, and life slips by like a field mouse, not shaking the grass." Since nothing was as pleasurable as being with my wife and children, that satisfaction always appeared to be fleeting.

To intensify the experience of being in a family, we took off to places where the four of us could be alone. We rarely said we took vacations. Instead we called them holidays like those celebrated all year. They were pilgrimages to look for and celebrate what we loved about being together.

We always had good luck getting away. Either we exchanged homes through Intervac, an international agency which has U.S. offices based in San Francisco, or we rented inexpensive properties. The French have a system of *gites*, the Italians have *agriturismo*, and the Swiss have Reka—all are made up of simple cottages or farms where people from the city can enjoy time out of town during the summer. It was possible to spend less than four hundred dollars a week. The Europeans, we came to believe, had a philosophy of leisure. One tenet is everyone has a right to be in the countryside during July or August. Another is that time spent in the mountains or by the sea is necessary to establish or maintain physical and emotional well-being.

This was before the Internet. We had to rely upon letters, phone calls, and a few photographs. Several months before Nicholas turned five and Madeline became eight, we had, as usual, a stack of catalogs on the kitchen table and no clear idea where to go. Most of the exchanges, farms, and cottages looked equally good or bad.

"Let's go back to Switzerland," I suggested. We had not returned since the month spent in Ticino after Madeline had been born. "The children are old enough to hike. We've always wanted to take them into the mountains. Let's stay on a Swiss farm."

"They're still too little to hike distances," said Laura, "but I wouldn't mind all that fresh air."

"It is clean and quiet," I said.

"Well, yes," she said, "but it's dull. Not that I mind dull. I work too hard. I wish my life *was* dull."

"I stayed on a Swiss farm one summer between my first and second years of college and I loved being outdoors all the time. It wasn't dull at all. I had to get up early and grind the oats, feed the horses and cows, clean the stables, pick cherries on tall ladders, harvest the hay, and empty cesspools."

"That sounds perfect for our family," she said.

"It was just an example," I said. "The point I wanted to make was it's beautiful in Switzerland, there's lots to do."

"I told you I'm not looking for things to do," she said. "Hikes would be enough."

"The Swiss specialize in that," I said. "They call them walks rather than hikes. And the children are the perfect ages."

The Reka catalog, written in German, is organized like many things in Switzerland: precisely, categorically, with the rhythms of a statistician. I love how the Swiss try to be systematic and enumerative. Their efforts make things look safer and more comprehensible than they are in reality. Italian and French guides tell only of a property's cost, its location, and the number of bedrooms and appliances. The Swiss list the type of farm—whether it has cows, pigs, goats, horses, or sheep; the ages and genders of children in the farmer's family; proximity in kilometers to mountains, public pools, train stations, and cities or towns; the farm's elevation above sea level; and whether or not guests are permitted to volunteer to work while visiting. This latter point is indicated with a picture of a tiny rake.

"Let's try and find a family that has children the same ages as ours," I said.

"I'd like to find an area where the hikes are easy enough for the children," said Laura. "Not the high mountains. But not flat either. Something the children will enjoy. We don't want to turn them off to hiking."

I had been to Switzerland several times before. I knew the geography well enough to suggest a farming region north of Bern. Sandwiched between Luzern and Bern, the Bernese Mittelland is known for its rolling hills, many farms, simplicity, and secular outlook.

"A farm sounds good," said Laura. "But why don't we find one in the French-speaking part of Switzerland?"

"I don't speak French," I said.

"Try something new," she said.

"Will *you* speak French?" I asked. "You're the one who studied it in school."

"Yes, I will," she said.

"I enjoy speaking German," I said.

"Well, I don't," she said. "It is an unpleasant language and it makes my ears ring."

"That's not possible," I said. "I bet if you tried you could learn German. It's very close to English, you see. Not like French."

"What if I don't want to learn German?" she said.

"Then you needn't," I said. "All I'm suggesting is that there's an advantage to going to a place where I can speak the language and act on our behalf."

"You had a fine time in Cannes, didn't you?" she said. "What has changed?"

"The fact that they all spoke French did not add to the experience."

"But it might one day," she said.

I promised to be open to looking at farms in the French-speaking region of Switzerland. Then I found three places in the Bernese Mittelland.

"These are all lovely," I said. "And the walks in the region are hilly and intriguing."

"How do you know?" she asked.

"I've seen hiking books," I said. "You sort of stroll through farms and say hello to farmers working as you pass by them. '*Gruezi!*' or '*Gruezi mitenand!*' "

"I know how to say hello in Swiss-German," Laura said. "And I know all about those gregarious, fun-loving Swiss."

"They are friendly," I said. "You just have to get to know them."

"They are not friendly," she said.

"Ursli and his family are friendly," I said. "And they're Swiss."

"I wouldn't call them typical. Besides they are not that friendly."

"It would be a good experience for the children," I said. "It would help prepare them for the world, which is not a friendly place."

"I do think the kids would love being on a farm," Laura said. "They could explore on their own. I just don't see why it has to be German-speaking."

"It doesn't," I said. "But the three farms I found appear to be more beautiful than all the others we've seen and they are in a relatively flat part of Switzerland. Besides, German is not so bad once you get used to it."

"And you like German," she said.

"I especially like the sound of Swiss-German," I said. "The language is full of diminutives and the Swiss sound as if they are going up and down with their voices when they speak. It is musical."

"German is not musical," she said.

"It is nearly musical," I said.

"German is nowhere near as beautiful as French or Italian," she said.

"Then why compare?" I said. "The farm is the destination. We are not going to Switzerland to immerse ourselves in Swiss-German language and culture. We are going so that the kids will have a chance to run around a farm without breaking things or getting into trouble."

"I agree that they're at ages when they want to explore," Laura said. "And they never get a chance in *this* neighborhood."

"We can take long walks, hold hands, and look at trees," I said.

"You are very happy there," she said.

"Well, it brings back memories of visits we took when I was a child with my parents and sister. And hearing German makes me think of my father."

"Uh-huh," she said.

"There's nothing wrong with that, is there?"

"Did I say there was?"

"You implied it."

"How?"

"I don't know," I said. "But you did."

"Honey, you're being paranoid," she said. She sang the words to pacify me.

"Staying on a farm is something we've both wanted to do for some time," I said. "And if we want real challenges, we can always head to the mountains, the Bernese Oberland, which are no more than an hour or two away."

"I'll admit it sounds lovely," Laura said. "I like the idea of being away from cities and crowds of tourists."

"But?"

"It's not just the language," she said. "It's the whole Swiss-German environment. It's rigid and judgmental. Swiss-Germans hate children."

"Oh, and the French love them?"

"No, but they're not mean to them. Not all the time, anyway. Only in restaurants. Look, children are loud and messy. Swiss-Germans love silence and cleanliness. There's certain to be conflict. Why don't we just go to Italy? Italians love children."

"We can't hike in Italy in the summer. It's too hot. And I don't want to sit around a pool getting fat. At least in Switzerland we'll be active."

"Fine," she said. "Tell me about the farms."

Each farm was described as "family-friendly" and "inviting." The one that stood out was depicted in the catalog as a classic Bernese Bauernhof, which meant it was old and built of wood, had several floors, a sloping roof that looked like a pageboy haircut, and numerous windows with red geraniums in flower boxes.

"And look," I said, "it has a *kinderfreundliches Eseli!*"

"You know I don't speak German," said Laura.

"They have a little, child-friendly donkey," I said. "I suppose that means the children can take rides on it. Maybe they hook it up to a cart and trot around in circles until the children get so dizzy they fall over."

"What about the rooms?" she said. "The donkey rides can wait."

"It doesn't say much," I said. "There's a flat in the farmhouse for rent with two rooms. The house is two hundred fifty years old. The farmer and his wife are named Peter and Elizabeth Zulauf. They have pigs, horses, ducks, chickens, and cows. The house is 1,250 meters above sea level. It is near the village of Rohrbach. That means 'babbling brook' in German. I'm sure it will be fine. Rustic, but fine. We'll be outdoors hiking, anyway. These old, traditional farms have a great deal of charm."

"You seem to forget what happened the last time we were in Switzerland. The rooms have to be comfortable. If it rains, we will be indoors most of the time."

"If it makes you feel better, I'll phone Ursli and ask him to contact the farmer and get more information."

"That's no guarantee," she said. "He doesn't seem to have the same standards we do."

"I'll tell him we want something of quality."

"What's the cost?"

The price was in Swiss francs.

"Based on the current exchange, it's a little under three hundred dollars for the week," I said.

"How nice can it be for three hundred?" Laura asked.

"It will be simple," I said. "But clean and practical."

"You start to sound Swiss whenever we talk about Switzerland," she said. "There's more to a holiday than clean and practical. Isn't that a starting point?"

"The farms are romantic," I said. "Even if it rains, the area is flat and we can take walks with hats and umbrellas. This farm is on the border of the Emmental. I've been before. Not to the same village, but close enough. The farm where I worked was in Luzern, the next canton over. We wouldn't be isolated, but we wouldn't be surrounded by tourists, either."

"I would love to get out of the city," Laura said. "Sure. Give Ursli a call and see what he can find out."

I contacted my friend and explained what we were after. Nothing fancy, but not primitive either.

"Clean and practical," he said.

"Right," I said. "But a bit more, too. Decent beds and a modern kitchen would be nice."

"Swiss beds are typically decent," he said. "And modern. Scott, this is a farm, not a condominium in Florida."

"I know that," I said.

Ursli always spoke to me in an aggressive tone, but I was surprised each time by how much I welcomed the sadness that came from being diminished by him.

"I am told many Swiss families enjoy going on these farming holidays," he said. "It is said to be perfect for young children like yours. I would find it dull, but you may not."

After Ursli phoned the farm and spoke with Frau Zulauf, he called me back.

"I think you will like it," he said. "Frau Zulauf is very sympathetic."

"Did you ask her about the rooms?"

"Yes, of course," he said.

"And?"

"They seem fine," he said.

"Well, that's what I told Laura," I said. "But she seems to want to know more. After all, we will be there for two weeks with two young children."

"I don't know what more I can tell you," he said. "There is a child-friendly donkey."

"I know," I said.

"The rooms are in the farmhouse. They have a cottage they rent on the property, but it is booked. You have been to a Swiss farm before. You know what it is like."

"How bad can it be?" I said.

"Exactly," he said.

Madeline and Nicholas were delighted when we told them they would play all day with a donkey, cows, pigs, horses, chickens, and ducks and live in a farmhouse. They asked the usual questions most of which had to do with whether or not they would be allowed to feed the animals, milk the cows, and play in the hayloft of the barn. It was not what they said that mattered, but what they didn't say. They were confident and secure.

Unlike most of the other young parents we knew, Laura and I

rarely discussed our emotional needs or those of the children. We explained things rather than said how we felt about them. We are not unemotional people, but we found talking about feelings to be dull in comparison to taking action based on how we felt. And most of the time we felt good and lucky.

Laura's reticence about feelings was one of the most attractive things I observed about her when we first met. She wanted to live rather than talk about how it felt to live. For a long time I attributed her ability to get things done without wasting time talking about how it feels to get things done to her being a doctor, but now I see it has more to do with her being the daughter of a woman who lived in London during the Nazi Blitz and a father who was wounded in combat in France during World War II.

I had been brought up by a survivor of the last *Kindertransport* to leave Nazi Germany and a mother who experiences emotions like an intellectual regarding ideas.

Both our families had made decisions about how we were brought up based on feelings informed by the large traumas of their past. Laura and I had found from the outset that making a family of our own was best when we did things without talking or explaining ourselves to one another, the children, or anyone else. We were raising the children to follow our shared ethos.

When visiting homes in Cambridge we ate lengthy dinners of spaghetti squash and curried lentils and heard our friends talk about their feelings. They had changed since becoming parents. People I knew from college who had taken artistic, intellectual, and personal risks were now pudgy in their thinking. Nothing seemed to get done properly as a direct result of introspection.

During the meals, their children would intrude and rather than be sent to sit in front of a video, they were asked how they felt about nearly everything: what they ate, what time they wished to go to bed, where they would like to go for vacations, who they wanted to play with, and so on. Encouraged by their parents to use their feelings to guide decisions they were clearly incapable of making, the children refused to put on clothing for nursery school, bathe, eat anything green, or cover their mouths when coughing. It was all seen as marvelous. Any effort to interfere was viewed as harmful to their self-esteem.

Our friends associated discussion of emotions with a guarantee of future happiness. They believed that asking their children about their feelings meant they were good, empathic parents. I frankly didn't see these connections. I figured we stood a decent chance of raising happy children as long as we showed them our love, provided a safe home, acted reliably and loving toward one another, and didn't ask too many personal questions.

Ironically, as someone who made a living as a psychologist, I was bored by feelings. I had enough of that sort of nonsense at work. I certainly did not want to spend evenings doing what my friends did—"processing," "interpreting," and "bonding." Our culture has convinced people that talking about their feelings makes them better, but it isn't true. I knew what had made me better—not therapy, meditation, or blathering on about how I felt. One decisive act that created change. Having children with a woman I loved and being responsible with her for their well-being.

We flew into Zurich and picked up a rental at the airport. Then we drove toward Rohrbach. The farm was said to be on its outskirts. Over an hour later we were still searching for the property. No sign read "Family Zulauf," we had not been given a street address, and none of the buildings we drove by resembled what we had seen in the catalog.

"Why don't you ask that farmer over there for directions?" said Laura.

She indicated a man with a bushy white beard by the side of the road. He wore dark blue overalls. Beside him stood a tiny, gnarled woman who must have been the local witch. The couple was ancient, but worked with more vigor than teenagers. He wielded a scythe to cut tall grass and she raked up after him.

"They are too busy to answer my question," I said.

"You said if we came here you would speak the language to help us," Laura said.

"I don't want to interrupt their rhythm," I said.

"I'm sure they wouldn't mind," she said. "You might even save their lives. They are too old to be working. They should be at home watching TV and eating chocolate."

"You promised we could have chocolate," said Nick. "You said Switzerland is famous for chocolate. When do we get chocolate?"

"We just got here, Nicky," said Madeline. "We'll have chocolate later."

"But it has to be at least today," he said.

"The sooner we get to the farm, the sooner we eat," said Laura. "But your father refuses to ask directions so we will have to starve until he changes his mind."

"It's not my fault," I said. "The problem is we're in Switzerland. If those two stop working, they would be accused of loitering and given huge fines and years of imprisonment. Swiss are idle only when sleeping. Even then they feel guilty about the necessity of being dormant and in the morning ask one another how they have slept: 'Hast du gut geschlafen?' They assume everyone sleeps poorly. If they stop working, they lose their fragile mental equilibrium."

The children asked Laura if I was telling the truth and she said I wasn't. Then we drove up and down other roads where we saw families planting or harvesting vegetables, picking cherries, riding tractors, working on machines, hanging out washing, and sweeping. It was like watching ants.

"If we lived here," I said. "We would have to work as hard as they do."

"I wouldn't," said Nicky.

"You would have to," I said. "Or you would be arrested and put in jail. You wouldn't like that would you?"

"Mommy wouldn't let them do that," he said.

"Of course not, honey," she said. Then she spoke to me. "If you don't ask the next person we see for directions, you're in big trouble."

"I'm looking for the right person," I said.

"Over there," she said. "In that field. Go ask her."

We parked beside a ditch. A few feet away, a woman and her three children were digging up potatoes. Piles of dirt-covered potatoes filled wooden baskets at their feet. I got out of the car and walked over.

I apologized for interrupting. They stared at me. The look was one of remorse rather than anger. I supposed they were filled with shame at being unclean. They were the dirtiest Swiss I had ever seen.

"*Gruezi mitenand*," I said. My greeting was returned. Then I continued on in my Swiss-accented German. "Do you know the Zulauf family? We are looking for their farm."

"Herr Peter Zulauf?"

"Yes, exactly," I said.

We were less than a half mile away and had driven by the farm several times. The photo in the catalog had been of the courtyard and principal entrance. The back of the house faced the road.

We drove over and parked beside the barn. As usual, we had enough suitcases of belongings to stay until winter. I unloaded the car while Laura and the children stood around looking picturesque. A small, black-haired woman wearing eyeglasses came out of the house next to the barn to greet us. She held an infant in her arms and was tailed by two small boys.

"Frau Zulauf?" I said. I imitated the formal language I had heard for years whenever Ursli met strangers. I introduced Laura and the children in German and we all shook hands. "Greetings. We are the Haas family from Boston. We have finally found your house and are very happy to be here."

We spoke a bit about traveling, the weather, and our families. Her husband was working. She told us that we would meet him later.

Then she said, "Let me show you the rooms."

Frau Zulauf looked like an elementary schoolteacher in her mid-twenties. Unlike my Swiss friends whose style was brusque and even aggressive at times, she was gentle. Most of the Swiss I had observed over the years were like my friends: blunt, judgmental, and aloof. By now I considered those features to be fundamental to the national character. So perhaps, I wondered, being maternal had changed Frau Zulauf the same way becoming a parent had changed me. When her children were older perhaps she would become Swiss again.

We paused long enough to take in the courtyard and house. It really was just like the picture we had seen. The farmhouse was huge, dark brown, pristine, and filled with big windows and geranium pots. To the left were a vegetable plot and the barn. We heard the cows shuffling and mooing. The horses snorted. The donkey moved slowly in a track tethered to a pole with a long rope. To the right of the house were a walnut tree and a metal sty in which a drift of gigantic, gray hogs grunted. The aromas of the barnyard inspired happy thoughts. I find it impossible to be irritable when I am on a farm. I think it must be in my blood, as my father's roots were in farming communities.

"Can we explore?" asked Nicky.

"Don't you want to see the rooms?" asked Laura.

"Later," he said and then he took off.

"It's really fine," said Frau Zulauf. She didn't speak a word of English. "He cannot get in trouble."

We climbed narrow stairs above her kitchen and the sty to reach the apartment. Doors were rarely locked in Switzerland and she pressed the handle down to let us in. The top half of the door was made up of six glass panels in a wooden frame. An old curtain behind the panel hid the interior from view.

"It is small, but cozy," she said.

"*Ganz gemütlich*," I said. Very cozy. I wanted to let her know how happy we were to be here. It was as if her happiness mattered more than ours. I had the strange fantasy that we were visiting relatives. These thoughts and emotions occur to me whenever I speak German. Being in Switzerland is as close as I can get to imagining what it would have been like to have met my father's family in Bavaria who did not survive the war as Jews. I relate to the Swiss as if they are that lost family. It makes no sense, but few things of this nature do. As always, I kept these sentiments to myself.

We took the tour. The rooms were as clean as a hospital ward. They smelled of flowers. All of the ceilings were low. The floors were made out of wood. The first room was a kitchen with a wooden table and four chairs. Then we passed by a bathroom with a shower and toilet before walking into a bedroom with four beds. We hadn't known we would all be sleeping in one room.

"Wow," said Madeline. "All of us in one room! Yeah! Great! Hooray! Wait until Nicky finds out." She jumped on a bed by a window. "I call this bed! Yeah!"

"Ah, two rooms," Laura said. "A kitchen and a bedroom. Not two bedrooms."

"No," I said.

"Is there a problem?" asked Frau Zulauf. She could see Laura's expression change and hear the annoyance in her voice even if she didn't understand what she was saying.

"No," I said. "No problem. Everything is in order."

"So," said Frau Zulauf. "Would you like my man to help with your baggage?"

"No," I said. "That's fine."

I followed her downstairs, shook hands, and began the first of several trips to fetch the luggage to the rooms. When I returned, Laura was alone.

"Where's Madeline?" I asked.

"Exploring," she said. "Isn't that what we wanted them to do?"

"Are you OK?" I asked.

"I'm fine," she said.

"Are you upset about the rooms?"

"No," she said. "Are you?"

"We will have to come up here during the day," I said. "Just the two of us."

"I thought we were hiking during the day," she said.

"Between breakfast and hikes, I mean."

"If there's time," she said.

"Right," I said.

"It certainly is clean," she said.

"And the children are happy about the four of us sleeping in one room," I said.

"They certainly are."

After carrying up the suitcases and unpacking, Laura and I found the children in the barn talking to cows. We put them back in the car and drove to the village to find a place to eat. The restaurants only served meals from twelve until two and it was nearly three so we bought groceries for lunch and dinner and returned to the farm for a picnic in the rooms.

"This place is great, Dad," said Madeline.

"It is, isn't it?" I said.

They ate quickly and ran outside again. It was a wonderful contrast to living in the city where they had no freedom.

"We're alone now," I said to Laura.

"I am taking a nap," she said.

"Why don't I join you?" I said.

"A nap," she said.

"Right," I said and went out to explore.

Madeline and Nicholas were now tossing grass at chickens that were roaming the barnyard. The birds ignored them, but the children were convinced they would succeed in feeding them if they threw bigger clumps. The oldest Zulauf boy, who was five years old, came over and stood next to my son. He glared at him for a while and then gave him a neat little shove. Nick fell over.

"Hey," I said. "Don't do that."

He walked away. His mother had seen everything from the kitchen window that faced the yard and came out to apologize.

"He gets like that," she said. "He will be punished. We are very sorry."

Then she went back in. Nick was all right, just startled.

"What is wrong with him?" he asked.

"I think he's frustrated about not being able to communicate with you," I said. "You don't speak German and he doesn't speak English."

"But that doesn't mean he has to push me," he said.

"No, it doesn't," I said. "But I bet he'll be your friend soon."

"I bet he won't," said Madeline. "I bet he's a jerk."

"Don't call people names," I said. "He's not a jerk. He does jerky things."

We threw more grass at the chickens and then went to see the hogs. Penned up and reveling in filth, the big, black creatures were cunning. They had been grunting as if having a discussion, but when we arrived they stopped and looked at us with beady eyes positioned narrowly between floppy ears as big as bat wings.

" 'All animals are equal but some are more equal than others,' " I said.

"What's that supposed to mean?" asked Madeline.

I told the children about Orwell's novel *Animal Farm* and how the pigs in that book had pretended to be fair, but had been unfair in order to control the lives of all the other animals on the farm.

"Animals wouldn't think like that," said Madeline.

"No," I said, "but imagine if they did."

"Do you think this farm is like that?" asked Nick.

"What do you think?" I asked.

"No," he said. "The animals look happy."

The hog pen was just below the living quarters of the farmer and his family. The farmer emerged from a dark space between the house and the pen. He was cheery like his wife. Young and robust, apple-cheeked and in overalls, he came toward us with great ceremony as if greeting dignitaries rather than tourists staying in his home.

"I am Peter Zulauf," he said and put out his hand. He did not speak English either. He had a broad grin. "And this is my farm. You are welcome to it. I see you are meeting our pigs."

"Yes," I said. "How many are there?"

"Oh, we have four hundred pigs," he said.

Then we looked at our feet, the pigs, and the house.

"*Ja*," he said. "*Ja, ja.* So."

"So," I said.

"*Ja, ja*," he said.

"*Ja,* so," I said. "The pigs."

"*Ja,* the pigs," he said.

"Four hundred," I said.

"*Ja*, four hundred," he said.

"That's many," I said. "A lot of work."

"Not so many," he said. "But it is work. All day working."

Then he said, "OK, then," shook hands, and went off to the barn.

"What a nice guy," I said to the children.

"But he didn't say anything," said Madeline. "How can you say he's nice?"

"He's nice," said Nick.

"He seemed nice," I said.

"You like people too much," said Madeline.

We followed the farmer to the barn and watched him milk cows. He did not use a machine. Milk squirting below the udders at first made a hard sound when it hit metal, but then as the bucket filled up the splashing was like the children playing in the bath.

That night Frau Zulauf knocked on our door and apologized for interrupting. We were seated around the wooden table in candle-light over a supper of melted Emmental, bacon, and boiled pota-toes. It seemed nothing we had ever eaten before had as much flavor. The old, cozy room was warm from the heat of the day, the stove, and our proximity to one another. We could pretend this was our house and that after a day of chores we were having a simple meal of what we had produced on our farm.

"I have for you a bottle of milk," Frau Zulauf said. "And in the morning would you like one left at your door?"

Laura and I had tasted fresh milk before, but nothing as good as what we had that night. It was creamy and smooth and had a faint smell of hazelnuts. We had two bottles each day after that. And when we left the bottle from the morning in our refrigerator, the cream rose to the top so that after a hike it was like drinking nec-tar. Now whenever any of us drink fresh milk, we think of our days and nights on that farm the summer the children were still so small they wanted to sleep with us and we were so young we didn't mind.

Laura was the first to hear the screaming. It was 4 A.M. The chil-dren didn't stir. They never stirred in their beds once they were asleep. Since having them, Laura and I no longer slept well. The slightest sound woke us up. It was as if we were on patrol and our job was to protect them even when unconscious.

"What is that?" she whispered to me. I was in the adjacent bed.

"Herr Zulauf is feeding the hogs," I said.

We were just above the hogs and the sound they made was thun-derous and aggressive—they were giving voice to their rage, impa-tience, and empty bellies. Four hundred of them were stamping their feet and repeating the howls in a rhythmic way that resembled a chant. Their protest seemed ancient in its purity and appeal. If we are not fed, their screams implied, we will riot.

"It had better stop soon," she said.

"It will."

Then as suddenly as it had started, the screams died out. The hogs were being fed and watered. We heard a few grunts and then the sounds of shuffling feet and munching. There was nothing left to complain about.

"We're going to have to hear this every night, aren't we?" Laura said.

"I think so," I said.

"How am I going to be rested for the hikes?"

"We'll get used to it," I said. "We'll sleep through it or we'll fall back asleep."

"I can never fall back asleep," she said. "You know that."

Then we just lay in the dark and said nothing for a few moments.

"Laura?" I said.

"No," she said. "Not with the children in the room."

"They're asleep," I said. "It's pitch black."

"Good night," she said. "Sleep well."

That morning after we had finished breakfast, I suggested to the children that they go out and explore the farm while Laura and I cleaned the dishes and put away the food.

"What if I don't want to explore?" asked Madeline. "I explored yesterday. I want to read."

"Go read outside," I said. "It's a beautiful day. The sun is shining. Go look at the flowers or feed the chickens."

"C'mon, Maddy," said Nick. "Maybe the farmer will let us milk the cows."

"He won't," she said. "Are you guys up to something? I thought there are no secrets."

"No secrets," said Laura. "Your father and I thought you might like to explore. Don't you like exploring?"

"Yes," she said.

"Then why not do it?"

"Are you planning something for my birthday?" she asked. Her birthday was a few weeks away.

"Yes," I said. "And it's a big surprise."

"Oh, OK," she said. She was still a little suspicious. "Then I'll go outside with Nicky."

"Yeah!" he said.

He loved being with his sister more than being with any of his friends. The two of them ran downstairs.

About a half hour later, we found the children in the barn and put them in the car. We had packed a picnic and would drive to the mountains. Each day would be as good as the first with blue skies and cool weather perfect for hiking. On the ride over we listened to bad folkloric Swiss music, which involved accordions and voices tempered by enforced happiness. The men and women sounded as if they would burst into tears the moment they stopped singing. My family insisted I turn off the radio as the cultural experience was less than the sheer awfulness of what we heard.

That morning we drove to the Stockhorn, a famous Alp about two hours away. At the base of the mountain there is an enormous cable car, which we rode up to the top. There we saw a range of mountains to the southeast and the lake of Thun to the east. Alpine ravens, spoiled by picking through food left behind by hikers, cawed overhead and bounced near us as we stood at the edge of a viewing platform. As a group, none of us had ever seen anything more beautiful so we said nothing and just held hands to mark the occasion. It was moments like these, and there were a great many back then, that convinced me that time could slow to the pace of a child's observation.

It became cold as we were exposed on all sides and above the tree line. So we made our way down the mountain. The trail, like most others Laura and I had been on in Switzerland, descended in an easy grade. Along the way we passed by benches put into key places meant for viewing. The Swiss regard the mountains as companions rather than as places of conquest or struggle. A nervous bunch, prone to organization rather than introspection, they use the Alps in order to try and calm down. I have rarely seen a Swiss hiker move quickly in the mountains. They prefer to take it all in as if the landscape was an analgesic or tranquilizer.

Up ahead we heard someone yodeling. At first I thought the yodeler was making a joke, but as he continued over several minutes his exuberance was made clear.

"We were lost once in the mountains," said Laura. Then she told the children about our hike years ago when Madeline was weeks old and, with her parents, we had been on a trail that vanished.

"We're safe now," she concluded.

In fact, we had never been safer. I knew the Swiss well enough to recognize that their edgy relationship to mountains was a lot like mine. But all of us, as a family, were able to join in and establish a connection that still lasts to the Alps through hikes like the one we took that day on the Stockhorn.

When we returned to the farm, Herr Zulauf led us to a nursery behind the sty and showed us nearly a dozen piglets born hours before. Blinking, pink, and adorable in their helplessness, they were an attraction.

Then the children watched him milk the cows, feed the horses, and clean the stables. A motorbike attached to a tiny cart pulled into the barnyard to collect big metal cans of milk that were then brought to a local dairy. There was no end to the activity.

Either we took long hikes through flat terrain in the farm's environs or we walked down mountains. It would be years before we made ascents. The region was filled with long, simple walks.

One especially clear, bright morning we took a route that started and ended at the train station in Rohrbach. The distance was a little over seven miles and according to my hiking guidebook, *Grosser Wander-Atlas der Schweiz* (The Big Wandering Atlas of Switzerland), it would take us three hours and thirty minutes. But we took all day. We walked through farms, past fields of potatoes, corn, and flowers, and into settlements of only a few houses. Joy unmitigated by circumstances other than what we experienced directly took hold of us. The places had exotic names: Zwanghubel, Chaltenegg, Chabisberg, and Längi. Most of the time we wandered across open fields in view of old trees. On a hill Laura saw an oak that resembled one which had featured prominently in a book we had read about the Black Death. We snuck into a field and dug up a few potatoes. Farmers, their wives, and children greeted us when we lifted the latches of waist-high, wooden doors and stepped through their yards.

"I wouldn't mind buying a house here," I said.

"We need a house in Cambridge first," she said. "How much longer can you live on Gillis Court?"

"I could stay there forever," I said.

"What's wrong with our house?" asked Madeline. "I like our house."

"It's a nice house, honey," Laura said. "But the neighborhood is run-down and . . . it's not that nice. The house is not that nice."

"Look over there," I said. "We could buy that house."

A few hundred feet away was another traditional farmhouse. It had a vegetable plot and near its entrance were two chestnut trees.

"I am not buying that house," Laura said. "Besides the Swiss won't sell to foreigners. You may love them, but they don't love you."

"I will admit my affection for Switzerland is a little one-sided," I said. "But that's OK. You know what Saul Bellow had Mr. Sammler say about the Poles: 'I think on the whole I like them better than they liked me.'"

"Oh, wonderful," she said, "let's live in a place where people don't like us."

"They don't dislike us," I said. "They don't think about us."

"That boy pushed me," Nicholas said.

"It was an accident," I said.

"It wasn't an accident," he said.

"I am not buying a house in Switzerland until we buy a new one in Cambridge," Laura said. "It's depressing coming home from these trips to Gillis Court. Sometimes I don't see why we leave home when we have to return to that house in that neighborhood."

"I don't want to live here," said Nick.

"We wouldn't live here," I said. "We would just visit in the summer."

"Every summer?" asked Laura. "You could come back to Rohrbach every summer? Of all the places you've been or want to see one day, this one is the best?"

"My father was the same way," I said. "We would go on vacation and he'd want to buy a house. It drove my mother crazy. I think it must have had to do with his having been taken from his home due to the Nazis. It wasn't that he wanted a home wherever he felt at home, but instead I think he was always imagining what it might be like to have to flee again. He lived like a refugee, always scoping out what could be his next residence. People travel for all sorts of reasons. That must have been one of his."

"It takes a long time to get here," said Madeline.

"That's why it would be wonderful to have our own place," I said. "We could leave clothing here. We could visit whenever we liked."

We continued on our way. The walk was like others we would take in years to come: a time to talk and listen to one another without much judgment or confusion. It wasn't like other family activities such as skiing, bicycling, or rollerblading. It wasn't even like hiking. We walked with deliberation and Laura's pace and observation set the even tone. It was as if we were walking through life, as if the panorama of what we saw and heard and remembered took on more importance than anything else preceding or still to come.

These walks in the country forced us to establish a good marching rhythm that was specific to our family. Each year we walked a little faster until as adolescents the children came to outpace us. Every family has its own pace and way of doing things that can be discovered only by walking together without being in much of a hurry.

As usual, a few days before we were to return home, Ursli came to visit. He seemed more comfortable and robust than he had been in Cannes. He took on an authoritative position as he walked the grounds of the farm and got close to the animals. He interviewed the farmer about the size of the property, the number of liters of milk produced by the cows, the breed of pigs being raised, the future of the farm, and so on.

"Your farmer is quite handsome," he said. "I don't see why he would be interested in his wife. She is rather plain."

Ursli spoke about men and women loving one another like a ten-year-old boy. He didn't get much of it and what he did understand he seemed to find icky. He would never change. His eternally youthful outlook appealed to Laura and me as we were changing each year due to our relationships to the children.

He and I walked from the farm to a beer hall nearby. Ursli *was* calmer than before.

"I have accepted the situation," he said. "And I am traveling more often on my own without Rolf. We are still one another's principal relationship, but now I am meeting new people. Over the winter I met a nice guy in Moscow—his name is Abdurazak—and next month he and I will go hiking in Slovenia. Perhaps you would like to join us."

"It would be difficult to return to the States and then fly back again," I said.

"It was last minute," he said. "We should have planned ahead."

"Perhaps next summer," I said.

"Yes," he said. "That would be good." He paused. "You know,

the odd thing is I don't know if Abdurazak is gay or straight. I met him at a conference. I have been to his flat. He talks about all the girlfriends he has had in the past, but he does not have one now. And I get what you would call 'vibes' from him. I think he likes me."

"Why don't you ask him?" I said. "Have you thought of that?"

"Oh, you are very conventional," he said. "No, no. It is just not done."

"What's not done?" I asked. "Asking someone you have a crush on whether or not they're gay or straight?"

"I do not have a crush on him," he said.

"Fine," I said. "But aren't you curious?"

"Does it matter so much? A person's sexuality?"

"Not to me," I said. "I thought it might to you."

"It has not come up in the conversation yet," he said.

And he followed that with a round of America-bashing that had to do with what he regarded as our base, puritanical ways of seeing the world. He seemed to mistake the puppy-dog honesty that can characterize conversations made by Americans like me with a rejection of the traditions that are necessary for civility. At the time, I was sufficiently in tune with this form of the European mentality and so began to apologize for trying to learn more by asking questions rather than waiting like Ursli, who clearly was struggling with affection for this man from Moscow. I think he enjoyed not knowing. The tension added to his desire for him.

"I just like being with him."

We finished our beer and headed back.

"This farm was a discovery," I said. "The children have been very happy."

"I can imagine," he said. "Have they taken many donkey rides?"

"Not one," I said.

"Is it that he is unfriendly?"

"No, the donkey is friendly," I said. "He just doesn't want to move. You put a kid on top of him and he stands there. He's not interested in working."

"Not very Swiss," he said.

Getting things done was a way of life for these people. The conversations over the years with Ursli had centered on facts. There was always some kind of a plan or a program to follow. Even when I visited him at his grandmother's cottage on a remote lake some summers, the talk over dinner had been about "the program for tomorrow." There always had to be something to do. I admired the ambition of the Swiss. They were no happier for it, but they managed to move forward as on a long walk with no end in sight. It was a lot like being in a family full of conundrums and the daily heat of intimacy. That effort to create and maintain our pace would be a project lasting all our lifetimes. At least I knew that.

After supper in the flat we made a plan for the next day's walk. Ursli drove to an inn. The children had been delighted by the gifts he brought with him. He always carried things made out of wood. This time it was a Swiss game the size of his palm that had to do with moving blocks to form a kind of puzzle. The game had no point and was based entirely on repetitive manipulation, but Madeline and Nicholas were good at whatever they needed to be good at in order to succeed. In that way, they were practically Swiss.

We walked until the early evening and ate fresh food by open fields while looking at the farms where generations of the same families had maintained their hold on the land. I wondered aloud about what might have happened had not my father's family been so gravely interrupted by the murders of the Holocaust.

"You and your family would be fluent in German," Ursli said, and then we made plans to return home.

SYROS

Evelyn would sit on a bench beside the outdoor track at the high school while her husband Max jogged with other couples. This was how they spent Sunday mornings. Evelyn used to run, too, until arthritis in both knees, tolerated secretly for years, put an end to that. I missed my mother-in-law's vigor.

At the insistence of her family, Evelyn decided to have knee replacement surgery. But in preparation for treatment, doctors ran routine tests and found she had lung cancer. This came as a huge surprise to everyone since Evelyn had never smoked or been unhealthy.

Evelyn was a real Pollyanna. It was the thing most of us who knew her loved most about her. She'd lived the entirety of the Blitz in London and tried to make the ordeal sound like a party in the Underground. Evelyn had a knack for lying to others, to make them feel good about themselves, and through that effort managed to make a confectionary world where what actually went on about her mattered less than how she felt about it.

It took her two and a half years to die. She carried the burden better than any of us who loved her. She knew what was happening while we could only imagine what it was like. The dying was catastrophic. The children, nine and six years old when the diagnosis of cancer was first made, looked to us as gauges. There were long periods of time when the poor woman would sit in the living room of our house with her daughters and husband and no one would say a word.

As her daughter and as a doctor, my wife was in the position of mourning the impending loss while navigating for the family with her mother's physicians. During the time of her mother's dying, Laura slept poorly. She suffered with us and at work and, of course, began to change. It was as if she were dying, too. I had never seen anything like this so I had no idea what to say or do that might be of use to her. All of us went a little crazy. Hopes predicated on fantasies seemed real, moods changed according to thoughts having nothing to do with actual observation. We tended to be miserable and frightened.

We did all we could—the children and me—to distract, comfort, and entertain Laura, but of course we failed. Often we should have said nothing, but that was impossible. There was this impulse to help and another to figure out what was happening when in fact silence would have been best. But who knows? Maybe if we had said nothing that would have been horribly painful, too. There was no way out.

The final six months of her life, Evelyn was in and out of the hospital. Laura was often absent during this time. In New Jersey with her mother or so preoccupied at home with us she couldn't think straight. I don't suppose there is any way she'll ever get over the loss. When a volcano explodes or there's an earthquake, nobody expects things to look the same again.

Evelyn died at home surrounded by her three daughters and her husband who, by that time, was genuinely confused.

"I was the one with all the heart problems," he said. He'd had surgeries and so on.

She had drifted in and out of consciousness in the few weeks remaining, sustained by morphine, and seemed to everyone to grow more beautiful. Her skin got softer and rosier and she at last was kind of calm.

To try and escape the impact of Evelyn's illness, we had continued over the two summers when she was sick to leave town. We knew the plans might be cancelled at the last possible moment and were prepared to come home early. She must have seen how much she meant to us so she said it was OK to go. Probably it was best, she said, to get rejuvenated and then come back stronger. We had no faith whatsoever in what she was saying.

We went far from home and no one followed us, but these places were modern and if necessary we could return to be with Evelyn in less than twenty-four hours.

Two women in Maui traded their home with us one of those summers. We were perched on a hill above Wailea, overlooking the Pacific and cut off from the tourist settlements on the coast.

When we tired of the water and lolling in the garden or bedroom or deck, we made a trip to Haleakala and spent three days and nights hiking inside the volcanic crater.

Then we drove to Hana. In one day we swam at four different types of beaches: black sand, green sand, red sand, white sand. The black-sand beach had been formed by relatively recent volcanic eruptions and had rocky coves and tidal pools. Then we swam with old, naked hippies at the red-sand beach. We hiked in a bamboo forest so dense we couldn't see daylight. We had no idea how we felt surrounded by all this beauty. But who does in the tropics? We were captivated. Overpowered by what we sensed around us, we paid less attention to ourselves. The landscapes and sea were violent and capacious. Our awareness of our emotions got much smaller.

The summer before Evelyn died, we traded homes with a minister and his family living in Luzern, a much-photographed Swiss city on a lake bordering four cantons. The river Reuss cuts through Luzern and its banks are lined with shops and hotels as perfectly arranged as the idea of a city rather than the place itself. Everyone looks healthy and the air smells of soap.

The first time I'd been to Luzern was in 1969 when, after visiting the village and towns in Bavaria where my father is from, my parents took my sister and me to spend a few days in Chateau

Gutsch, which is a posh hotel on a hilltop above the city center. We had arrived late and the clerk said that according to his records we didn't have a reservation. My father, screwy from visiting his home where almost everyone he knew had been murdered, flipped out and seemed to threaten the hotelier with murder if rooms couldn't be found for us. The remedy was provided. Two suites, overlooking the lake, with private terraces. I must have taken hundreds of pictures of the room, the terrace, pots of geraniums, turrets, and balustrades.

From the terrace, I took more photos. Mountains, the river, and the lake. I had never seen anything so beautiful. The hillsides and Alps looked as if they'd been sculpted and freshly seeded. Nothing appeared to be placed at random. The world is out of control, but the Swiss had purpose. They derived life's meaning from geography.

And to look down on the dull, orderly, spotless city was to recognize architecture that is practical, toylike, stripped of personality or imperial motive, and designed to convey a muted response to the Alps. The outside world might do what it liked, but Switzerland would remain the same, forever, no matter what took place. The country is dull, but dull the way a patient mother is dull. No surprises, no effusion, no noise whatsoever. Such a mother exhausts a child.

We had been miserable the moment we had arrived in Germany. We drove through all these places familiar to my father, but now the buildings had different functions. Everyone he knew had been deported and killed or long gone. It was like looking at things none of which had the right labels. Everything was tinged with regret and desire so we couldn't see clearly. We pictured things as they once were, not as we saw them. No one we spoke to and nothing we saw seemed connected to the past. So at last we were left alone with our sentiments, the four of us, driving through the agricultural landscape and then past factories. In the cities, too, the walks we took as a family lacked a good pace. We walked too slowly, linger-

ing in front of places that meant something to my father and nothing to us, or we walked in haste. We were never normal, whatever
normal is, and we were certainly not like ourselves before we left
home.

Evelyn's cancer got worse, it got better, but no one could face
the facts. Laura was on the phone with doctors. No one had anything good to say.

Arriving in Switzerland while Evelyn was dying back home
made us more keenly aware of how much we loved her. Sitting next
to a woman we loved had been unbearable and we had struggled
then not to think of how much losing her would mean to us.
Sometimes only physical distance from those we love can encour-
age us to recognize their importance.

Once in Switzerland, we recalled hiking with her in the Ticino
when Madeline was about eight weeks old. I could picture us walking by Lake Lugano. But above all it was the silence that magnified
her importance. And the things about Switzerland I had once found
annoying were now restorative. Obsession with cleanliness, need for
decorum, how people mourn and celebrate without fanfare.

The minister's house was austere and near the lake and river. We
went to the marvelous cheese market. We swam and hiked. The
children were old enough to walk great distances and twice we
went deep into the mountains, going from inn to inn, taking the
opportunity on these marches to talk about Evelyn. She wasn't all
we talked about, but inside a glacial bowl or on top of a ridge, she
was in our thoughts in a way that the distractions at home made
impossible. We were very unhappy.

We had started taking the children on hikes when they were
only weeks old. For years, we had carried them in a Snugli or a
backpack. By the time they were able to walk, they thought hiking
was normal. The summer we visited a Swiss farm had convinced
them of that. When they complained, we gave them chocolate.

We went through a lot of chocolate. It was necessary to be out all day, as much as the weather allowed, and hear what the kids had been thinking while Evelyn was dying. They rarely said anything. I suppose they didn't want to upset us. But the opportunity to enjoy long walks together had to be enough. We felt rather Swiss in our avoidance. We thought about Evelyn, but it was the scenery—the magnificence of the Alps—we spoke about most.

One day we hiked to a remote inn in a valley near Kandersteg where the proprietors and staff and other guests only spoke Swiss-German. The inn had no lights. At night we read by candles in our beds, under thick eiderdowns stuffed with goose feathers, with the windows open to let in cold mountain air.

"This is very romantic," said Laura, putting down her book.

So we blew out the lights.

When Evelyn died, none of us knew what to do. The funeral was on a Thursday. A lot of people drove in from out of town. Laura made a speech at the service because neither of her sisters had her medical training. She was accustomed to talking about the dead with compassion and detachment. One of the things she said had to do with Evelyn's childhood on Great Portland Street in London:

"My mother used to say when we were growing up that she thought as a child that she lived in a neighborhood filled with princesses. She would see these gorgeous women—in big, colorful dresses, perfectly coiffed hair, and lots of makeup—stepping out of big, black London taxis. Night after night. Later she discovered that the women had been prostitutes. But that was Evelyn. Always seeing the best in people."

A lot of the mourners came up to us to tell us how they felt. One man, an oncologist who had been her friend before she got sick, did a pantomime. He rocked back on his left heel, spread out both arms with a sad grin, and then kissed Laura before taking a seat. We went back to the house and almost everyone sat on folded rental chairs. We ate cold cuts on paper plates and talked about stuff having nothing whatsoever to do with how any us felt. There wasn't any point.

The house was filled with her things. Evelyn collected antiques. English hunting prints, plates picturing the Queen, impractical chairs and tables, and dozens of clocks.

The clocks defined Evelyn's sense of interior design. Every room had at least three clocks. Not all of them indicated the correct time. There was a constant ticking sound and a lot of bonging and gonging at different hours. It was like living in a factory. The noise was so deafening that the first night I spent at the house years ago I got up at 3 A.M. to sleep in my car in the driveway. Laura had spent her childhood in a house of clocks.

"Where are you going this summer?" Evelyn's friend Seymour asked us.

Laura's family called him The Frozen Banana King. Seymour and his wife said they had invented the world's first frozen banana, dipped in chocolate and sold in Asbury Park.

"We're going to Greece," I said, "but we have no desire to go anywhere."

"Greece," he said. "You're gonna love Greece."

Seymour spoke with authority. Say what you like, his manner implied, I'm the one who made the fortune selling bananas. His arrogance was based on fruit.

"We went to Greece years ago," he said. "Beautiful. Very, very beautiful. The ruins, the beaches. You'll love it."

"We've never been," I said.

"We were on a cruise," he said, "and spent a couple of days in Athens. It's a big city. But the islands, oh boy, they're something else really."

"We're going to Syros," I said.

"Which is?"

"One of the islands."

"I don't know it."

I gave Seymour the rundown. Syros, center of the Cyclades: not as beautiful as Santorini, not as hip as Mykonos, not as historical as Rhodes, not as remote as Limnos or Lipsi or Tilos, but instead, we had heard, more authentically Greek and unspoilt than any other island due to its large, year-round population.

We were exchanging homes and cars with a retired military couple from the United States who had been based in Germany for decades and then bought a cottage on Syros for their retirement.

"I'm sure they're CIA," I said. "I just hope no one blows up their car while we're in it."

"Oh, come on," he said.

"I'm sure we'll be fine," I said.

I told Seymour why I thought Gladys and her husband were CIA. All those years in Germany, I explained, "administrative work" in Moscow, flights to visit "friends in Virginia," the way her e-mails seemed coded. When Seymour asked me what I meant by "coded," I couldn't explain.

"But it's pretty obvious," I said.

"Uh-huh," he said.

He looked around the room for someone else to talk to, but the others were engaged in conversation and, anyhow, it would have meant getting up, which is difficult to do after eating frozen chocolate bananas for half a century.

"At least I think they're CIA," I said.

"It sounds exciting," he said. "You'll have fun."

"I'm sure we will," I said. "I bet being on the CIA payroll all those years provided Gladys and her husband with a pot of money. I figure it's a guarantee that the house will be well equipped."

"Have you seen pictures?" asked Seymour.

"Sure," I said. "Over the past three months Gladys sent dozens. She's an amateur photographer and just bought a digital camera. So we received pictures of the market, the town square, views from the garden, and of course the house. It's on a cliff overlooking the

Aegean and Gladys says you can see boats going to and from Piraeus."

"You'll visit other islands."

"Sure," I said. "Other islands. You bet. I've done research. Mykonos, whatever. We have time."

"We enjoyed practically everything," said Seymour. "You will, too."

I expected Evelyn to step out of the kitchen holding a tray of things to eat.

"I hope so. I don't know if we will. We probably will. I think we probably will. I wonder. What kind of place would CIA officers find attractive?"

"It will be very nice," said Seymour.

"We're looking forward to it," I said. "But is it right? Maybe it is right."

"What kind of right or wrong?" asked Seymour.

"We never knew whether or not we'd be going," I said. "If Evelyn hadn't died yesterday . . ."

"Of course not," he said.

"What if she had lived another month or two?"

"No, no, she was too sick. You know that."

"We're scheduled to leave Wednesday night," I said. "So what would have happened if she had lived longer? Would I have left with the children? Would we all have stayed home? Gladys and her husband are arriving the day we leave, they're taking our house. So we would have had to leave. We would have had to come here. And now what are we supposed to do? Get on a plane five days from now? Does that make any sense? Laura's in no shape to go. None of us are."

"The cold cuts come from a local guy," said Seymour. "Larry something. We've used him for other affairs. I think they do a nice job. Don't you?"

"Greece will be nice," I said. "Don't you think? Laura deserves a rest. There is nothing to do where we're going. Only swim and see ruins."

"You know? I wish I was going on a trip," said Seymour. "But we're not."

"What will you do?"

"We have a place down the shore," he said.

"Right," I said.

"It's nice there so we like it. Friends will come to see us. Maybe Max will also visit. That would be nice."

"I bet he will," I said.

"You never know with Max," he said.

I kept waiting for Seymour to tell me not to go. But either he thought we should go or he wanted to say what he believed would be most conducive to my sanity, or most likely he had lost so many people he loved he knew it didn't matter. I resolved to tell Laura we couldn't go.

The flight from Boston to Athens was indirect. We landed in Zurich and waited two hours for the next flight. Then we got on another plane.

All I expected from Athens was dirt and chaos. I wasn't disappointed. The only thing I hadn't anticipated was just how bad it would be.

Greeks regard smoking as a social obligation. Living in Cambridge my family regarded smoking as second only to child abuse.

"This is disgusting," said Madeline.

We were in the airport terminal. She held her nose.

"I can't breathe," she said.

"What's disgusting?" I asked.

"The smoking," she said.

"I have no idea what you're talking about," I said.

Her brother lay prostrate and performed what in ideal circumstances would have been a superb and convincing imitation of a drowning child. Where had he learned to do this? Was this what he was being taught in the private school where we sent him? How to entertain adults? I thought him marvelous. The twenty grand we spent each year to have him educated was well spent.

"Get off the floor," said Laura. "It's filthy."

Hundreds of cigarette butts lay near Nick.

"Yes, get off the floor," I said. "We're guests here and you're making a spectacle of yourself."

All of us were exhausted. We stood by the carousel waiting for our last pieces of luggage. An hour had gone by and we'd just about given up.

"C'mon, Dad," Nick said. He stood up and brushed ash off his knees. "You have to admit smoking is disgusting."

"I don't have to admit anything," I said. "Why should I? I hadn't even noticed the smoke until you mentioned it."

I had bought a box of first-rate Cuban cigars at the Duty Free in Zurich and intended to smoke every single one of them that month.

Another troubling fact became apparent. Greeks find it necessary to congregate in well-packed masses. What cultural purpose is served, I wonder, by crowding in? Is this a calculated move to overcome the boredom and loneliness which accompany standing alone? I doubt it. But whatever the reasons, if there are any, the four of us were soon hemmed in by hundreds of Greeks returning home. Unable to breathe, exhausted, miserable, and still without luggage, our mood turned homicidal.

Before we began to say things to one another—cruel and insightful things we were certain to regret having said for the rest of our lives—the carousel came to life. A mad scramble started. We were shoved aside and stepped on.

"Aren't you going to fight back?" asked Nick.

"No," I said.

"Are you a wimp?" he asked.

"I can't do this right now," I said.

"Can't do what?" he asked.

"Can't have this conversation."

"Why not?" he asked.

I made my way to the other side of the carousel. Madeline came along. Nick stayed with his mother.

"Well, this is starting out well," Madeline said.

"Don't you start," I said.

"Start what? I haven't done anything."

"What's that supposed to mean?" I asked.

"You're insane," she said.

"I don't mean to be," I said, weakening suddenly.

Of all the people I have known, Madeline is the one who causes me most to reconsider my reactions to what goes on around me. Laura and I spent more time at home than in offices for many years after the children were born. Madeline and I were together more than we were apart from her birth until she went to nursery school and I think I learned from her what people I love want most from me.

"Just calm down then," she said. "It's bad enough."

Being scolded by a twelve-year-old forced me to realize that as the organizer of the holidays it was my duty to face forward at all times and never to complain. It was easier to accept criticism from Madeline rather than her brother, as she meant what she said as an act of reform while he was toppling over busts of Stalin.

"Mmm," I said, which was becoming my answer to everything.

At last the bags arrived. We made our way to a stand of tiny taxis. A driver managed to stuff his trunk with our luggage. Then we piled in.

"Grande Bretagne," I said. My voice deepened with pride. I sounded stuffy, elongating the "grande" and going up on the "Bretagne." The luxury hotel was originally built as a palace. During World War II the British high command had made it their headquarters and before that the Nazis had done the same. I had booked two rooms for our first and last nights.

"Wha'?" said the driver. At least he meant "wha'?" But of course he used the Greek equivalent: *Ti*.

"Grande Bretagne," I said again. "You must know it. Grande Bretagne. Grande Bretagne? Grand Bretagne!"

"Wha'?"

I wrote the hotel's name down and handed him the slip of paper. He studied it. Then he sighed and looked out the window.

"Grande Bretagne!" I said. "Grande Bretagne! Grande Bretagne!"

"Don't lose your patience, honey," said Laura. "You know what happens when you lose your patience."

"No, what?"

"It only makes things worse."

"Oh, really?"

"Hang in there, Dad," said Nick.

Squeezed into the front seat with several pieces of carry-on, more aware of heat and fatigue than I had been in years, I was ready to get out and find another cab.

"I quit," I said.

I was having thoughts best managed through resignation rather than expression of sheer rage. After all, I was unfamiliar with the Athenian legal system and had no wish to spend the holidays tied up in the courts.

"You can't quit," said Laura.

"I can," I said. Indeed, it was a pleasure to indulge myself after a long flight over by getting rid of the burden of being a parent and returning instead to the more familiar turf of being a bad child.

"You're acting like a child," she said.

"Hey," said Madeline, "that's unfair!"

"And disrespectful," said Nick.

Their private school had convinced them, through years of

propaganda cleverly disguised as classroom instruction, that "self-esteem" was more important than learning how to read and write. It saved the administration thousands of dollars in the long run. As long as the children felt good about themselves, they had no explaining to do.

"Pull yourself together," said Laura.

A short period of time elapsed. No one stirred. Then I found a photograph of the hotel.

"Here," I said. "Grande Bretagne."

"Ah, *Grande Bretagne*," he said. Hadn't the Greeks been the first to turn irony into art? "OK, no problem."

That was the moment I realized with quiet terror that the next month would be more of the same. A calculated incomprehension tempered by deceit and faulty national infrastructure. I recognized the pattern. Before the children had been born, I had come across this sort of nonsense in Mexico, Mali, and Nicaragua. Why hadn't we been warned? I would have prepared. But now, in the taxi zooming into traffic, narrowly missing pedestrians, spewing black clouds of exhaust, it was too late. No getting around it. We were in the Third World where nothing works.

I try not to judge my circumstances. Where I live, everything is considered relative. All cultures are equal, the saying goes in Cambridge, and standards don't matter nearly as much as people's feelings. Above all, don't hurt anyone's feelings! That is the one standard.

On the ride into town, I therefore struggled to remind myself that no matter how bad it got—and I knew for certain it would get very bad—life was far more terrible for locals than it would be for us. After all, we knew what it was like to be in a place where things actually functioned. Yes, we would become frustrated by the inefficiency we were sure to encounter, but *at least we hadn't gotten used to it*. We had not given up. Nor would we give up here, I decided. Being stuck in traffic gave me a lot of time to think.

Then the driver took turns at forbidden speeds and ran many

red lights. He smoked a lot, too. Driving was an excuse to smoke. He smoked better than he drove.

On the straightaways he hit speeds that previously had been unimaginable. We glimpsed the sea, but it was a blur. Most Greeks live in a blur. They can only look back. They had invented civilization. So why bother with trying to make things work today?

The Grande Bretagne is on Syntagma Square, in the center of the city, within steps of the Parliament and the first McDonald's to open in Greece. When we pulled up to the entrance of the hotel, a tall, amber-colored man who looked Egyptian got some boys under his command to unload the taxi. All the hotel employees had on dark green uniforms and military caps. They looked as if they were playing at being soldiers.

The lobby was cool, clean, and filled with big bowls of flowers. The place stank of lilies. A John Coltrane tune played through hidden speakers. We were as far removed from what I'd seen to be daily life in Athens as the moon is from the earth.

Laura passed out a few minutes after stretching out on the bed in our room. I took the children to see the Acropolis. We walked up a long alley lined with shops selling backgammon sets, obscene T-shirts, plaster replicas of ruins, and many other things with the words "Athens" and "Greece" printed on them. I found a nice pair of oven mitts.

It was early. Vendors outnumbered tourists. Salespeople we encountered had the sleepy, guilty look of the few who fool the rest of us. They had no confidence in what stuffed their shelves and windows—even a chimp could see it was junk—but selling it hour after hour, day after day, for years on end, had enabled them to experience an altered state of consciousness. They paid rent, utility bills, car payments, insurance, for food, clothing, appliances, boats, and automobiles; for vacations and visits to the dentist—all from selling horrible little souvenirs. They obviously didn't believe in what they were doing, but that was the wonder.

Normally, I had been informed, the line to enter the Acropolis is long, but we had no trouble getting in. A couple of elderly German groups followed their guides, who kept them in order by holding up an umbrella and shouting out explanations. I thought of the scene in an Indiana Jones movie where a Nazi's head explodes after he steals secrets from a crypt.

"I want an ice cream," said Nick.

"There is no ice cream," I said. "These are ruins. Maybe there was once ice cream here, but not anymore."

"I know that," he said. "I'm not stupid. I saw ice cream across the street from the entrance."

"You did? Oh, right. That place. That place looked awful. And expensive. What was it? Four dollars for a single cone? Outrageous."

"So what? I'm hungry. I didn't eat on the plane."

Ever since I had praised Madeline years ago for rejecting an airline meal, she and Nick had refused all solid food while flying. They always arrived irritable and famished.

"Tell you what," I said. "Why don't we walk around the Acropolis for about an hour and then I'll buy you a treat?"

"What if I decide I don't want anything?" asked Nick. "Does that mean we can leave now?"

In the fall, entering fourth grade, Nick would study ancient Greece for the year. But his third grade curriculum—called the "central subject" at his school—had been the ocean. It had consisted primarily of feeding tropical fish in an aquarium in the classroom. Then each one of the children took turns saying how they felt about feeding the fish. At the end of the year, the teacher took them on a whale watch. Then they had returned to the school to draw pictures of the whales. Some of the pictures looked like whales. All of the children were told they were delightful, which of course they were. The Acropolis had as yet no meaning for him.

"No," I said.

The wind blew dirt and dust in our eyes so we sat down.

"I've always wanted to see the Acropolis," I told the children. I read to them from a guidebook purchased back home. "Can you imagine what it was like thousands of years ago? And now this is all that's left."

"The Greeks may have died out," said Madeline, "but they left their culture behind."

We experienced the wonder that visitors to the Acropolis have always known. We lacked with them the words to describe what we observed, being more aware of what we felt than of what we saw. Our critical faculties were ruined by the audacity of it all. We had been reduced to tourists.

Then exhaustion overcame us. We made our way back to the hotel. I bought Nick ice cream near the Agora and then complained to him about how much it cost.

We woke Laura up and told her she had to see the Acropolis that night before it closed. The children said they didn't want to go back, but I told them they had no choice. They said I was stupid and Laura asked why I woke her up to hear arguing. I said it wasn't my fault. The children were bad. We had bad children. The children said they weren't bad and then Laura threw us out.

While she showered and dressed, I watched CNN with Nicholas and Madeline. JFK, Jr., had just gone down off Martha's Vineyard. I know he's not his father, but I felt an enormity of sadness which utterly surprised me.

Then I went downstairs and had a martini. The bar was elegant. Polished wood and lots of glass.

On the walk over, Laura didn't seem to notice the vendors.

Inside the Acropolis, she said, "These must be the most beautiful buildings I've ever seen."

Then for over an hour Laura looked at what remained. The children said they were hungry and tired and that got her mad, but in the end Madeline and Nicholas wouldn't leave her side. I think Laura could have spent days inside the Acropolis.

That night we ate a good meal of grilled fish and vegetables and boiled grains at O Platanos, a restaurant with outdoor tables I'd read about. It was becoming more difficult to satisfy my hunger. Everything tasted the same or had no taste or lacked any connection to the place where it was prepared and to the people who did the cooking. The restaurants we saw in Athens that night were filled with tourists. But we had been lucky to find a spot with originality serving food that had flavor.

We flew to Syros the next morning. We were met by a friend of the CIA couple. She was originally from Australia and had moved to Syros after marrying a local who then left her the year before in order to marry another Australian. He went to Athens to manage a hotel. She was raising their eleven-year-old boy, which wasn't easy. He missed his father terribly. Did we know of any jobs in the States? Would Nick be interested in playing with her son some afternoon? We learned these things on the twenty-minute ride to the house where we were staying.

Then she showed us the bedrooms, storage closets, the kitchen and bathrooms, and how to operate appliances.

The house had been built on a bare hill overlooking the sea. Its exterior walls were painted white and the roof was the color of clay like all the other homes on the island. To reach the front door, we had to walk through a garden with a grape arbor above a table and chairs. Nearby was an outdoor shower.

We put things away. Then I looked for clues around the house that would reveal intimate things about its owners. I was unable to find any equipment which might be used for spying. The only personal item in the place was a book on how to quit drinking. But why start? Then the children began quarreling about who got to sleep in which bed and I had to put away the question for later in order to resolve their dispute.

Laura met me in the garden. We looked out at the water. She appeared sad, but defiant and very beautiful. To the east and north were barren land and a few houses. To the west, past a cove, stood two hills on which nine metal frames for houses had been built. The Australian had explained to us that the laws in Greece had changed and that as of last year no new construction was allowed on the coastlines of the island.

"So a wealthy Athenian lawyer quickly built the nine sites," she said. "It will take years before the construction is completed. But when it's done, she ought to make a fortune, I reckon. That's how it is in Greece. They all play around with the law. They regard the law as a joke."

The nine unfinished sites looked like a conceptual art project, the black metal cubes on cement platforms symbolizing something and the rust-colored hills symbolizing something else.

"I'm so glad we came here," said Laura.

She was no one I knew anymore. I was trying to convince myself I didn't mind the change. Not that what I thought mattered. Whatever made her miserable made me miserable, too.

"I had to do it all," Laura said. "I had to negotiate with the doctors. She was in a lot of pain at the end, but I think she was finally ready to die. She let go."

We talked some more about depressing things. Then we went into Hermoupolis, the capital of Syros and the center of the Cycladic islands. Due to its large year-round population, working harbor, and shops which sell practical and useful goods, tourists don't matter as much as its residents. We parked at the end of the harbor and walked past about a dozen cafés and restaurants before reaching the daily market which is held in an alley off the main square.

On the way, we passed by wooden racks inside meshed wire cages. Octopi were left to dry on these racks. Purple, white, and black, their tentacles stretched to the asphalt. We were told the fishermen beat them against rocks and then dried their bodies out. The animals later appeared on restaurant menus doused with olive oil, vinegar, salt, pepper, and parsley.

At the entrance of the alley where the market was held, we stopped inside a shop we then went to daily. Fresh feta, bowls of yogurt, local wines, caper berries, olive oil, and preserved olives.

Past this store were open-air, wooden palettes of figs, watermelons, eggplants, onions, peppers, tomatoes, and fish. There was a barber to the right and a few butchers on side streets who sold lamb, chicken, and pork.

Just beyond the market were a bakery and a shop selling roasted seeds and nuts. Islanders lined up to buy a variety of breads. Across the alley was a café. The side streets, alley, shops, and cafés were filled each morning.

Visits to the market became the high point of our day. The produce and fruit were positively second-rate: spoiled, dull in flavor, and soft in texture. Sardines or anchovies were usually the only fish available. Meats were fatty. But the breads, seeds, cheeses, and olives were delicious and besides, we told ourselves, this was local and indigenous culture, a chance to rub elbows with Greeks who did not live in comparison to tourists.

We didn't understand anything beyond *kalimera* (good morning) and *efcharisto* (thank you) and *parakalo* (please). We couldn't read well either. I recognized letters from fraternity signs. I'd bought cassettes to study the language, but what had I learned?

After shopping, we went to the town's main square at the end of the market alley. The square, the size of a football field, is made up of huge, smooth marble slabs and lined by cafés and restaurants on three sides and a beautiful city hall along its entire length. At midnight the square fills up with hundreds of families. Each morning we had it to ourselves.

We fell in love with Hermoupolis. It didn't have ruins and most of its shops and restaurants were awful, but the harbor, narrow streets, steep hills to the upper city, and even the residents provided us with a sense of what Greece must have been like before it became inundated with tourists and chucked everything in order to cater to them.

Nicholas raced each day in the town square, like a Greek child, and Madeline took it in. Laura moved slowly. As usual, her passion for observing was greater than her desire to remark on what she saw. Her quiet had of course deepened since Evelyn got sick and died, but not just from despair. It was as if she had developed a carapace like a beetle.

We would often stop at the first café on the square. Then the children began to tell us about the year at school. Now as always they hardly mentioned Evelyn. So much of family life takes place in what's not said.

On our first drive back to the house, we stopped at a fruit and vegetable store and in pantomime asked for charcoal and lighter fluid we needed to make fires in the grill. But that night we ate at a taverna in the cove below us.

It was simple, well-lit, and no more than fifteen yards from the water. The menu was printed in Greek and English. We ate in a room without windows and Laura and I drank large bottles of beer.

Everything seemed good at first, but after the first bite we realized it all tasted the same. Salad of tomatoes, onions, lettuce, and feta cheese, tiny fried fish, crispy and salty, yogurt and fish roe, some big beans in tomato sauce. The dominant flavors were of salt or olive oil.

When we left at midnight to climb the hill to our house, people were just arriving. We'd been the only guests not speaking Greek.

Soon we adapted. We ate at ten or eleven at night and then talked and played Hearts under candlelight in the garden until one. Stars were visible through the arbor. I thought of the ancient Greeks making war and navigating with that canopy and those constellations, how by naming the universe they could better pretend to outlast the short terms they'd been given.

Then we did not get out of bed before noon. After a drive to town, we swam in the cove and returned home to nap.

The beach was littered with cigarette butts and clouds of smoke above the bathers. I read John Cheever's journals and tried not to think about the smoke and dirt. But we thought about the smoke and dirt. So we stopped swimming each day.

Then what were we supposed to do? It was too hot to do anything. We started to go to Hermoupolis to eat lunch, but the restaurants served horrible food. How could anyone delight in salads of soggy tomatoes, discolored onions, sour-tasting feta cheese or tiny, greasy fish the size of baby fingers fried in cups of reused oil or thick, fatty chunks of grilled lamb, all washed down with pine-resin-flavored wine? Whose idea was it to put resin in the wine, anyway? We heard resin had been added hundreds of years ago in order to keep invaders from drinking the wine. The Greeks had a plan. They would develop awful-tasting cuisine no one else could tolerate. Their entire gastronomy was based on a conspiracy.

The children began to weaken.

"We're never coming back," they said. "We hate it here, there's nothing to do. How can you eat the food?"

"Don't be silly," I said. "Everything is delicious."

"It's not," said Nicholas. "You don't like it either."

"I love it," I said. "It's the best food I've ever had in my life."

"This is why I don't talk to you," he said. "I'm going to tell Mommy."

"You go ahead," I said. "She'll tell you the same thing."

"Nick," she said, "there's nothing we can do about it, honey. Let's make the most of it. Let's try to have a good time. We're on vacation."

Within a week of our visit, Laura had limited herself to eating Greek salads.

"Let's explore the island," I suggested. "There must be food somewhere. It will be an adventure."

"It will not be an adventure," Nicholas said. "It will be hot and stupid."

"Oh, you say that now," I said, "but wait. You'll see. It will be magical and unforgettable, the experience of a lifetime. Who knows what we'll find? We're on an island. Maybe we'll find buried treasure."

"I doubt it," he said.

But he was softening.

We piled into the beaten-up station wagon Gladys had left us and drove to Kini, a fishing village where the CIA couple had friends. It was odd how the beauty of the island—its bare hills and stark vistas and long views of the sea—contrasted with a cuisine that failed to take flavors into consideration. Were the Greeks so awestruck by the magnificence of their world that they had no time to spend in kitchens? But France and Italy were beautiful, too, and they had good food. No, that couldn't be it. They were simply lazy.

The couple in Kini denied any affiliation with international spying, which came as no surprise really. I hadn't expected them to come out and admit to anything. But what I hadn't anticipated was the way they pretended to be ordinary innkeepers with hobbies and eccentricities. I had thought they might hint at their history of espionage and covert action, to be unable to contain their enthusiasm for subterfuge, to let slip some fact that would reveal their origins and occupation. But if they really were spies, they were awfully good at concealing the truth.

First of all, they were thrilled to see us. Life on Syros was so without meaning that the arrival of complete strangers was cause for celebration. They took us into their home and told us every single detail of their life stories. This enterprise included, but was not limited to, rummaging through shoe boxes of filed photographs. We knew we were really in it for it when they staged a mock fight about how they had met.

Then Helga, a former Tyrolean, took us on a tour of the village, which was made up of run-down cafés, a grocery store selling German foodstuffs, and a filthy beach.

"It's paradise," she said. She spread her arms wide to make the point. "I have found heaven!"

Her accented English, marking her forever as a German speaker by birth, made it undeniable. What she saw had to be preferable to a childhood spent eating sausages and potatoes in a mountaintop village, for indeed she sauntered around the decrepit surroundings as if in Valhalla. I saw beer bottles on the street, stray dogs, brimming garbage cans, and clouds of cigarette smoke. She saw angels and fairy princesses and smiling faces and baskets of manna. It was uncanny how she greeted the unshaven shopkeepers. I found the whole exercise depressing. Both the circumstances I observed as well as her monumental delusion. I began to wonder if she was psychotic.

Then she said, "I must show you the cats."

She told us about the cats with something beyond pride, in a tone more indicative of the sort of hubris I associate with historically validated figures like Napoleon or her own countryman, Herr Hitler.

"I am the cat lady," she said.

And although she had no costume or brochures to substantiate the title, it soon became clear she was telling the truth. We had left her inn and made an abrupt turn down a street away from the harbor when we came upon a warehouse. She slid open its doors to show us huge bags of cat food.

"I sterilize them," she said. "In this way, the stray cat problem of Kini has been solved! Greece, you see, is overrun by stray cats. They are everywhere! Inhabiting doorways and town squares, along the beaches, everywhere you look you see them. Cats!"

She took a measuring cup and began to fill stainless steel bowls at her feet. Then she lined up a dozen bowls on the cement loading dock attached to the warehouse. We circled her and waited.

"Mr. Schminki!" she cried out. "Oh, Mr. Schminki! Mr. Schminki is my favorite. He is my favorite love cat. I call him my love cat. I love Mr. Schminki."

"Dad," whispered Nick, "what is wrong with her?"

"Shh," I said, "we'll talk about this later."

"Mr. Schminki," she said. "Blinky! Osiris! Blue Bells! Hydrangea! Poodles! Here, Poodles, Poodles, Poodles! Pss, pss, pss, pss."

Within moments we were surrounded by over two dozen cats. I had never before seen a pack of cats. More aggressive when in a group, they came up to us and began to nip and paw at our feet.

"They are perfectly harmless," said Helga. "Oh, look, there he is! Mr. Schminki!"

Her love cat was the largest of the pack. A tom that had to be over twenty-five pounds. He prowled and banged into the others to get to her side.

"I put sterilizer into the food," said Helga, stooping to pick him up. Her back hunched forward from the weight. She and her husband had never had children. I am certain that late at night she dressed the cats up.

It was getting dark and lights or reflectors cannot be found on most roads in Syros. Helga had suggested we all dine at a restaurant operated by the former mayor of Kini. We left at once.

"What do you think is wrong with her?" asked Madeline on the car ride home.

"She is insane," I said.

"That's not nice," said Laura. "And not true. She is helping the cats survive. If she didn't sterilize them, the cats would starve. There are too many."

"So you think she sterilizes cats because she's nice?" I asked.

"Of course," she said. "Why else would she do it?"

"Because she's insane," I said.

"That's harsh, Dad," said Madeline.

"Well, anyway, it's what I thought," I said.

Then we argued all the way home and ate dinner and went to bed angry at one another.

"We have to get off the island," I said the next morning.

"Fine," said Laura.

"Don't *you* want to see other islands?" I asked.

"It doesn't matter what I want," she said. "You've already made up your mind."

"No, I haven't."

"Fine," she said. "I do want to see other islands. Is that better?"

We drove to Hermoupolis to buy tickets for the boat ride. Lining the picturesque harbor were several little family-run travel agencies. They were identical and each consisted of a desk, a fan, a calendar, posters showing islands and ruins, a cash register, and an agent smoking a cigarette.

"We want to go to Santorini," I told an agent.

"When do you want to go?" he asked.

"As soon as possible," I said.

"You must give me a time," he said.

"Fine," I said. "Today."

"That's impossible," he said.

"How about tomorrow morning? First thing tomorrow morning."

"No, no boats tomorrow," he said.

"When are there boats?" I asked.

"When do you want to go?"

"It doesn't matter," I said. "Day after tomorrow?"

"No, I'm sorry."

"Is there a schedule?"

"Of course there is a schedule," he said. "What do you think?"

"So when do boats leave from Syros for Santorini?"

"When do you want to go?" he asked.

"This week," I said. "This week would be fine."

"You must choose a day," he said. "I cannot choose for you."

"Oh, how about Monday? And if Monday doesn't work, just go to Tuesday and so on until you get to Sunday."

"There are no boats on Sunday," he said.

"Right," I said. " 'Never on Sunday,' right?"

"You are making a joke?" he asked.

"No," I said.

"I am a busy man," he said.

"I can see that," I said. "How about Monday then?"

"Fine," he said. He began to flip pages through a binder that looked like a real schedule book. Just like where we stood looked like a real office. Just like the agent looked like a real agent. "Tomorrow there is a boat at nine in the morning. Good?"

"I thought you said there were no boats tomorrow."

"Do you want to go or not?" he said.

"Fine," I said. "Perfect. Tomorrow is perfect."

I had the name of a posh hotel on Santorini I had read about and so I booked rooms for three nights.

We arrived the next morning at the designated dock.

"No, no," a stevedore told us. "You must go to *that* dock. Hurry!"

He pointed across the harbor. We ran to the dock he indicated. Then we saw a boat arriving in the harbor and heading toward the first dock. We ran back with our luggage and joined a crowd. Old locals, men dressed in traditional island garb, drinking retsina or ouzo despite the early hour, pointed and laughed at us. Most of them had no teeth. Reaching the point of embarkation, we were pressed together tightly in an area cordoned off with ropes. Movement was impossible until the crew on board lowered a ramp and screamed at us in Greek. Then all the Greeks pushed forward and in the midst of them we got on the boat.

The boat was sleek, white, and modern in appearance.

"Wow," I said to my sleepy, angry family, "a hydrofoil. I've always wanted to ride a hydrofoil."

"What's a hydrofoil?" asked Nicholas.

"I'm not sure," I said, "but somehow it hovers above the water as it picks up speed. It's sort of like flying."

We took seats downstairs. Passengers sat on plastic, turquoise chairs bolted into rows as at a movie theater. A TV screen was on. It would show a steady blur accompanied by a garbled soundtrack in Greek all the way to Santorini. As soon as the boat left the harbor, people began smoking. Then we reached the open seas. I tried to think about the romance and heroism of the ancient Greeks. Madeline and Nicholas got sick. As it was the first time they had ever complained of the effects of motion sickness, we had not come prepared with medicine. They lay on deck like gasping fish.

"Isn't this marvelous?" I asked Laura. "Can you picture the Greeks returning home from Troy?"

"They wouldn't be returning home from Troy," she said. "We are heading south."

"Are you trying to pick an argument?" I asked. "Please don't start with me."

" 'Don't start with me?' Isn't that what your father always says? *You* are turning into your father."

Laura and I had agreed years before that I would never compare her to her parents and she, in turn, would never compare me to mine. The agreement had followed a set of comparisons.

"What's that?" I said. "Are you comparing me to my father?"

"Yes," she said. "And what are you going to do about it?"

"I am not going to do anything about it," I said.

"I didn't think so," she said.

"Not now, anyway," I said.

"Are you threatening me?" she said.

"Please stop fighting," said Madeline. She lay at Laura's feet and spoke in a drowsy voice. "I'm sick."

"I'm sick, too," said Nicholas.

"We're not fighting," I said. "We're having a discussion."

"It sounds like you're fighting," said Nicholas.

"I know that," I said. "But we're not. Sometimes discussions sound a lot like arguments. The difference is often subtle."

The boat catapulted forward and bounced up and down and then side to side. We saw the horizon and the water as if they were circling unsteadily on a TV screen. I clutched the railing and watched the children slide on the floor.

"We'll be there soon," I said.

At last we saw Santorini. The island is the rim of a volcano that exploded about thirty-five hundred years ago. Smaller bodies of land are visible off its center and the northern tip: Thirasia, Nea Kameni, Palaia Kameni. What had once been the volcanic crater is now a harbor. Cliffs go down to the water from the rim. Nothing could have prepared us for the beauty of what remained. A dream of a place rather than the place itself, sheer, narrow rouge-colored cliffs that fell almost as if an embrace of the sea. The size of everything geological had been reduced. We were only seeing the remnants of a larger, greater world. A lot is left to the imagination. What is missing is as significant as what is seen. When the volcano exploded, it caused a tsunami. These two events destroyed everyone and everything. We were getting pleasure from the effects of a disaster.

A man from our hotel met us at the landing. Except for the tuxedo he was wearing, he looked poor. He took our things to a van and drove us to the hotel.

On the way, we passed by dozens of holiday homes and garish hotels. The road went beside a cliff. Our hotel was next to a cluster of whitewashed houses that had once been a village.

"Welcome to Villa Vedema," said a thin fellow at the hotel's entrance. He looked as if he would be more comfortable doing anything else. He looked embarrassed to be working. "Why don't you follow me?"

We felt at once we had no business being there. He showed us into a cavernous room and instructed a woman to serve us drinks.

Then we were asked all sorts of silly questions about our trip to Santorini. They were surprised we hadn't flown over. I kept wondering whether the champagne would be put on our bill.

Two more servants entered and suggested we follow them. They took us past many perfect pools of water, Jacuzzi baths, outdoor bars, a café, and two restaurants. The place was huge. We encountered few people. Some were servants. Others, who were wealthy, moved and spoke in ways that implied they were accustomed to being observed. They gave away nothing intimate.

The rooms we were shown formed a duplex apartment. Its temperature was as cool as an early spring day, its floors polished marble, the recessed lighting meant to inspire seduction. I had encountered luxury before, but nothing quite like this. More than a luxurious hotel, this was a way of life.

We sent the children off to swim so we could unpack. Then we made love. I don't know if sex is in fact better in elegant rooms.

"It took you a long time to unpack," said Madeline. She was lounging poolside, sipping a fruit drink that cost more than a complete dinner at the taverna next to the house in Syros.

"You had a lot of clothing," I said. "Next time don't pack so much."

"Right," she said. "Blame me."

Nicholas was seated at the bar listening to the bartender telling an ad executive from Long Island how he was going to open a club in New York. The club would have three floors, a private VIP room, a café, several bars, and two restaurants. As he spoke, he poured Nicholas a tall, colorful drink I knew would cost a fortune. All he needed were backers.

"How many of those have you had?" I asked.

"C'mon, Dad," he said, "there's no alcohol in it."

"I didn't ask you about alcohol," I said.

"Honey," said Laura, "why don't you relax? Let the kids enjoy themselves. We're on vacation."

"Yeah, Dad," said Nicholas.

"Oh, all right," I said. They were right. How middle class of me to worry about the children racking up a huge tab at the bar by or-

dering countless drinks that cost a fortune! I needed to relax. I
needed to try and fit in.

A French couple frolicked in the pool beside the bar. They wore
brilliant sunglasses while swimming. Neither one had on much
clothing. They were familiar with pleasure in ways I can almost
imagine.

I got in the water and then Laura joined me.

"Do you think we look like them?" I asked.

"Oh, yes, absolutely," she said.

For a huge fee, the chef would cook a meal in our apartment, but
we ate with other guests. Why not? At breakfast we dined on
scrambled eggs and crème fraiche, fruits, and bread. Lunch was also
simple, but perfect. Dinner was served, grown-ups only, in a former
wine cellar, with candlelight and music: grilled lamb, etc. All the ingredients were fresh and first-rate. No wonder the markets and tav-
ernas in Syros had been awful. The best stuff went to upscale hotels
and restaurants.

We took the shuttle to the hotel's private spot on a black-sand
beach. A servant set up deck chairs and umbrellas and gave us cool
drinks and thick, white towels and robes. The beach had been
formed thousands of years ago by the volcanic explosion. The
morning's activity was then made up of wading into the sea and
asking one another whether or not the beach was the most beautiful we'd ever been on.

Had we remained inside Villa Vedema, we would have been im-
mersed in luxury. But I had read up on Santorini and I insisted we
see the sites. The children preferred the hotel's setting to everything
else we proposed, proving once and for all that at their school they
were learning social climbing rather than multiplication tables and
how to spell properly.

We rented a car for one day in order to visit the ruins. A driver
showed up at the hotel and handed me the keys. I didn't have to

sign anything. We had no idea what anything cost. It was like being in a movie. Each day is a movie for the rich. We are extras.

Then we drove to ancient Thira and saw what had once been a thriving community on a hill above the sea. The remains looked like big bones. Madeline and Nicholas griped as we walked on paths alongside waist-high stones where buildings had once been. The heat was oppressive and our children couldn't understand why we had left the hotel. We didn't do a good job of explaining. We were all disappointed in one another. We wanted the children to appreciate history. They wanted to swim and play and drink fruit shakes. I remembered being their age, but the memory was vague, rather like a frog recollecting being without legs.

Afterward we went to the archaeological museum, which is housed in a huge building resembling an airplane hangar only its floor is dirt and there are no lights. We felt as if we were in a warehouse. Handed some tattered, photocopied guides written in barely comprehensible English, we then filed past rows of artifacts stacked on wooden platforms. Few things had labels. A plaque in the museum marked the spot where decades ago the chief archaeologist had slipped, fallen, broken his neck, and then died. What did it all mean? The effect depressed us. I believe this had been the intention of the curator.

Within walking distance of the museum, behind a cliff, was a narrow strip of rocky soil where Germans sunbathed and boats dropped off excursionists for a brief swim. It was early, however, so we found a spot.

"This is not as nice as the hotel's beach," said Nick.

"Nothing is," said Laura.

"So why are we here?" he asked. "We could be there."

"To see new things," I said.

"But everything we've seen is old," he said. "If you want to see new things, we should have stayed at the hotel."

"This beach isn't old," I said.

"It is compared to the hotel," he said. "And it's crowded."

"Fine," I said. "Let's go. Let's order expensive fruit drinks and sit next to rich people."

"Boy, you're in a bad mood," said Nick.

"No, I'm not," I said. "I'm in a good mood. A great mood, in fact."

We stayed a while longer and then returned to the hotel in order to spend more. We weren't happy unless we were spending lots of money. Even though we had already rented a car, we hired a driver and a second car that night. The driver was necessary, we figured, since driving at night on cliff roads without streetlights or guardrails was treacherous.

Then we had him take us to Oia. We had been informed by a reliable guidebook that it would be possible to view sunsets over the caldera we might remember years later.

"Thira was not always like this," said our driver on the way over. He used the Greek name for Santorini.

"Like what?" asked Laura.

"All these homes and hotels and tourists," he said.

"Doesn't he know we're tourists?" whispered Nicholas. "Why is he insulting us?"

"We're not tourists," I whispered back. "We're visitors."

"No, we're not," he said. "Who are we visiting? Why are you afraid to call yourself a tourist?"

"We're tourists, Dad," said Madeline. "Face it."

"I can't hear what our driver is saying," Laura said.

"It hasn't been ruined completely," said the driver, "but Thira was once more beautiful. Then the corruption started and the government in Athens allowed anyone to build who had money."

At this he increased speed. Then we saw we were inches away from a cliff's edge. From there it was hundreds of feet down to rocks and the sea.

"So what happened was everything changed," he said. "The

island emptied of people whose families had been here for centuries. Shops were sold to rich Athenians who open them only a few months of the year during tourist season. Then when the tourists have left, it is very difficult to buy anything. The only jobs on the island are working for tourists in hotels or shops. Prices for food are too high. The restaurants are terrible. They cater to tourists who don't know our food. Rents are unaffordable. No one can buy land. The price of petrol is crazy. And most of the talented or skilled people have left."

But of course he loved Santorini and would never leave.

Then he pulled into Oia. Hundreds of tourists jammed the main street and walkways in front of tacky, useless shops. Some were middle-aged and camera toting, but most were in their twenties. Many faces looked with anticipation and interest for something that might attract and then hold their attention for more than a few minutes.

Our hotel had reserved a table for us at a restaurant with a French name. We reached it by entering a long alleyway so filled with tourists we could do no more than inch forward. Lights came on in display cases of gold in jewelry store windows.

The restaurant had a garden behind walls we walked through to reach the main room. Torches burned on posts at the entrance to the main dining room. Most tables were empty. Customers were dressed formally.

"I don't want to stay," I said. "It's empty, everyone's a tourist, and the menu looks ridiculous. Why would I eat escargot in Greece? Or coq au vin? We're not in France. So why are they serving fake French food?"

"Don't do this," said Laura.

"Don't do what?" I said. "The place looks awful."

"It's just a meal," she said.

"Just a meal?" I said. "How can you say that? Every meal is important. Food reflects history and culture. And besides it has to taste good."

"You've never eaten here," said Nicholas. "Maybe the food is good."

"I can tell it will be terrible," I said.

"Oh, really?" said Laura.

"Yes, of course," I said.

"Well, we want to eat," she said.

"This place is not perfect," I said.

"It doesn't have to be perfect," she said. "It's just dinner."

"It's not authentic," I said. "The menu is French."

"So what?" she said. "It might be good."

"It won't be," I said. "It never is. Besides there's no view."

"We can have drinks at a place with a view and then come back," she said.

We hurried to a café and found the last table available that had a western view. The management played a Bob Marley song. When the sun set, everyone cheered.

Then I refused to go back to the restaurant.

"I am not walking for hours while you look for a restaurant that doesn't exist," said Laura. "We're all hungry. So decide where you want to eat, but do it quickly."

"It shouldn't be my decision alone," I said.

"Oh, but it is," she said. "This is your thing. We're happy eating anywhere."

"You mean to say you're happy spending a lot to eat terrible food? Why? Why don't we try instead to find an authentic Greek restaurant?"

"Because they don't exist," she said. "We haven't had one decent meal out since we've been in Greece."

"That's not true," I said. "What about the taverna next to our house in Syros?"

"You hate the taverna," she said. "You refuse to go back."

"You're right," I said. "I do hate it."

"At least the French place will have good ingredients," said

Madeline. "If it's a fancy place maybe they'll spend more on the food."

We stood in front of the bar where we had had sunset drinks. The volume of noise from stampeding tourists was deafening.

"Let's eat at the hotel," said Nicholas.

"*That* will cost a fortune," I said.

"So what?" he said. "At least it will be good."

But instead we wandered through Oia. The lights used by shops to advertise their stuff were so bright we might as well have been indoors. The alleys were narrow and identical. With the push of tourists, we were pressed up against display cases. At last I saw a one-room taverna that appeared to be authentic. Then we ate bad food with families from Holland and Germany.

The next day no one wanted to leave the hotel. We lounged by the pool and swam.

"How long can we afford to stay here?" Madeline asked Laura.

"A week or two," said Laura.

"But what if we sold everything?" asked Nicholas.

"We don't have much to sell," said Laura. "Just our house and the cars."

"I know that," he said.

"Really?" I said. I had been about to doze off. I opened my eyes. "We happen to have a lot. We're very well off."

"Are we millionaires?" he asked.

"Lower your voice," I said. "Yes, of course we're millionaires."

"We are not millionaires," said Laura.

"Why don't we sell everything and live here?" Nick asked.

"Fine with me," said Laura.

Then Laura and I silently added things up while the children waited.

"OK," said Laura, eyes half-closed, "if we sold everything we could stay here for three years."

"Does that include meals?" asked Madeline.

"I forgot about meals," said Laura.

We recalculated.

"Two years at most," Laura said, "and then we'd have to start our lives all over again."

Syros looked shabby when we returned. We saw the house for what it was. Cluttered with doodads and prints of Greek fishermen weaving nets in villages that no longer existed. The beach in the cove below us was worse than ever. We were approaching the peak of the summer. By noon every available spot was taken by Athenians who ate and drank and smoked constantly.

We went to the market in Hermoupolis to amuse ourselves, but the supply of food wasn't enough to meet the demands of the summer tourists. Now everything on display was completely rotten. Bruised eggplants that looked as if they had been punched, moldy tomatoes, and onions soft to the touch.

Nicholas decided as we walked through the market that he needed to get a haircut at the tiny booth of a barber who worked facing a stand of stinking fish.

"Bzzzz," said Laura. She made a fist with her right hand and made curved moves in the air to suggest the type of cut Nicholas wanted. "Buzz cut. Bzzz, bzzz, bzzz."

"Ah, bzzz, bzzz," the barber said.

He was a small old man, nearly bald, and he understood. All the Greek boys Nick's age had buzz cuts, too. After the haircut, we realized we had done everything there was to do on Syros and that we had to leave at once.

"Four tickets to Mykonos, please," I told the agent who had booked us to Santorini.

"Yes, of course," he said. "When do you wish to go?"

"As soon as possible," I said. "Tomorrow morning."

"That is no problem," he said.

He was delighted by his own efficiency. He took an enormous

ledger out of a desk drawer and began leafing through it. We gave him our names.

"And we will stay for three nights," I said.

"Of course," he said.

"I'd like to book round-trip," I said.

"Not possible," he said without looking up.

He was embellishing our names with curlicues and switching different colored pens for adults and children. His work was either a hobby or a form of therapy recommended to him by his psychiatrist.

"No?" I said.

"I'm afraid not," he said.

He stopped writing, extinguished his cigarette, and lit another.

"And why not?"

"You must book the boat back to Syros in Mykonos," he said. "We don't have the schedule of boats returning. Everyone knows that. It is obvious."

"No, it's not obvious," I said. "It's not at all obvious."

"Honey, you're raising your voice," said Laura.

"No, I am not raising my voice," I said. "I realize it seems as if I am raising my voice, but I'm not."

"Sir, it's no problem," the agent said. "You go to Mykonos and then you buy the ticket back to Syros. I cannot sell you a ticket from Mykonos to Syros because I do not know the schedule of boats."

"Well, I do," I said. "Or I did. Look, back in Boston I saw the schedule of the shipping lines posted on the Internet. You could check on the Internet, get the schedule, and sell me tickets."

"But we don't have a computer," he said.

"I see the computer behind you," I said.

"Oh, that," he said. "That is not for checking schedules."

"What's it for then?" I asked.

He ignored me.

"Do you want these tickets or not?" he asked.

"Down the road I saw an Internet café," I said. "If I went there and got the schedule of boats coming back from Mykonos, could you then sell me tickets?"

"No, absolutely not," he said.

"Why not?" I asked.

The next morning we ran between piers in Hermoupolis. One group of stevedores directed us one way and another sent us back. On the ride over, the boat shook as if it was having a seizure. We arrived in Mykonos to see lovely, whitewashed homes and Greek people dressed up to look old-fashioned in a fishing village. Several of them directed us to shops and restaurants where their relatives would sell us useless things, but we walked on a busy highway to our hotel. All the taxis had disappeared. On the road, cars spewed exhaust and blew dirt into our faces.

The hotel was secluded with panoramic views of the harbor and the sea. Laura took a nap. I swam with the children at the pool. We were in motion. It was important to be doing something.

The next day was Madeline's birthday. We celebrated by taking a boat to see the ruins on the island of Delos. Nothing original occurred to us as we walked in the heat past what remained of temples, sanctuaries, houses, and statues.

On the boat ride back, wind speed picked up and the water was the roughest it had been since our arrival in Greece. The cabin was enclosed and people smoked with fervor.

"You're turning green, Dad," said Madeline.

"Don't talk to me," I said. "I'm concentrating on not being sick."

I held onto the wooden back of a long bench secured to the floor. All around us people groaned, got sick, or passed out.

We had booked a table that night at Chez Katrin, a terrific little restaurant on an alley behind the town square. It was filled with laughing patrons spending money with the enthusiasm of counterfeiters. We got a glimpse of what Mykonos once must have been: a cool, gay scene.

"Sir," said the waiter, whose smile vanished when the check arrived, "really, you must try these."

He displayed several trays of oily fish and vegetables.

"That's a great idea," I said.

He spooned out a few morsels onto each of our plates. Only later did we learn that we had been charged thirty dollars a plate. But this was Greece. We were on holiday. We were having fun! When the main courses were brought to us, no one had an appetite, but we felt obliged. After all, the cost was remarkable. By the time the evening was over, we had spent over three hundred dollars in a restaurant where the scene had been more interesting than the food. The restaurant owner understood that nothing he charged would be too much.

After lolling by the pool at our hotel for a couple more days, we prepared our return to Syros. The shipping office was a mile from the hotel. I walked there and then stood in line for an hour. Back-packers from all over the Western world were trying to buy tickets. I paid a clerk and he said the tickets would be issued by my hotel. I asked him why I hadn't been able to buy the tickets from my hotel in the first place and he said he didn't know.

"When does the boat leave?" I asked.

"At four o' clock this afternoon," he said.

"And where will it leave from?"

He pointed to a pier below the office.

"Be there at three o' clock," he said.

We arrived at three, but there was no boat so I got back in line.

"The weather is rough so the boats are cancelled," he said.

"When will they leave?" I asked.

"We don't know," he said. "Maybe today. Maybe tomorrow. It's hard to say."

"When will you know?" I asked.

"Later," he said.

We conferred as a family and decided to redeem the tickets and stay another night. I returned to the office of the shipping company.

"We can't give you money back for the tickets," the clerk said.

"Why not?"

"You must get the money back at your hotel," he said.

We walked back to the hotel.

"We cannot give you money for the tickets," a clerk there told me. "I don't know why they told you that. They know better. You have to go back to the office where you paid for the tickets."

The family went swimming and I walked back to the office and got in line.

"No, no," the clerk said, "you must go back to your hotel. They will give you the money."

"I am not going back to the hotel," I said.

He took a slip of paper, wrote something down, and handed it to me.

"Here," he said. "Take this."

"What is it?"

"The address of the company that supplies the tickets to us. It is a central agency."

The office was two miles away behind the center of town. I walked past cheap hostels and arrived at a colorful booth where a young, bearded man sat at a desk covered with ledgers and ticket books. He wore beautiful clothing and gold jewelry and looked robust. I wanted to know where he ate, but instead I showed him my tickets for the boat that would not be leaving the island.

"This is not customary at all," he said. "I am not giving you any money."

"Yes, you are," I said. "Or I will call the police."

He laughed.

"The police? What will the police do?"

"I don't know," I said. "But you and I will find out. Do you really want to take money for a boat that doesn't exist?"

I seem to attract people who want me to pay for things they cannot deliver. I had been through this with a mad pizza chef years ago when Madeline was a baby. I reveled in the conflict.

"You are making me very angry," he said. He gripped the sides of the desk and then he and I exchanged threats. Then his German girlfriend slithered out from curtains and said something to him in Greek.

"Here," he said. He slapped money on the desk and shoved it toward me. "Take your money and get out."

Back at the hotel, Laura informed me the hotel had no rooms for the night.

"What are we going to do, Daddy?" asked Madeline.

"We will sleep on the streets," I said.

"We will not sleep on the streets," said Laura. "We will find a nice hotel room."

"You will find a nice hotel room," I said. "I got the money. Now it's your turn to come up with a plan."

We walked back to the shipping office to see when the boats might be running. I stood in line and Laura and the children waited outside. I was about to speak to a clerk when Laura ran in to get me.

"Quick," she said. "Hurry! Hurry up! The boat is leaving!"

"What boat?"

"The boat to Syros," she said. "C'mon, let's go! Hurry!"

She pulled me out and the four of us ran to the pier.

"I thought they cancelled the boat," I said.

"Never mind," she said. "It's leaving and we have to get on it."

"But what about tickets?" I asked.

"Don't worry about tickets," she said. "Just get on the boat."

The next morning in Syros we were restless again. Only an idiot could fail to see the connection between our inability to sit still and the misery brought on by the death of Evelyn, but we didn't get it. Nor did we recognize how our irritation with normal Greek life was in part an expression of grief. So I went to town and bought tickets to leave a day later for Amorgos, an island in the southeastern corner of the Cyclades.

We went through the rituals of buying one-way passage, running back and forth from pier to pier, and then feeling horribly sick on the long boat ride over.

We had heard that in the late 1960s and up until the mid-1970s the dictatorship of the Greek colonels had banished their enemies to Amorgos, but pictures we had seen of the island appealed to us. We liked its rough geography and isolation.

We arrived late in the evening in a busy harbor. The hotel had informed us that a driver would be there to fetch us, but of course he wasn't. We phoned the hotel and the receptionist pretended to be surprised we were waiting. I was about to hire a taxi when the driver showed up. He was small and wizened and the whole time he drove to the hotel he told us stories of no interest whatsoever about his life in Paterson, New Jersey, where he had lived for many years doing repetitive factory work.

The owners of the hotel were the man, his daughter, and his son-in-law. We learned rather quickly that they all hated one another and were convinced that each was cheating the other. To assuage their suspicions, they charged the guests exorbitant prices for everything. They had what the son-in-law called a "guest workers program" at the hotel, too. This program was made up of beautiful, young Norwegian women who came for the summer to clean, cook, wait tables, and serve at the bar.

One afternoon I spoke to a guest worker from Bergen. I had been to her hometown years ago. Then I went to the front desk to get my room key from the son-in-law.

"What did you talk about with her?" he asked me.

"What do you mean?" I asked.

"You are a guest here," he said. "You should not be speaking with our staff. What were the two of you talking about?"

"None of your business," I said.

"But it is my business," he said. "Everything that goes on in this hotel is my business."

"May I please have my key?" I said.

"First you must tell me what you were talking about with the girl."

"Oh, for goodness sakes," I said. "We were talking about Bergen."

He handed me the key.

"Don't talk to her again," he said.

The hotel had a pool table, but when Nicholas and I picked up cues and started to play we were told that playing pool was forbidden in the evening. During the day we went to swim in the hotel's salt water pool, but were told the children were not allowed in unless an adult went in with them. We called a taxi to take us to a beach, but were told the taxi would not be coming. Instead, the father-in-law drove us for a fee twice that of the cab. He also recommended that we visit Moni Panagia Chozoviotissa, a monastery built into a cliff.

In order to enter the monastery we had to climb hundreds of steps up. Then we entered a dark, musty foyer that smelled of body odor where we were required to put on black smocks to cover our bare arms and legs. A dwarf monk took us on a tour of the monastery's rooms and then into its library. On the table were rows of glasses filled with sweet wine, a tray of cookies, souvenir booklets for sale, and a collection box for donations.

After we left the monastery, we swam in brilliant coves below the cliff. Nearby was an outdoor restaurant where we bought tiny fried fish and yogurt flavored with fish eggs.

"I can't eat this food anymore," said Madeline.

"We don't have a choice," I said. "You don't want to die of starvation, do you?"

"Of course not," she said.

One day the daughter suggested we visit another beach where she had a friend who ran a good restaurant.

"My children like the food there," she said with the conviction of a pathological liar. "It is really quite delicious."

The father drove us to the restaurant, which was at the end of a long dirt driveway that led to a simple house behind which was a garden, a few tables, and a path to the beach. Normal looking people sat and ate food that looked good. And when we ate the food— chunks of eggplant swimming in orange-colored oil, huge butter beans with some kind of root vegetable, and a whole fish covered in a green sauce—it actually tasted flavorful. A few hours later we all had severe stomach cramps.

Back at the hotel that night I met a round and pleasant man who identified himself as an Athenian lawyer. He told me he came to the hotel every year with his wife and son.

"I love Amorgos," he said. "It is simple here. Not like in Athens. Athens is like New York."

No, it's not, I thought. Athens is like Calcutta. But I smiled to show sympathy.

"Tell me, please," I asked, "have you found a decent place to eat here? We haven't had any luck."

"Of course," he said. "You know we Greeks like to keep our little secrets. Because otherwise they become spoiled. Ruined by tourists. But, yes, of course, I have heard of a place. My sister who told me about Amorgos has been there many times. Say . . . why don't we all go tonight? It's a wonderful place. Very simple, a real Greek taverna."

"Perfect," I said.

We hired the father to bring us to a village in the hills above the hotel. He was rather reluctant since he and his daughter and son-in-law preferred that guests eat at the hotel in the evening. We had done this once. That night the chicken cutlet served to Madeline was actually frozen. A large, thick slab of chicken parts was brought to the table drenched in tomato sauce and a sort of cheese product.

We followed the Greek lawyer through some alleys in the village. A cool breeze blew steadily. No junk existed here yet, just flats and homes in front of which old men and women sat on wooden chairs looking at us as if we were tax collectors.

At last we reached the taverna where the last remaining seats at a long table had been reserved for us. There were no menus and my new friend told us what was available.

"The specialty is goat intestines stuffed with meat and vegetables," he said. "My sister has told me it is almost as good as our mother's."

"No! How could it be?" I said.

"*Almost* as good, my friend," he said and smiled. "*Almost!*"

"Well, we have to have that," I said.

"Of course," he said.

Then he ordered more stuff I knew nothing about and lots of retsina.

The big deal about the taverna was its live music. Two little old men would play string instruments while we dined. The Greeks knew the songs and joined in when the choruses came around. The themes concerned old men tricking young women into having sex with them, old men whose virility completely overwhelmed their wives or girlfriends, and old men who shocked and thrilled their young brides on their wedding night because of their enormous penises. Although they had heard these dull songs since they had been children, the crowd laughed and applauded with enthusiasm that was appalling.

"How are your goat guts?" asked Laura.

"Delicious," I said. "You should try some."

"What do they taste like?" she asked.

"Impossible to describe," I said. "Fantastic. Really fantastic. Amazing."

In fact, the guts were working their way into my central nervous system in ways which were immediately apparent. I felt as if I would survive the experience, but just barely. I could picture my car with a handicapped sticker dangling from the rearview mirror. People would say: He's sweet and he understands more than he can put into words.

We left the taverna past one, just as things were getting started. But the children had had enough. Of course, I was sick the next day and the day after that, etc.

I would have left the island without eating again, but the children needed to be fed so on our last night before departing we dined at the hotel again. Things came to the table resembling what we'd ordered, but the magnitude of the kitchen's hostility toward food was so great that the cooks managed to destroy simple dishes like soups, noodles, and salads.

A French family arrived as we were leaving. They looked exhausted, but happy. This was the beginning of their holiday and when they sat down and began to examine their menus with the forensic attention of diners from France, tears came to my eyes. I should have warned them, but didn't. Let them have a few moments of happiness, I thought, before the food arrives.

We made it back to Syros. We remained another five days. During that time we ate pasta at every meal with a sauce of tomatoes stewed in butter and an onion. The sauce is for children, the feeble, and the old. It nearly restored our health.

"I never want to come back to Greece," Madeline said during our last meal in the garden. "I hate it."

"There was nothing to do," said Nicholas.

"Oh, come on," said Laura. "How can you say that? It's beautiful here, don't you think?" She gestured with her arms to indicate the expanse of the sea and the night sky.

"You didn't like it either," said Madeline.

"I did, too," Laura said. "OK, so the food was a problem."

"*Yeah*," said Nicholas.

"And the boats were a problem, too," Laura said. "But it's so peaceful here. I love this house."

"I can't eat Greek food," said Madeline. "If I have one more Greek salad, I'll scream."

"We didn't come for the food," Laura said.

"Why *did* we come here?" asked Nicholas.

"Next year you're studying Greece in school," Laura said. "You'll see. All the places we visited—you'll learn about them."

"So?" he said.

"It's history, Nick," she said. "So many things started here. The civilization we live in today has its roots in Greece."

"Uh-huh," he said. "Fascinating."

"Didn't you like Santorini?" Laura asked.

"That was only for three days," he said.

"How about the ruins?" she asked.

"They were OK," he said.

"I liked everything we saw and did," said Madeline, "but I would have had a better time if we'd gotten decent food."

"I love the quiet of being here," Laura said. "Sitting in the garden right now means a lot to me. I can see the stars and hear the sea. Probably it was like this for the ancient Greeks when they went on their great sea voyages. Just listen."

We returned to the Grande Bretagne the next day. Athens was more chaotic than before. Tourists were everywhere. Greeks not on holiday were in a foul temper. Taxis rocketed through the streets and the restaurants that remained open in the summer heat were staffed by thieves.

"We have to hurry up," I told the family.

We checked in quickly in order to get to the national archaeology museum and still have time to visit the Acropolis. Most of the significant items taken from ruins we had visited were in the museum. We got a taxi and then ran up the steps to the entrance. But a sign on the massive doors read: Closed due to the heat.

"How can they close a museum because of heat?" asked Laura. "It's always hot here in the summer."

"I thought you loved Greece, Mom," said Nick.

"Oh, this is so irritating," she said.

"Fine," I said, "now we have more time for the Acropolis."

But the children were hungry and instead of touring we went to Lykavittos Hill. I had heard restaurants in this upscale neighborhood served good food. Most of them were closed for summer holidays, but an hour or two later we got to the St. George Hotel. Then we returned to the Acropolis.

We left Greece the next morning for Zurich. Our flight to Boston was delayed for six hours. Swissair gave us vouchers to go into town.

"We are so sorry," the clerk said.

"Sorry?" I said. "This is thrilling!"

The train departed and arrived according to schedule. We were at the main train station in precisely eleven minutes.

"We can breathe again," I said.

Hardly anyone was smoking. The exhaust from cars was minimal.

We walked along the Limmat river and then passed by zum Ruden, a medieval structure where Laura and I had dined on our honeymoon. The sun was shining and the river was pale blue and white so we crossed over a bridge to eat in the gardens of Hotel zum Storchen.

"Oh, at last to be back in a country where things work," I said as we crossed the bridge. "Everything functions: the boats and the trams and the trains. Isn't it wonderful to be in a country where things are clean? Is that so bad? Why is that a bad thing? We can eat anywhere we like! Good, fresh food. Not animal organs or fish parts swimming in oil."

"Let's come here next year," said Madeline, "if you love it so much."

"Don't you love it, too?" I asked. "Don't you all love it?"

"We were here last year," said Laura. "Do you really want to come back every year?"

"Absolutely," I said.

"I don't," said Nicholas.

"Why not?" I asked.

"I just don't," he said.

We ate beside the river and then strolled down Bahnhofstrasse, the city's exclusive walking street, until we reached Sprungli, a shop that sells beautiful truffles.

"Only the dark ones," I said. The woman behind the counter used silver tongs to pick up the chocolates. "And please leave four in a bag."

We ate our truffles as we walked past the distinguished Swiss on the way back to the station. Laura stood a long time in front of shop windows looking at watches and clocks.

"Being here is like being home," she said. "Do we have to go back?"

BELLA ITALIA:
THE HOLY FAMILY

The children love Italy and so do we. Art and architecture, cities rich in history, gastronomy and viniculture, kind people, beautiful clothing, and an appreciation for living life slowly.

The problem is *everyone* loves Italy. We'd started visiting as a family in the 1980s and without kids a decade before. Each time we returned, we found more people, complete strangers, weighted down by photo equipment and other gear, in line to enter museums and churches, clogging up the roads, filling tables at favorite restaurants, touring wine cellars and eager to tell us how much they loved Italy, how much they adored the food, the people, the art, the architecture, the sensibility, the fashion, the whole damn way of life. It was enough to make us sick. This was our country, after all, where we felt at home. Who were *these* people? Where did they all come from? Why didn't they go home?

We had at first taken the children to Tuscany, staying then at houses we'd rented or in the homes of friends who needed us to keep an eye on their property while they were away. But then the places we loved got overrun. Florence became a theme park. We heard more English spoken than Italian in Siena. San Gimignano, Lucca, Cortona, Gaiole in Chianti—they all lost their charm. There was no place to park, the food began to taste bland, and how many times can you hear someone say how much they love Italy before you think of hitting them? It was really enough.

We recalled with fondness the early days of travels in Italy: Jesus

Christ, only a baby, is held in his mother's arms while she fixes him with adoration in her gaze and through her posture. Mary is more devoted than millions of believers. Her love is the purest sort, meant not just to inspire, but to instruct. It's an advertisement for the Church, but it's also a "how to" illustration. This is a visual aid, after all, the painting hanging in the Uffizi, showing ordinary men and women how to do it. See Mary hold the infant Jesus? See how she's really calm? She's not walloping him. She wouldn't dream of whacking the Son of God. Don't spank Jesus! You've got to love Him. But not just Jesus, you've got to love your own sons and daughters. Don't beat the hell out of them! Got it?

Nick is fastened to my chest in the Snugli and Laura is holding the pint-sized Madeline's hand as we stroll through the museum's galleries. The rooms are hot and poorly lit, but at least there are not many visitors.

Suddenly a boy who appears to be twice Madeline's age, which makes him about eight, cuts off from a school trip and stands between me and some painting of Madonna and Child. There are dozens. It's as if we're in an aquarium, but instead of fish, we've got Jesus and his mother.

"*Che occhi!*" he says. He's amazed. "*Che belli occhi!*"

"Huh?"

"*La bambina,*" he says, "*o il bambino. Che occhi! Che belli occhi!*"

What is he talking about? My son's blue eyes—his *occhi*—are *belli*—they're beautiful. So what? Why has the boy left his friends to tell me this? I can't imagine an American kid of any age showing this much interest in a stranger's baby. But his expression is calm and his pleasure is genuine.

"*Quanti mesi?*" he asks. How many months? He's got on one of those cute desk-sized backpacks almost as big as he is.

"*Tredici,*" I say. Thirteen months.

"Oh," he croons, "*che bella!*"

Nothing I do can convince the boy to go away. He wants to tour

with us. We smile and nod and he murmurs, "*Che belli! Che belli!*"
We take a few steps, so does he.

"OK, *ciao*," I say. "*Ciao, ciao.*"

He won't budge.

"Why is that boy following us?" asks Madeline.

"He thinks Nicky is baby Jesus," I say.

"He does not," says Laura.

"*Che bello bambino,*" he says.

"*Ciao,*" I say again. "*Ciao.* Buzz off."

"*Che bello!*"

"Don't be mean," says Laura.

"He has no idea what 'buzz off' means," I say. "Buzz off. See?"

"MARCO!"

One of his teachers has run into the room and grabbed Marco by the wrist. From her expression, it's easy to imagine that Marco's done this sort of thing before.

Italy is nuts about kids. In a café the owner asks if our children want warm milk. At a restaurant, the chef, a woman in her seventies, runs out of the kitchen to wish Madeline a happy birthday. In an open market, we are sold the best fruits, vegetables, meat, and fish. On earlier visits, before Madeline and Nicholas were born, Laura and I were usually given rotten stuff.

Toy stores, *gelati* vendors, and fresh fruit are everywhere. The children love the promise of tiny, colorful berries, which look more like beads. Their first words in Italian were *lamponi, fragole, mirtilli*—raspberries, strawberries, blueberries. Italy is a nation that understands the power of a bribe. We can get the children to go to museums, churches, vineyards, fabric stores, and cheese shops just by promising them a toy, an ice cream, or fruit afterward.

And naps. This is a country that believes in sleep. After a two hour lunch made up of the most delicious food imaginable, we hurry home to go to bed.

But we quit Italy for awhile. We felt spurned. How could our lover surrender to those tourists when she had us? We weren't tourists. We were visitors. And we *genuinely* loved her. Not like the others.

Years went by. There would be a lull in the conversation. Then one of us would say something about Italy.

"You know, I miss pasta in Italy," said Madeline as she stared at a plate of sausages and boiled potatoes in a horrible little place, deep in the Swiss mountains, that had no reason to be called a restaurant. "Why can't we go back there?"

"I miss the art," Laura would say over drinks in a neon-lit bar in Hawaii. "I miss all that culture."

"I wish we could go back to Italy," Nicholas said in the supermarket. "I love the berries and the pizza and the French fries."

"What French fries?" I'd ask. "Italy does not have French fries."

"It doesn't?"

"Well, it does, but it's not famous for them."

"Then I don't miss them," he said. "But I do miss the berries. I loved going to the market with you in the morning before Mommy and Madeline woke up. If we go back to Italy, can we do that again?"

"Absolutely."

"Can we go to cafés, too?"

"Sure."

"Just the two of us, OK?"

"What about Maddy and Mommy?"

"But not all the time."

"We'll see."

We needed a plan. How could we return to Italy and avoid the tourists? At first we thought we would be fine if we went outside of Tuscany. We would search for an isolated region or village and discover the real Italy.

But the more we heard, read, and saw, the more we realized no matter where we wanted to go, tourists were everywhere. Sicily,

Naples, Rome, Florence, Siena, Bologna, Genoa, Alba, Milan, Venice. The islands, the beaches, the lakes, and the mountains—all jammed. Centuries ago pilgrims had journeyed, followed by artists, writers, and poets. Nowadays buses and carloads of vacationers arrive to tour churches and museums, eat bowls of pasta and plates of pizza, soak up the sun, snap photographs of hilltop villages or volcanic islands, olive groves and vineyards, tombs and statues, frescoes and fountains, big-eyed, dark haired Italian kids playing with hoops in a piazza, old peasants in cafés staring vacantly, gatherings of *ragazzi* in soccer uniforms, priests on hillsides—these images and experiences of Italy had been inculcated by history, but also by the tourists themselves—they had created the Italy of their dreams, they had invented a place that didn't really exist. They had imagined Italy and Italy had responded: "OK, that's what you want? Fine, that's what we'll be." But where was the real Italy? How would we find it?

Even this, we discovered, had been going on for centuries. Everybody had always wanted to know: Where is the real Italy? Even the Italians wanted to know. *Especially* the Italians. Where beneath the show put on for visitors was the Italian soul?

We despaired. We didn't want to join a cavalcade. But we wanted to return to the one place on earth that made us feel most cherished as a family.

We were about to give up until late one night, examining a brochure picturing another place that looked a lot like every other place, Laura and I realized it wasn't important where we went in Italy, but *how* we went. What if we infiltrated? What if we stepped through the mirror that was Italy and found ourselves inside looking out? What if we were able to blend in? It suddenly hit us: our complaints about the tourists, the towns, the restaurants, the loss of the traditional way of life, the search for the Italian soul—*Ecco!* These were exactly the things Italians complained and worried about. We determined to become more Italian than the Italians.

And the way to do that was not to avoid centers of tourism, but instead to go to them. After all, if we rented a house in a remote village in the Dolomites, we'd be the American family condescended to by locals. But if we went to a popular spot, we'd be compared to thousands of tourists who didn't have a clue about local rules and customs.

Tuscany was still out of the question. It fit the criteria of being spoiled by an influx of tourism, had cities and villages stripped of character and tradition, contained many restaurants that served bad food, and had replaced local businesses and craftsmanship with industry designed to cater strictly to tourists. We could easily have rented a house and complained the entire time. But Tuscany was missing two things that over years of holidays together as a family we knew were essential: water and walks. The children needed a place to swim. We also did not want to get in a car each day. Renting a house with a pool was too expensive. Being in a town or a city during a Tuscan summer is brutal—besides the heat, the insects are terrible.

We headed further north. Italy's lake district—Garda, Como, Maggiore—is ideal. But it took us a long time to find anything. Either gorgeous, antique villas or simple flats in lakeside villages had rental prices jacked up to accommodate the Swiss and German tourists who, unless they are paying twice what a property is worth, don't feel as if they are having a real holiday. Finally, we came across a house in the annual catalog sent to us by the agency through which we had swapped homes in the past.

The black and white picture next to the listing was wallet-sized. It showed a tiny island in a lake surrounded by mountains: Isola San Giulio in Lago di Orta. An arrow had been drawn to indicate that one of the island homes—we could barely see it—was their property.

We made contact with the owners by mail and were sent more photographs. The lake was about eight miles long and two miles wide. The village of Orta has a lovely old piazza framed by an arcade of shops, two turn-of-the-century hotels, a few cafés, medieval streets, and a long quay filled with rowboats and water taxis. The island, about four times as big as an average high school gym, was dominated by a monastery and rimmed by villas centuries old. Their villa, built in 1634, had renovated bedrooms, a modern kitchen, and a huge living room that looked like a section of a palace. Their garden, abutting the lake, had a grape arbor, a palm tree, bougainvillea, and stone tables and benches for dining *al fresco*.

The owner, an Italian who lived in Milan with her English husband, explained that the house had been in her family for close to two hundred years. Before that she thought it had belonged to the church and served as a residence for a priest. She and her husband had spent years fixing it up. They went in the fall or over Christmas. They weren't interested in an exchange, but would we want to rent it?

Everything was so old-fashioned and charming. Orta was smaller and not as well known as Como, Garda, or Maggiore. The lake, the village, and the island all appeared to be covered in fog. In travel brochures the copy was sure to read that Orta was "shrouded by the mists of time." We knew at once we would find ourselves surrounded by cognoscenti, tourists who would arrive with guidebooks to the "real" Italy and the "hidden" Italy. But the Italians would say of them: They don't know nothing.

We could settle in, then row into the village, strut around a bit, and return to our villa to swim and lounge in the garden and make fun of the tourists. That the tourists would be sophisticated would add to our pleasure.

My suspicions were validated by research.

Famous writers had been to Orta. Nietzsche had visited with Lou Andreas-Salome. The place would be overrun by Germans retracing his steps, reading loudly from *Thus Spake Zarathustra* as they walked through Orta's alleys, ordering the wrong kinds of meals in cafés, speaking loudly, acting with aggression, buying souvenirs manufactured in Sri Lanka, eating at the wrong time of the day, not knowing any basic words in Italian—all this and perfect swimming, too.

Besides the Germans, we would find hundreds of real pilgrims who had come to Orta to find salvation. The island's monastery was a holy site. Two other sacred sites were nearby, too. Above the village was Sacre Monte, which is a centuries-old series of more than a dozen chapels filled with statues showing the life of Saint Francis. And more recently, a miracle had been discovered in Orta. Faded paint on the wall of a building had suddenly assumed the face of Padre Pio—mystic, saint, priest!

"It's going to be crowded," said Madeline.

"No," I said. "That's the point. It will be crowded in the village, but from our house we'll be in the perfect position to observe all the chaos. We'll be above it all."

"We're never above it all," said Laura. "We're lucky if we can keep up."

"You're being negative, honey," I said.

"And we'll be stuck there," said Nicholas, "with nothing to do."

"How can you say that?" I said. "We'll go swimming."

"And then what?" he said. "Swimming is fun, but then what?"

"The house comes with a rowboat," said Laura. "We can row for fun. See? That's not negative."

"But you were a moment ago," I said.

"Now who's being negative?" she said.

"I'm just responding to what you said."

"No, you're not."

"We'll have to row to the village," I said.

"Can I row?" Nick asked. He was ten years old.

"Of course," Laura said.

"It will be hard," I said.

"I said he could row," she said.

"I want to go someplace where there's miniature golf," said Nicholas.

"We'll look for miniature golf," I said.

"And can I get a *Herald Tribune* every day?"

"Every day?" I asked.

"I want to check the Red Sox scores."

"The paper's very expensive, Nick," I said.

"You can get the paper, sweetheart," said Laura.

"I think we should discuss this," I said.

"Oh, really?" said Laura.

"And can I have ice cream every day?" Nick asked.

"Not every day," I said.

"Ask me, honey. Your father will spend hundreds of dollars on a meal in a restaurant, but nothing on the normal things every child deserves."

"That is not true," I said.

"Oh, but it is," Laura said.

"The garden looks beautiful," said Madeline.

"It is beautiful," I said.

"How do you know?" asked Nick. "You haven't been there."

"It *looks* beautiful," I said.

I could picture us in the garden, on chaise lounges, drinking local wines, reading long, old novels, and griping about the northerners and the superstitious pilgrims. It was promising.

We flew into Lugano via Zurich in order to rest for one night before driving to the house. Nothing seemed to have changed from earlier visits when Madeline and Nicholas had nearly been babies. The stasis was appealing. We could imagine we hadn't changed either. It wasn't that we had lost innocence or that life as a family was easier back then. But at the beginning the children were at our mercy. Now they had points of view, personalities, negotiating skills, and standards in conflict with ours. We didn't want to return to the early years of being a family. Just having back the confidence that comes from complete, unquestioned authority over every aspect of their lives would have been enough.

While Laura napped, I took the children through alleyways in the old part of town and then down to the lake. Crowds of people filled the streets. A big jazz festival was in swing. We ate at a café in view of American performers on a bandstand. I remembered a walk Laura and I had taken with her mother Evelyn years ago in the public gardens on the way to Villa Favorita. Madeline had just been born. Evelyn had talked about the trees for almost an hour. She was fascinated as well as knowledgeable. Now whenever I think of Lugano, the most emotional memory is of Evelyn and the trees. She was happy then. She spoke during those first weeks with so much attachment to Madeline it seemed as if she were the one who had brought her into this world. She kept saying "my baby" this and "my baby" that. But on the walk, it was clear she was beginning to reconcile herself. She talked about trees with the same intensity as she had when speaking about Madeline. As if the trees were her babies, too.

We returned to our hotel. Principe Leopoldo was an insanely plush property on top of *collina d'ora*, "the golden hill." The hotel resembled a castle. Once belonging to a Hapsburg prince, through the years it had added to the fame of its origins by hosting writers like Hermann Hesse and scores of wealthy and aristocratic Europeans. The rooms were practically gilded, the hallways wide enough to drive a golf cart through, and the egg-shaped pool movie-star quality. The whole place was designed to give you the willies.

Properly intimidated, feeling out of place, we behaved like the other guests. We knew that if we spent a lot, we'd fit in. We drank champagne in view of the lake and mountains. We ordered a dinner of summer truffle risotto, Breton sea bass baked in salt, and then for dessert some sort of big chocolate thing. We washed it all down with white wine from Burgundy and then looked at the bill. We obviously belonged. This was, I reckoned, our kind of place.

The next morning the children announced they had no intention of leaving. After a brief struggle involving threats, but no force, they packed up their bear and dog, stuffed animals they had possessed since birth, and agreed to get in the car.

"You are so cheap," said Nicholas.

"It's not polite to talk about money," I said.

"I just don't see why we're leaving. Italy. Who wants to go to Italy? There will be nothing to do. I'm going to hate it."

"No, you're not," I said.

"Yes, I am," he said. "You don't know. You're not me."

"Why don't you stop complaining for five minutes and look out the window? We're driving through beautiful countryside and all you do is complain."

"Let me handle this," said Laura. "The two of you are impossible."

"He's impossible," I said. "I'm trying to drive. What's he doing?"

"See?" said Nicholas. "See, Mom? He always puts me down."

"Daddy's tired, sweetheart, and he has to concentrate on his driving. He doesn't want anyone to talk until we get there."

"That's not true," I said. "I just don't want to hear constant complaining."

"Nicky wasn't complaining, were you, honey?"

"No," he said.

"He was just expressing his point of view. Right, darling?"

"Yup," he said.

"I don't appreciate this," I said.

"You need to relax," Laura said.

"How can I relax? It's hard to drive on these roads. Have you looked out the window? We're on mountain roads. Cliffs! If I don't pay attention, we could all die in a flaming car wreck!"

"We're behind you 100 percent!" she said.

"It's true, Dad," Madeline said. "You're doing a great job."

"Be positive," Laura said. "You always tell me to be positive."

"OK," I said, "I will try to be positive. Maybe if I explained a little bit about where we are, why it's so special, certain people would stop complaining constantly, acting entitled like their friends at the namby-pamby, pandering private school we send them to!"

"Honey. Honey, that's not being positive. How do you expect Nicholas to be positive if you put down his friends and school?"

"Which he does all the time," Nick said.

"OK," I said. "I'm sorry."

"It's like this all the time when you're not home, Mom," Nick said.

"Oh, it is not," said Madeline. "You're exaggerating, as usual."

"Daddy's girl," said Nick.

"You should talk," she said, "Mr. Mommy's boy."

"Oh, is Nicky a girly man?" I asked.

"MOM!"

"OK! That's it, not a word out of anyone for ten minutes," said Laura. "I have a headache and I'm exhausted. And you! You're the adult!"

"I'm sorry," I said.

"Ten minutes, I mean it," she said.

Squabbles with Nick had an athleticism about them that invigorated us both. He wasn't weak. One more reason to admire my son.

Nick and I were members of the father and son club. In speaking with other fathers and sons we discovered our arguments were the secret handshake that got us in. We also belonged to one another through our disagreements. It is a part of how we make necessary contact.

There has been lately a trend among social workers posing as doctors to suggest that men need to talk more and argue less. Should they succeed in their efforts to reform men, we can expect to see more games end in a tie.

Soon we were in the outskirts of Locarno. We had driven north in order to take the road toward Stresa. Driving this route was difficult, but going directly south from Lugano would have been worse. I checked my watch. Time's up!

"We're in the Ticino," I said, "which is the Italian-speaking part of Switzerland. Eighty years ago, philosophers, artists, and writers came to form free-spirited communities based on love, music, dance, and creative expression. Isadora Duncan, Carl Jung, Hermann Hesse, and James Joyce visited. The area was also home to movie stars. Paulette Goddard lived here. She was once married to Charlie Chaplin and starred in his movie *Modern Times*. I think she came because the region has a unique micro-climate. There are subalpine hills and mountains, but it's also tropical. Palm trees grow here. The villages are made of stone. They are filled with campaniles, alleys, and the homes of shepherds. And the people are Italian. They joined the Swiss confederation in order to get military help against a possible conquest by Napoleon. They remain Italian in their approach to life. That's what I love about the Ticino. It has Swiss order, but the Italian way of life."

"We came here on our honeymoon," Laura said.

"Wasn't that when you were chased by sheep?" asked Nicholas.

"Yes," said Laura.

We had hiked through what we thought was an abandoned collection of ruined shepherds' stone huts. Then a flock of more than a hundred sheep suddenly appeared. At first they surrounded us. Then they pursued aggressively.

"But we survived," said Laura.

"It wasn't easy," I said. "We had to fight them off."

"With what?" asked Nick.

"Rocks and tree branches, at first, then I found a cache of firearms in a Swiss military depot. Have you ever tasted the meat of an animal you've killed? It's delicious. We grilled lamb chops over an open fire that night, drizzled with olive oil, fresh rosemary, salt and black pepper, and lemon juice."

"That sounds good," said Nicholas.

"It was good," I said.

"That never happened," said Laura.

"We weren't surrounded by sheep?" I asked.

"No, the part about shooting them. And I don't think it's funny to joke about guns. Do you know how many people die each year from handguns?"

"These were rifles," I said.

"I'm being serious," she said. "You should think about what you're saying. The children believe you."

"They should believe me," I said.

"Why is everything I say considered a joke?" she said.

"I want ice cream," said Nicholas.

We were in the center of Locarno. I had taken a detour to show them the town.

"Swiss ice cream is not as good as Italian ice cream," I said. "Which is surprising, don't you think? When you consider how good Swiss milk is, you'd think the ice cream would be of high quality. But it's not."

"Mom," said Nicholas, "why can't we stop for ice cream?"

"We've been in the car less than an hour," I said. "I want to get to the house."

"It's so pretty here," Laura said. "What's the point of driving through? We should walk around."

"No," I said. "I don't want to stop."

"You're not the only one to decide," Laura said. "We all want to stop."

"Madeline," I asked, "do you want to stop?"

"I don't care either way," she said.

"Two against two," I said.

"Oh, pull over," said Laura. "Don't be so difficult. Besides you like Locarno. Remember how much you loved it here on our honeymoon?"

"Omigod," said Nicholas. "OMIGOD!! OMIGOD!!!!"

He was shouting now, tantamount in Switzerland, a nation that prizes silence and decorum, to urinating out the window.

"What is it?" asked Laura.

"Mini-golf!" said Nick. "Look!"

A bright sign indicated that three hundred yards up ahead there was a course.

"Unfortunately, we don't have time for mini-golf," I said. "Sorry."

"We're not on a schedule," said Laura. "We're on vacation."

"I hate mini-golf," said Madeline.

"Oh, it'll be fun," Laura said.

"No, it won't," she said. "It never is."

We parked the car in a public garage and bought ice cream before renting clubs and balls. The course was the standard Swiss sadistic set of links. Eighteen holes of impossible runways, manufactured from hard plastic, with loops, crests, angles, gaps, and one windmill, all designed to aggravate me. The caretaker kept interrupting our game by sweeping away leaves and twigs that landed on the runways. We all cheated and after the game was over we got back in the car and drove to Italy.

Most of the drive to Orta had been through Switzerland where the pristine countryside is protected by law from development. Crossing into Italy we faced landscapes pocked by shopping malls, garages, and factories. Italy has taken the cliché "it's who you know" as national policy on the environment. Money had changed hands. Developers built whatever they liked wherever they liked. We passed dozens of statuaries where plaster had been poured into molds of Roman gods, Jesus Christ, Saint Francis and other saints, Disney characters, the Holy Family, and wildlife. Getting closer to Orta we came across many sink and toilet manufacturers.

"This is beyond ugly," said Laura. "This is oog-lee."

"I'm sure the lake and the house will be beautiful," I said.

Omegna was the last town we drove through before reaching Orta. Then along the road we passed by marshes and unfinished homes. It looked as if everyone had run out of money or was on the verge. In contrast to the opulent surroundings of lakes Maggiore, Lugano, Como, and Garda, here we saw pink and purple discothèques and motels. Then we turned right at the candy-colored tower of Villa Crespi, which is a luxury hotel resembling Mother Goose's house at the Storyland theme park in southern New Hampshire. We took the road down to the village to meet the owners of our rental. They brought us to the island in a rowboat powered by an outboard motor.

Even if we hadn't been exhausted from the flight and bickering, in search of a place we could call home for a month, Orta would have had a calming influence. Life, in general, was weary and repetitive in Cambridge, a sinewy layer of school and work, where being together as a family was limited to eating a few meals each week. We were all getting older. The children spent most of their time studying or with friends. Laura and I worked harder than ever to meet expenses. On the ride to San Giulio, an island regarded as sacred by the Church, we saw salvation.

The shoreline was relatively undeveloped. We saw a few old villages, grasslands, villas, hills, and medieval towers used to warn of invaders.

As we sped by Orta, we glimpsed its piazza and the dozen or so three-story dwellings, arcade, cafés, and hotels that formed its borders. Middle-aged men dressed like sailors manned beautiful wooden boats used as water taxis. The architecture was turn of the century, outdated and impractical, suggestive of a time when people were forcibly more connected to their immediate circumstances.

"There will be nothing to do here!" shouted Nicholas over the wake. "I bet it sucks!"

"Sucks is not a nice word," I shouted. "You bet it stinks!"

Then I smiled apologetically at George, the owner of the house, who was doing his best to maneuver us and our eight suitcases across the lake. The craft we were in was best suited for two.

"It's all right," he shouted in an accent from a working class neighborhood in the north of England. He was a retired banking administrator who'd spent most of his adult life in the Middle East. "I worked with an American chap years ago in Dubai. Same thing. You Americans are like that. Y'know. Always wanting to be entertained." He tapped his head with his right forefinger. "But it's all here, isn't it? What you make of life."

"I can't hear you!" I shouted. Typical, I thought, English expat explaining Americans to Americans. That's what *he* makes of life. "What's that you say?"

We docked in a small private bay that had been built of stones beside the house and garden. Then we unloaded our bulk. George removed the engine from the boat and pointed to a pair of oars.

"We never use the engine unless it's to bring our stuff back and forth," he said. "But if you want, I'll leave it on. Only you'll have to pay us an additional eighteen thousand lire per day."

We decided the rowing would be good exercise, paid the owners our rent, and settled in. The house was far more beautiful than we had imagined.

"Easily the loveliest place we've ever rented," said Laura.

While centuries-old stones had been preserved on the exterior, the villa's rooms were modern and spacious, their furnishings elegant, ceilings high, beams exposed, the kitchen practical. The garden, about six feet above water level, was filled with tropical plants and bordered by knee-high stone walls facing the water. Other sides were enclosed by walls nearly ten feet tall. We could swim whenever we liked. The lake was clean. The water temperature was perfect.

"It's paradise," said Madeline.

"I have to admit it's nice," said Nicholas. "Just don't say, 'See, I told you?' "

"I would never say that," I said. "I don't know what makes you say I would. Why would you even suggest such a thing? Typical! You think I'm always being critical, don't you? But I'm not. Why don't you admit *that*?"

"I'm not admitting anything," he said.

After a swim, we walked around the island. There was one loop, a stone path, wide enough for two people to walk side by side, between the monastery and the villas, along which posted signs, written in four languages, extolled the virtues of silence. The monastery, of the Benedictine order, was huge and white with dozens of tiny windows big enough to frame a face. It had been built on a crest and towered over us.

"Do you know why this island is called San Giulio?" I whispered.

"Can I please walk in peace?" said Laura. "The signs say we have to be quiet."

"The church sanctified Isola di San Giulio to honor Saint Giulio," I said. "He was said to have killed a giant, evil serpent on the island centuries ago. This was before people realized giant, evil serpents do not exist. Saint Giulio was not in the big leagues, like Saint George or Saint Patrick, but he did a good job of repressing sexuality through the metaphor of his slaying of the giant, evil serpent so the church built the monastery in the 1840s to say, 'Thanks, Giulio, good job! Good for you! We are so proud!' The monastery closed in 1947 and reopened in 1973 to become home for the Benedictine order of nuns."

"You are being very disrespectful," said Laura. "And you're setting a bad example for the children."

"But it's all true."

"It is not true."

"Oh? What part did I make up?"

"It's your tone," she said.

We were told the nuns were not allowed to talk or be seen. They could sing, but they could not talk. The entire month we were on the island, we never saw any nuns.

We never met any of the other residents either. Each villa was surrounded by stone walls like ours. The only way to see anyone or anything was from the water.

Tourists passed by us on the walk. They came on ferries or water taxis. They walked the loop, went inside a church attached to the monastery, and sometimes ate at the island's one restaurant.

The restaurant had a beautiful outdoor garden where mosquitoes had established a large and ambitious colony. We ate there once, but I complained the whole time about the food and when I suggested we try it again and said that I was sorry, no one would go back with me.

The only sounds we heard on the island were bells ringing, water lapping against its shores, whistles and horns from passing boats, and the voices of people as they swam, motored, or paddled by. Every day tourists came over, but they landed on the other end of the island, did the walk, visited the church, and ate in the restaurant so we never saw them unless we made the loop, which was something we avoided.

Going to the village of Orta was necessary, but not desirable. The best thing about the trip over was being in a rowboat, just the four of us, making the crossing of about fifteen hundred feet in ten or twenty minutes, depending upon who was rowing. Everybody had a lot to say.

We would dock at a stone rampart next to the ferry landing and near the row of water taxis. Just above us was a verandah with tables and chairs that belonged to the Leon d'Ora hotel. Metal rings had been cemented on the shore to tie boats up.

"It's like being on a horse," said Nick. "Tying him up while we go in a saloon."

Then he would take off in search of a paper. Only two shops sold any and neither carried *USA Today* nor the *International Herald*

Tribune every day, so Nick would return glum about half the time. Either we spent the rest of the morning trying to cheer him up or we heard details on the Red Sox which included not just ERAs, scores, and batting averages, but the favorite TV shows of players, their superstitions, wives' recipes for brownies, and number and type of cars owned by the infield.

"What's Nomar's mortgage?" I asked as we walked through the piazza. "One year adjustable? Or thirty year fixed?"

"All *you* talk about is food," he said.

"I do not," I said. "Say, look! The bakery's selling fresh gnocchi!"

"See?" he said. "That's all you care about."

"You like to eat, too," I said, paying for the gnocchi. "These will be delicious with a butter sauce and preserved black truffles."

"That does sound good," Nick said.

"I told you," I said.

"But that's not *all* I care about," he said.

"No, you care about sports. If there's a ball in motion, you'll watch it," I said.

"That is so mean," said Laura.

"And it's not true," said Nick.

"He's rebelling," I said. "I like sports. I have nothing against sports. But there's more to life than sports. What about books? What about art and literature? What about gastronomy?"

"You're ranting, honey," said Laura.

Italian men do not walk. They strut with their hips thrust forward. Their arms swing at their sides as they move forward. Their chests are thrown back and their feet are parted slightly to imply their balls are too big to fit between their legs. They resemble boxers entering a ring. That's how I was trying to move through the piazza.

"He's a ten-year-old boy," Laura explained. "Ten-year-old boys don't care about literature."

"I did," I said.

"That's because you were a loser," said Nick. "I saw pictures of you in your old school yearbook. You were on the swim team, right? You looked like a little white worm. You were totally out of shape."

"Let's sit at a café," suggested Madeline.

We got a table and ordered *cappuccini* and *spumante*. Laura and I knew how Nicholas had developed a passion for sports. He and Madeline were never allowed to watch TV unless a game was on: football, baseball, basketball, soccer, it didn't matter.

"We have created a monster," I said.

"This piazza is beautiful," said Laura. "I think it must be one of the most beautiful I've seen in Italy. I love the way it's bordered on one side by the lake. And I love the lamplights and the colorful old buildings."

A contest was underway to see who had the best display of geraniums. Numbered white placards were nailed to flowering balconies, making it easier for judges to provide scores.

"Can we play mini-golf this afternoon?" asked Nicholas.

A course had been built next to the parking lots above the village.

"I don't want to row back to town after we go home this morning," I said.

"Then let's play now," he said.

"It's too hot," I said.

"C'mon, be a dad," said Laura.

"Oh, all right," I said. "We'll take the ferry back later."

Laura and Madeline rowed back to the island. Nick and I went up through back alleys to the links. It was getting late in the morning, nearly eleven, when tourists typically arrived to shop for souvenirs, see the island, eat lunch, and visit Sacre Monte.

The mini-golf course was in a lot with few trees next to an ice cream stand. Each hole was impossible, as is typical in my mini-golf experience, but it was good to exercise in the fresh air with my son.

"I wouldn't exactly call this strenuous," said Nick.

"That's because we're so good at it," I said. I lowered my voice. "See that German guy and his son?"

"Yeah?"

"They're drenched in sweat. They're exhausted."

The Germans were not playing by the customary rules. Not only were they not permitting any do-over's, but instead of a five-stroke limit per hole, they played until the ball was putted in.

"They'll be here all day," I said.

They let us play through. We finished in less than an hour. We would have been done sooner, but we argued a lot. Then we ate ice cream and walked back through the village. On our way down, we passed by the façade of paint that resembled Padre Pio in profile. A crowd gathered daily to take pictures.

"Why's he famous?" asked Nick.

"He cured sick people with the power of faith," I said.

"Really?" he asked.

"No," I said.

"But why do people believe it if it isn't true?" he asked.

"That's part of the miracle," I said.

"See?" said Nicholas. "I'm not just interested in sports."

"I know," I said. "I'm sorry for giving you a hard time."

"That's OK."

"No, it's really not," I said. "I don't know what comes over me. I just get mental."

"Your father isn't interested in sports either," he said.

"That's no excuse," I said.

We turned down the long, medieval alley that led from Padre Pio to the piazza. Shops selling useless goods lined the way. We had a choice of paintings of the island and the lake, jewelry, dried ham and porcini mushrooms, *limoncella*, and wine. The salespeople were in foul moods since they had to pretend to be proprietors when, in fact, they worked for the two families who owned the hotels.

"Can we buy some grapes?" asked Nicholas.

We were passing below the one shop in the village where fruit and vegetables were sold.

"As long as you do all the talking," I said.

"Sure," he said.

We went in. The woman knew Nick. He stopped by almost every day on his own. We would sit at a café and wait for him to return.

"What else can we get?" he asked.

"Whatever you want," I said.

"You feel badly about being mean to me for what you said about sports," he said after buying most of the fruit in the shop.

"Absolutely not," I said.

"She's nice," he said.

"Who?"

"The woman in the shop," he said. "I was in there yesterday and she spoke Italian to me and English to some tourists. Do you think she thinks I'm Italian?"

"Maybe," I said.

"But what do you think?"

"No," I said. "I don't think she thinks you're Italian."

"Do I look Italian?"

"Oh, definitely," I said. "Your dark hair and blue eyes make you very handsome."

"But do I look Italian?"

"Sure," I said.

"That's cool," he said.

On the way to the ferry we were greeted by the owner of a shop where local textiles were sold. We had bought tablecloths from him and during the transaction mentioned we wanted to see a big soccer match. Italy was playing France in a European final. We had no TV. Did he know where we might see the game?

The game was being broadcast, he had explained, on a huge screen in the courtyard of his sports club in a hilltop village. Why not join him? The four of us drove up that night. The clubhouse was a small one-story building filled with gaming tables, a long wooden bar, and trophy heads of deer. Rows of metal chairs had been set up outside. We took seats. Laura and I drank beer and the children ate potato chips. Everyone in the crowd was Italian except for us. We all cheered for Italy. They scored a goal early in the game and led one to nothing up until the final twenty-five seconds when France came back and tied it up. Then France won in overtime. The crowd had planned a spaghetti dinner, but everyone left in silence and anger without eating.

"I am ashamed of our team," the shopkeeper told us. He was about to burst into tears and tear his garments. "I am so ashamed!"

"Don't say it," said Nick on the way back to the island.

"Say what?"

"Oh, c'mon, you know," he said.

"No, I don't."

"He thinks you're going to compare the Italian team to the Red Sox," Madeline said.

"Maddy!" shouted Nick.

I grew up in New Jersey. I love the Yankees. Nicholas is growing up in Boston. He loves the Red Sox.

"I think we found the Italian soul," I said as Laura rowed back home in still waters and under moonlit, overcast skies. I had stretched out and was stargazing, only there were no stars. "In that courtyard. The soccer match symbolized Italy: People were so busy celebrating being ahead that they didn't notice how lackluster the players were until it was too late. And then the sincere disappointment everyone felt! The loss upset them, but more than that they felt—they feel—they could have done better. That's why that guy said he was ashamed. He must wonder, like a lot of Italians: Why doesn't the country make more of an effort? But it's not easy. Because think how hard they have to try! The standards here are so high—the history of the Roman empire, all the sublime art and architecture—that each day, no matter what they do, they fall short of centuries-old standards. So I think after a while they must say: 'Why bother?' But then they feel horrible and ashamed when they realize how little they've accomplished."

"Is that really what you think?" asked Nicholas. "Dad. Please. Honestly. It was a soccer game. That's all it was. Do you know why Italy lost? They had no defense. And because France's goalie Zidane is amazing. That first goal? French defense broke down. And Italy was lucky. Super lucky. Italy tried. But they lost because France is better."

"Oh, really?" I said. "Is that what *you* think?"

"If you knew how soccer is played, you'd say the same thing. But unfortunately you don't."

"I played soccer in junior high school," I said.

"You stank," he said.

"I was a wing," I said. "I was very fast."

"Then you should know that what I'm saying is obviously true."

"Nick, I was talking about the game as a symbol for Italy. I wasn't talking about the game itself."

"Was Daddy always like this?" he asked Laura.

"What's that supposed to mean?" I said.

"I can't talk now," she said. "I'm busy rowing."

Laura was working hard to get us across the lake. She had on an ankle-length turquoise-and-dark-blue dress, which resembled a *burka*, and was in no mood to entertain questions. The lake resisted her overtures, but when it yielded I could see the pleasure she took. She was, typically, of the moment.

We docked the boat and went to bed. All that silence made us reflective and appreciative of one another. I don't know if the island really was magical, but sleep always came easy.

Soon we left only when we ran out of food. Huge supermarkets a short distance away had a dozen aisles of 100 percent Italian ingredients that in Boston and Cambridge cost much more in snotty gourmet shops. So we loaded up carts and bought tons of stuff. Other times we drove to restaurants deep in the countryside where it is still possible to find authentic Piedmontese cuisine. These places are family-owned affairs. The husband cooks and the wife runs the front of the house or the other way around. We sat for hours in the afternoons eating and drinking. In the kitchens and wine cellars, I interviewed chefs and sommeliers. These remain some of the best meals any of us have ever enjoyed. It's worth mentioning since the gastronomy is disappearing, a victim of progress, and the passion to carry on in the gardens and rooms where we dined is an effort to preserve community. I don't think any other cuisine is as simple and loving as Italian.

Once we climbed the hundreds of steps to Sacre Monte. The views from the parapet by the entrance were of Alps, hills, villages, and the island. When we entered the sacred grounds, we came across many open chapels displaying painted, wooden mannequins telling the story of the life of Saint Francis. The explanations of each scene were elaborate and pontifical.

"In this scene," I said, "we see a little boy born with wings begging a surgeon to remove them even though his health insurance has run out. But the doctor won't budge. He is insisting on both the co-pay and the insurance. The people around the surgeon and the little boy are a panel of experts trying to determine if he can fly. The boy says he can fly, but he wants the wings removed because he is afraid of heights. The title of the diorama is: *The Uninsured Girly Man*."

"That's Saint Francis entering heaven," said Laura.

"How do you know?"

"The sign says so."

"Really?"

"You read Italian. Tell the children what it says."

I read the brass plaque.

"*The Uninsured Girly Man*," I said.

"I don't understand how you can be so disrespectful," Laura said. "This is religious art."

"It is not. It's kitsch. Honestly. Do you find any of this spiritually uplifting?"

"No," she said, "but that doesn't mean I'm going to put it down."

"Why not?"

"Because other people believe in it."

"No one can hear us," I said.

"The point is to respect others," she said.

"But what if the statues showed devil worshippers sacrificing cats? Where do you draw the line?"

"It's very beautiful here, children," Laura said.

Like her mother, Laura knows the names of trees. She began pointing them out.

"And peaceful and quiet," said Madeline.

The most splendid place of all was our villa and its garden on the lake. I would look up from a book and see Nick's extraordinarily handsome face: his fair skin, dark blue eyes, and black hair. He occupied most of the day bouncing a ball against the villa's walls until told that one more time and I would throw the ball so far into the lake that he would never find it even if he spent the rest of his life looking. I was trying to read, I explained, and how could I with the sound of the ball bouncing? He was keeping score, he explained impatiently, a major league game was on, with hits and outs. I didn't see how that was possible. Laura told me to leave him alone. I have never loved a boy more than I love Nicholas. It was possible on the island to see the world as he saw it: in motion and filled with people and things he loved. He has more confidence and charm than anyone I've ever met. And then to look over at Madeline and Laura dozing or reading in canvas chairs beneath the grape arbor or palm tree. All this filled me up in a way that made me keenly aware of how empty I'd been before them, but also how many promises had been kept by their arrival. This was the family I wished I'd been born into and grown up with. In our corner of the island, with views of the village, and access to the lake, we had surfeit as well as room for possibility.

The more time we spent at the villa and in the garden, the more we convinced ourselves we were turning Italian. Certainly it was true that we cooked and ate like our friends in Italy. Pasta each day after a long swim and dishes made up of fresh, seasonal ingredients. Fried zucchini blossoms. Pan seared swordfish sliced thin like a *vitello di mare* and drizzled with olive oil, lemon juice, loads of salt, and cracked black pepper. Tomatoes and buffalo-milk mozzarella and basil. And when we weren't eating, we talked about eating, comparing meals at restaurants with what we cooked, discussing the merits of a flavor, planning the next lunch. We sat, talked, cooked, ate, drank, and loved for hours. It was indolence raised to an art form, what the Italians call *dolce far niente*: sweetness doing nothing.

In late June, when we had arrived, a few water taxis and ferries motored by each day and boatloads of tourists would snap pictures and make videos of us as they circled our villa. By mid-summer, boats came by as often as four times an hour. There wasn't much distance between us and them, just fifty feet or so, and the low stone wall at the edge of the garden on the perimeter of the lake provided nothing in the way of privacy. They'd wave to us and we would wave back.

"They think we're Italian," I said.

We wore Italian clothing and moved the way we saw Italians move. Paradoxically, with intention and lethargy, as if it might take us all day to cross from one end of the garden to the other. We had gone undercover and infiltrated this most passionate of cultures. For what else was there to do on that small piece of land and in that lovely, old home, but be passionate with one another? Wasn't that the crux of the Italian soul? The knowledge that family is all we've got. Our one hope of salvation.

"We have accomplished what we set out to do," I said to my family. "We have crossed over. We are at home here. We have found the real Italy."

"What's that, honey?" said Laura. "Did you say something?"

"I said, 'We have found the real Italy.' "

"Oh, that's nice," she said.

"I'm serious," I said. "Do you think it's easy to find a place like this? I did tons of research! And logistics! Finding good restaurants! First-rate markets! Recipes for delicious food! All so we could discover the real Italy, the Italy even Italians look for, but often don't find."

"Children, tell your father how much you appreciate him."

"Thanks, Dad!" said Madeline.

"This group is very ironic and I can't say I appreciate it," I said.

"I wasn't being ironic," said Madeline. "I do appreciate what you do. Really."

"Well, thanks," I said. "That's nice of you."

"I'm not ashamed to be American," said Nicholas.

"Are you saying I am?" I asked.

"Well, *yeah*," he said in a tone implying I would need his help to feed myself.

"I have no idea what you're talking about," I said. "I am not happy to be an American. I'm thrilled."

"No you're not," he said.

"He's not," agreed Laura.

"I thought you were reading," I said.

"Why would you want people to think you're Italian?" Nick asked.

"Didn't you want to look Italian the other day at the fruit store?" I asked.

"I'm not as bad as you are," he said.

"We're in Italy," I said. "Don't you want to blend in? Don't you want to find the real Italy?"

"I like Cambridge," he said. "I like it here, too, but this isn't home."

"It is for now," I said.

"For you maybe," he said. "But would you live here? Would you move here, I mean?"

"No question about it."

"You're more pathetic than I thought," he said. "How could you give up Cambridge? Baseball? Our schools? My friends? And what about the dog? What about Bear? Wouldn't you miss him?"

"If we moved here, I would bring the dog to live with us," I said.

"I'm not moving here," he said. "I don't care what you say."

"Your father's just talking," said Laura. "We're not moving."

"Good," he said.

"Yeah, but if we could afford to buy this house, Nick, you'd do it, wouldn't you?" asked Madeline.

He looked to the lake.

"Maybe," he said. "I do love being on this island. And the dog *would* like it here."

"Like it here?" I said. "He'd love it!"

"And I admit it's cool that people are taking pictures of us," he said. "It makes me feel special. Do they really think we're Italian?"

"*Si, certo*," I said. Yes, of course.

Another boat went by. Its railing was lined with over a dozen tourists waving to us and snapping photos and making movies of our family.

They waved to us and we waved back.

"Hello," we said with our hands. We waved backwards, our palms facing us. Like Italians. Like the Pope.

THE UNITED STATES:
MANHATTAN,
SAN FRANCISCO, GEORGIA,
DISNEY WORLD

MANHATTAN

"Is 'feckin' the same as 'fucking'?"

"Yes," I said, "now lower your voice, please. People can hear you."

"SO ALL THIS TIME THEY'VE BEEN SAYING 'FUCK-ING'?" he shouted.

I walked to the other side of the lobby. His mother could deal with him. Nicholas had led the way out during intermission at the Atlantic Theatre Company. Although he was only ten years old, Nick had acquired a useful vocabulary. Only my father was as skilled at embarrassing me.

I had bought hard-to-get tickets to see *The Beauty Queen of Leenane* knowing nothing of what the play was about. I'd heard London critics praise the work. And I'm always looking for plays to see at the Atlantic. Housed in what appears to have been a church, on a dark residential street of triple-decker, brick townhouses in Chelsea, the theater is distinctive enough to be a character in per-formances held in its interior.

I hadn't known the dialogue would consist of saying "fucking" a lot. And when the lead in the play began to whack her palm at the end of the first act with a poker, Laura and I exchanged glances in the dark and whispered "uh-oh," knowing of Chekhov's remark:"One must not put a loaded rifle on the stage if no one is thinking of firing it."

During the intermission, other audience members, most of whom I took to be New Yorkers by the contrast between their bland, I've-seen-it-all expressions and stylish dress, took time out from their meditation on the play to express their irritation with me for bringing our children to the performance by scowling, clucking their tongues, and shaking their heads with disdain when they looked in my direction.

"What had you heard about this play?" Laura wanted to know. The children were outside, on the sidewalk, with the smokers.

"I heard it was good," I said. "Aren't you enjoying it?"

"I'm thinking about the children," she said. "Do you think it's appropriate for them?"

"In retrospect, no," I said.

"We're not in retrospect," she said. "We're only past the first act."

"It's not as if they haven't heard bad language before," I said. "I could call them over right now and say 'fuck.' What difference could that make?"

"It's not just the language," she said. "What about the poker? What do you think she's going to do with that?"

"The poker does have me worried," I admitted. "I do have a bad feeling about that."

"Would you please do a little bit more research before you buy tickets in the future?" she said.

"Look," I said, "there's Ricky Jay!"

Ricky Jay was across the lobby in a *Late Night with David Letterman* jacket. He had just finished a sold-out run on Broadway of a magic show and was recognizable at once from his many appearances in films.

"Don't try to change the subject," she said. "Where?"

We got cups of water and stood near Ricky Jay. Then the lights dimmed and we brought the children back in. The mother of the beauty queen was slumped in a rocking chair with her eyes open. The beauty queen walked around the stage and talked about her mother. Then she gave the rocking chair a little shove and the woman in it fell forward. Blood spilled out her mouth. Later we learned the daughter had bludgeoned her mother.

"Anyone want to get something to eat?" I asked the family on the street after the play was over.

But no one was speaking to me. We found a cab and headed back to the apartment we had rented for the weekend on the Upper West Side.

"That was terrible, Dad," said Madeline. "Really terrible."

"I'm sorry," I said. "Are you upset?"

"Of course I'm upset," she said. "I shouldn't even be talking to you right now. That was really bad."

"I said, 'I'm sorry.' " I did feel terrible. "I have an idea: Why don't we get some take-out Chinese and watch *Saturday Night Live*? Get the taste of that play out of our mouths."

"I keep thinking of the blood coming out of her mouth," said Nick.

"Right," I said.

"That wasn't real blood, was it?" he asked.

"No," I said.

"It was still pretty horrible," he said.

"This is the worst night of my life as a parent," Laura said.

The cabdriver looked at us in the rearview mirror.

"No, it wasn't," I said. "You're exaggerating."

"What was worse?" she asked.

"I'm not going to try and think of a worse night," I said. "Why would I try to think of bad things? I feel bad enough."

"That's because you can't think of anything worse than what just happened," she said.

"We didn't actually see her get killed," I said.

"No, but she was killed," Laura said.

"It was just a play," I said. "It was theater. They were actors. No one was hurt."

"I don't want to talk about this," said Madeline. "You're upsetting me. Please stop."

"I know she wasn't really killed and so do the children," Laura said. "That's not the point."

"Think of it as an experience," I said. "We just had an experience at the theater."

"It was a bad experience," said Laura.

"I know that," I said.

We cut across Twenty-third Street.

"Hey, look," I said, "you can see the lights of the Chelsea Hotel! Wow! Sid Vicious died there . . . no, wait. He didn't die there. No, that's where he killed his girlfriend Nancy."

"How did he do that?" asked Nicholas.

"I think he stabbed her to death," I said.

"Dad, please stop," said Madeline.

"Who was he?" asked Nick.

"Bass player for the Sex Pistols," I said.

"You're not making anyone feel any better," Laura said.

"This is history, Laura. It's important to tell the children about famous things that happened here. Please."

"But why does it always have to be morbid?"

"What's 'morbid' mean?" asked Nick.

"Whatever your mother disagrees with is morbid," I said.

"Are you trying to start an argument with me?" she asked.

"No," I said. "I'm sorry. 'Morbid' means sad, horrible, and unpleasant."

"Like the play tonight," said Madeline.

"Oh, come on," I said. "You enjoyed it for a while."

"Yeah, like for the first five minutes," she said.

We reached Forty-second Street.

"Hey, look," I said. "That's where a guy pulled a knife on me! I was in town with a friend from college and this guy came up to me in front of that fire station you see on the corner. See it?"

"Wow," said Nick. "How big was the knife?"

"About six inches, I think," I said. "But we ran across the street and he took off in the other direction. Do you know why they call this part of town Hell's Kitchen?"

"Didn't anything nice happen to you in New York?" asked Madeline.

"Oh, sure," I said. "Plenty. My mother used to take my sister and me to see Broadway plays at Wednesday matinees during our school vacations. She bought two-fer's at the TKTS booth in Duffy Square. We'd have lunch at a corny, wonderful place called Rene Pujol where they served old-fashioned dishes like duck à la orange or French onion soup. My dad used to take us downtown to the Strand to buy used books. And some Sundays we'd drive to Chinatown or the Lower East Side. But the city was different then."

I told them about what it had been like in the 1960s and 1970s. Hundreds of homeless men lined Houston Street in the Bowery. Transvestite prostitutes on Eighth Avenue hung out near the Port Authority Bus Terminal. Drug dealers filled Washington Square. Dozens of head shops in the East Village sold drug paraphernalia. And Times Square meant peep shows, strip clubs, and pornography movie houses.

"How is this helping?" asked Laura.

"I'm telling the children the truth," I said. "New York wasn't always nice. Part of its appeal was not being nice."

"You liked it better then?" asked Madeline.

"I love being here with you now," I said. "And I don't miss the crime and poverty. But I do regret not seeing the things I loved then. It was an odd place. Now it's normal."

"You say normal like it's a bad thing," said Laura.

"I remember being in bed late at night in New Jersey and listening to a New York radio station called WBAI," I said. "The city the announcer described is gone. Back then it was home to Allen Ginsberg and John Lennon. Now who lives here? Donald Trump."

"You're old, Dad," said Madeline.

"No, I'm serious," I said. "New York was a restless, dangerous, artistic city when I was growing up. Now look at it. Everything's commercialized and homogenized and sanitized."

"You're ranting," said Laura.

"I know it sounds like I'm ranting," I said, "but I'm not. I'm expressing my dissatisfaction with the ways New York has lost a lot of the weirdness and urgency that once made it so interesting. I mean, look out the window."

We were heading toward Columbus Circle and passing by one franchise store after another.

"These shops used to be individually owned! These streets were once filled with ordinary people who lived in the neighborhood! But who can afford rents nowadays? The city's gone corporate!"

"So why do we come here if you hate it so much?" asked Madeline.

"Well," I said, "In order to see plays like the one we saw tonight. I'll admit it was scary and kind of unpleasant, but from an artistic point of view . . ."

"You are such a Pollyanna," Laura said. "The play was completely inappropriate for the children! How can you even suggest it's why we come to New York?"

"It was art, Laura, and Brecht said art isn't nice."

"I never want to see a play with you again," said Nick.

"Me neither," said Madeline.

"Oh, come on," I said. "That is so mean."

"You have to promise the next time we see a play you will read about it before you buy the tickets," said Laura. "Or none of us are going."

"Fine," I said.

Then we reached the apartment and got out.

We brought the children to Manhattan several times each year. When they had been babies, we took them to see Broadway musicals and the dead animals at the Museum of Natural History. Each visit made something new possible. No other place we'd been presented us with the opportunity to choose things that conformed to our needs and desires as a family. If we went to a beach, we swam and sat in the sun and played and read books. But in New York, each occasion differed.

The only thing we *always* do in town is eat. At first we went to places I knew growing up, but since I started to write about food, we visit restaurants and shops owned by people I meet through work. Madeline and I spoke to Max McCalman, a man obsessed with cheese, at Picholine. Why, I wondered, does he sound just like a stereo components salesman? Then Nick got a tour of the kitchen at Daniel. We all ate for hours at Nobu. And when restaurateur Silvano Marchetto needed someone to write his cookbook, he called me. Then for over a year, each time we went to New York, the children saw what it really means to run a restaurant.

One night at Da Silvano, we shared a table with Patti Smith.

"Can I sit with you?" she asked. "You seem like a nice family. I miss mine."

But New York is home. We leave having changed little. We fill a cooler with sturgeon from Barney Greengrass, Nova from Zabar's, bagels from H&H, oysters and fish and dry aged beef from Citarella, and greens from the Union Square Market. The food is delicious, but feeling at home in Manhattan, acting like émigrés in Boston, signifies not only that we haven't left home, but that we return each visit.

SAN FRANCISCO

"$1 A HUG," read the sign next to a young woman on the sidewalk. We were in the Haight. She was seated near others offering hugs, too.

"Hey, man, want a hug?" she asked me.

"No, thank you," I said.

"Dad, are you blushing?" asked Madeline.

"Certainly not," I said. "I do not want a hug."

"Why is she giving out hugs?" she asked.

"Because she's broke," I said.

"Then why not let her give you a hug?" she asked.

"I'll give her a dollar and she can hug you," I said.

"No, thanks," she said.

"Same," said Nick.

"I think I'll give her a dollar," said Laura.

"No, don't," I said. "They have a system worked out. That would bring everything down."

"It would not," she said.

She gave the woman offering hugs a dollar. Then we passed by lots of shops where stuff like what I'd bought when I was younger was being sold: lava lamps, beads, buttons, posters, bongs, and pipes.

We were in San Francisco for the first time in my life. Laura had been many times before and now she was taking us on tour. Her love for the city was physical. She looked and sounded younger than before.

We started out seeing a few sights, but then planned days around eating and shopping for food. What had started out as an obsession and then turned into work was now an obsession again. It was exhilarating to go to City Lights, the bookstore and publishing outfit that had been home to the Beats, but just down the street was Molinari and Sons. So before buying books, we stopped by to devour huge sandwiches of Italian meat and cheese. Then we went to Yank Sing and made our way through a dim sum feast.

In less than a week we managed to eat at over a dozen cafés and restaurants I'd researched in advance of our visit. Before arriving, I had associated the city with the Jefferson Airplane, the Grateful Dead, Jack Kerouac, Lawrence Ferlinghetti, and the San Francisco shown in the movie version of *The Maltese Falcon*. But nowadays what I see is food.

"San Francisco is a microcosm of the political decline of this country," I told the family over a meal of Kumamoto oysters, shoe-string fries, and roast chicken at Zuni Café. I paused. "Is this the best food you've ever had in your life?"

"I love it here," said Nick.

"But isn't it remarkable?" I asked. "How a city once famous for political innovation and the birth of the '60s is now known for its gastronomy? Doesn't that bother anyone?"

"Dad, the '60s are over," said Nick, cupping an oyster to his lips and sucking it down. "Wow."

"These fries are great, I have to admit," I said. "And the atmosphere in this restaurant is perfect. Soothing and hip."

A huge fire was blazing in the oven behind us.

"It still bothers me that so much of the political and social energy of the past now is sublimated, you might say, in the cultivation of food and wine. I'm not saying I don't appreciate what we've eaten since we got here, but what about all the homeless? I've never seen more homeless people. And what about that woman giving out hugs?"

I pulled the fries closer.

"Hey," said Nick.

"You're eating all of them," I said. "Why is that OK? You're not the only one here."

"If you're so worried about poor people, why are we eating in all these nice restaurants?" he asked.

We had been to Delfina, LuLu, Chez Panisse, Ton Kiang, Postrio, and Jardinière. Laura had taken us to the markets in Chinatown, the Embarcadero, and Marin County. The day before we had driven to The French Laundry, mecca of the restaurant world in America, where I spent three hours in the kitchen interviewing Thomas Keller, its chef, and observing him work. On Sunday we planned to return for lunch.

"I'll admit it looks as if I'm contradicting myself," I said. "But

I'm not. I'm writing about food and wine, yes, but it's really a way to observe people and document my observations."

"Oh, please," said Laura.

"It's true," I said. "I don't care that much about food. It's just food."

Then they all laughed at me.

"Oh, sure, Dad," Madeline said. "Why not just admit you love to eat? There's nothing wrong with that, you know. Just because you love to eat doesn't mean you don't care about poor people."

"My thoughts exactly," I said.

"You always try to please Daddy," said Nick.

Then I asked for the check and we left. We were staying nearby in the Tenderloin. I had liked the name when booking rooms and geographically it was near Union Square. I had thought of a nice cut of meat. Laura was too busy with work to be involved in where we would stay and left it all to me. We were at the Savoy, a simple inn filled with Europeans looking for an inexpensive holiday.

The neighborhood we entered each morning was filled with people dying on the streets from the effects of heroin, alcohol, and sexually transmitted viruses. It made us miserable to walk past them with nothing to offer other than compassionate thoughts. I worked with people like this as a clinical psychologist and thought again of the shriek of the elephant man: "I am a man, I am . . . a human being!"

Our lunch at The French Laundry lasted about five hours. We had come into one of the restaurant's smaller rooms and everyone stopped eating and talking when they saw us enter. They were all adults. Civilians, tourists, no one involved either in the restaurant trade or the business of writing about it. Arriving with children, we were taken to be intruders on what they seemed to believe was exclusively an adult experience, like sex.

But the maitre d', a Corsican, was accustomed to rudeness and said loudly after we'd been seated, "Thomas has prepared a menu for you. Would that be acceptable? Or would you prefer to choose?"

Suddenly we were in, which brought with it a new set of problems. During the meal, one couple asked another how they had managed to get a table.

"Oh," one of them answered, "we had to call three months in advance BECAUSE UNLIKE SOME PEOPLE WE DON'T KNOW ANYBODY TO PULL STRINGS FOR US!"

Which was a lie since the restaurant only takes reservations two months in advance, but never mind, I thought. I had called in like everyone else rather than use my connections.

The food did not conform to the reality of what we expected from food or dining out. Keller's kitchen functions at a different, higher level than most others on the planet, now or before, and his passion for and knowledge of ingredients is matched by humor and love and poetic memory. Where else is it as good? Taillevent, L'Arpege, Ducasse, Auberge d'Ill. But Keller is an American, relatively unschooled, and certainly lacking in a family or cultural tradition that often informs an intuitive style of cooking. So his genius, lacking context, is even more interesting.

"Wow, what a great deal," I whispered to Laura when the bill came.

"Don't tell me," she said.

I gave the waitress a credit card.

"OK, how much was it?" Laura said.

"You said you didn't want to know," I said.

"Just tell me," she said.

"About seven hundred dollars," I said.

"How can you call that a great deal?" she asked. "That's infuriating. You're infuriating. I can't get our bathrooms fixed and you tell me that seven hundred dollars for lunch is a great deal."

"I liked the food a lot," said Nicholas.

"I did, too," said Madeline. "Thank you for taking us."

After discussing the relative merits of home repair and upscale dining, we staggered out. We had eaten nineteen courses.

Adjacent to the dining room is a splendid garden. The children had gone there between courses to let off steam. The chef was waiting for us.

"Had enough?" he said.

"Absolutely," I said. "Delicious, beginning to end."

"Are you sure you've had enough? Because we can go down the road to Bouchon and have a dozen oysters if you're still hungry."

"I'm in if you are," I said.

But we left and no one ate anything for the next twenty-four hours.

WASSAU: A GEORGIA SEACOAST ISLAND

Kitty's family owned an island off the coast of Georgia. She told us that a distant relation had won the land in a poker game that took place soon after the Civil War. Then about eighty years later, when governor Lester Maddux declared his intention to buy the property and build an amusement park on it, the family arranged a sale to the federal government on the condition that the land become a nature trust protected from development. What remained of the family's holdings was now a compound of six ramshackle homes, less than a dozen acres of lawns, and a dirt road to the beach facing the Atlantic. The original owner had been a wealthy, New England aristocrat, "with homes up and down the eastern seaboard, from Georgia to Maine," but now more than one hundred cousins, aunts, and uncles shared the property with love and rancor as no one had enough to pay for upkeep.

Nick knew Hazel, Kitty's daughter, from school and we'd all become friends.

We went in June after school let out for the summer. The drive down, through the Carolinas, was made interesting by visits to family-owned barbecue restaurants I had read about in advance.

The pulled pork sandwiches were tasty so we ate too many. We all liked being called "honey" and "darling" by the waitresses even though we knew they had no real interest in us whatsoever.

And the atmosphere in several restaurants owned by white people—their austerity, prim and proper customers, the whole perfumed and playhouse quality, the sanitized tables and floors—was appealing in its theatricality. The corny propriety of the white-owned establishments was designed to make clear to everyone that although soul food was being served, it was white people cooking and serving it. They did not want to be mistaken for being black.

After we got past Savannah, Kitty showed us a run-down collection of shacks beside the road.

"Pinpoint," she said. "Where Clarence Thomas grew up. It's one the poorest communities in the state. Clarence could barely read or write as a child."

"And then what happened?" I asked.

"Oh, he's a bad man," said Kitty.

Kitty is a Republican, but she abhors hypocrisy.

She shuddered and got back on the road.

Then we drove just a few miles away through an exclusive community of posh homes. Beyond this neighborhood a golf course had been built, a clubhouse on the water, and then a launch. We parked beside the clubhouse and servants took our things on a cart in order to wheel them over a boardwalk to a boat that would take us to the island. The servants were all young white men, well-scrubbed and in shorts, reeking of cologne, with the sort of ruddy, piggish appearances I associate with heavy drinking. They were awfully kind and very polite and had no feeling for what they were doing, but they demonstrated compliance fueled by anger, which is often the best kind since it is rigid as well as reliable.

Then we motored through wetlands. Dolphins followed the boat.

The heat on the island was brutal. It was heat that is soapy and blistering, perfect for the birth and development of bugs. In fact, insects, we learned quickly, regarded the island as a giant petri dish. I would walk to the beach in the morning with Madeline and our dog, but by ten o'clock could not do more than lounge on a couch and read old books. At five each afternoon, I would pour ice and gin into a metal cylinder in order to prepare martinis to be enjoyed with Kitty. Later, sleep was supposed to occur on relics of mattresses positioned in wiry frames that nearly touched the floor.

I was feigning sleep one horrible afternoon, a book on my chest, when Nicholas entered the house crying, covered in mud, and clutching his left arm. I could see at once that the arm was broken. The bone was pressed up against his skin in a way that was frankly alarming.

"Nicky fell out of a tree while we were alligator hunting," Laura said. She was right behind him. Nick was dripping mud and water onto the wooden floor. "We found a tree with planks nailed into its trunk and he climbed up them to get a better view of the swamp."

"Did you see any alligators?" I asked.

"No," she said. "Then on the way down the tree, Nicky missed a step and fell face forward into the mud. But I think he'll be fine."

"He doesn't look fine to me," said Jonathan, Kitty's husband.

Laura and I took Nicholas to the outside shower and cleaned him off. He looked like he was in an awful amount of pain. But one of the marvels of living with Laura has been the discovery that, as a physician, she never reacts with anything other than love at times of physical distress. Nothing must be allowed to interfere with the act of observation. She held Nick's arm closely and through her fingers and hands conveyed love when touching his skin.

"Why don't we wait an hour or so?" she said. "See how things go."

Laura's calm can have the effect, however, of panicking others around her unaccustomed to its purpose. Jonathan, for example, normally a man whose anxiety is most often seen in repetitive

behavior rather than fear, began to pace and raise his voice in unpleasant ways meant apparently to force us to take more immediate
action.

Then we had to take care of him for a while.

Soon it was obvious that it would be necessary to call the ma-
rina and get a boat to take us to Savannah. Nicholas cried the whole
way over and we hugged him.

The hospital in Savannah was poor and urban. We waited for a
specialist Kitty's family had called to meet us. A gurney went by. On
it was a man in a dark green uniform: Georgia State Penitentiary.
The prisoner was shackled to the metal bars of the moving platform
and then we saw he was accompanied by two state troopers.

"Look, Nick," I whispered. "A real criminal."

"Wow," he said.

"Don't point, honey," I said. "Just look."

"What do you think he did?" asked Nick.

"I don't know, honey. What do *you* think he did?"

"Maybe he murdered someone," said Nick.

"Maybe," I said. "Or stole something. Or broke into someone's
home. Or hid income from the government. Maybe it was more
than one thing."

"Will the two of you please stop?" said Laura.

"I'm trying to cheer Nick up," I said.

Then the doctor arrived and got ready to see us. But first he had
to treat a man in worse condition than Nick. The patient was
bruised and bloody. His face was discolored from internal hemor-
rhaging. He kept moaning softly. He could barely move.

"What happened to him?" I asked the doctor when it was our
turn to be seen.

"He was hang-gliding off the back of a truck and when the
truck stopped, he fell onto the highway from a height of about four
or five stories."

By the time Nick was ready to be examined, the manners he had been taught at his private school had kicked in. He said "please" and "thank you" and managed to smile. He only whimpered a little when his arm was examined. So the doctor thought it would be OK to move the bones back into place without first administering an anesthetic. After that Nick screamed and I thought of getting up to assault the doctor.

The next day was better. Nicholas had forgotten the pain associated with falling out of a tree, breaking his arm, and having the bones reset without an analgesic. He also enjoyed having a cast, his first, for others to sign and fuss over.

Then the dog developed a rash as a result of heat, salt from swimming in the ocean each morning, and bites of insects on the sore, salted skin. Why we thought it would be fun to bring a Bernese mountain dog to Georgia during the month of June is beyond me. The dog became increasingly lethargic by the hour. I would lift him in my arms and try and cool him down in a pool beside the house and that worked for awhile, but then he looked awful again. He stopped eating and only drank a little.

"He's dying," said Kitty.

"He's not even two years old," I said.

"I know that," she said. "But he's dying."

Laura decided to stay as planned, but I left the next morning with the children and the dog in order to drive back home before the dog died. We could have gone to a vet in Savannah, but figured if we got home in thirty-six hours he would be OK. The dog perked up in the air-conditioned car. Then we reached South Carolina for the night.

"I'm sorry, sir," said the receptionist at the motel over the phone in our room, "but we're going to have to turn down the A/C for awhile. It stresses out the generator."

We had checked in early and then made the room as cold as a meat locker. The sixth game of the NBA finals were about to begin. As there was no TV on the island, we had missed the others.

"But you will turn it back on, right?" I said.

"Oh, yes sir, absolutely," she said. "You bet."

We got ready for the game. I had spent over an hour driving on roads nearby in an effort to try and find food we wanted to eat, but had passed by only franchises where things were deep fried and then heavily salted before being sold.

"This looks delicious," I said. We each had on our laps rectangular-shaped paper boxes holding chicken parts.

Madeline took a bite.

"I can't eat this," she said.

"Oh, come on," I said. "Why not?"

"You taste it," she said, "and tell me what you think."

I had a bite.

"OK," I said. "I don't see a problem."

"Dad, it's all fat and skin," she said. "It's horrible."

"You're exaggerating," I said. "I'll admit it's not the best meal I've ever had, but it's not the worst either."

"I can't eat it either," said Nick. "I'm sorry, Dad."

"You're both being snobs," I said. "Besides we have no choice. We're in the middle of nowhere. We looked for a place to eat, but couldn't find one, could we? We're all hungry so we have to eat."

"I'm not that hungry," Madeline said.

"Same," said Nick.

"Fine," I said. "Don't eat. See if I care. I just can't believe I spent eight dollars for your dinners and you're not going to eat them. Man, oh, man. What a waste of money!"

"You always tell us to think about what we eat," said Madeline. "Well, I'm thinking about it."

"Fine," I said.

Nick turned on the game and then the air conditioning came back on. I took another bite.

"This does taste awful," I said. "Why, I can remember driving through the south twenty-five years ago and stopping in small towns to have great local food. And now look what's happened! Capitalism has destroyed gastronomy and local agriculture! Communities have been destroyed, too! To say nothing of the terrible effects on one's health of eating this stuff! Did you see the size of the people buying dinners tonight? They were enormous! What's happened to this country?"

"Dad," said Nick, "calm down. I'm trying to watch the game. Please. It's just dinner."

"Just dinner? 'Just dinner,' you say? It's not just dinner. No dinner is just dinner. No, this meal is a perfect example of the way tradition and history are being destroyed every day by capitalism!"

"See?" Madeline said. "So why did you give us such a hard time? You can't eat it either."

"I didn't give you a hard time," I said. "I was only encouraging you to eat."

"You gave us a hard time, Dad," she said.

"I did? Well, then I'm sorry."

"How can Kobe make those shots?" asked Nicholas.

"No one knows, Nick," I said.

Then we left the next morning and drove home. The dog was given antibiotics and skin cream and managed to survive nicely.

DISNEY WORLD

After the murderous attacks on September 11th, I had an overwhelming need to know what people hated most about America so we arranged to go to Disney World. The Disney Corporation had been the forbidden fruit in our household. I saw its theme parks as the embodiment of ruthless, gutless capitalism hell-bent on destroying the natural curiosity of children, indigenous cultures of the developing world, and a spirit of community I associate with generations of tradition and history. Replacing these values instead with an insatiable urge to spend, the Disney Corporation, it seemed to me, had succeeded in making desire the point rather than satisfaction. I thought Saul Bellow had got it right when he had Henderson the Rain King mutter, "I want, I want, I want," and it had become clear to me that Disney was the culprit, exploiting the consumerist mentality which fueled the U.S. economy, making it the hated symbol of ahistorical greed.

Madeline tended to agree with me on each one of these points, which I had made efforts to explain to her routinely since birth, but her brother, choosing his own path as usual, wanted to maintain parity with his friends whose families went to Disney World regularly and regarded the world as a huge playground. Laura took for granted that I was being argumentative and regarded my opposition as characteristic and without merit.

It took terrorism to get us to Disney World.

Laura found a medical conference on colposcopy that would be taking place at Disney World in March during school vacation for the children.

"I'm not going," said Madeline, who had turned fourteen a few months earlier. "Disney World represents the worst things about this country. It's totally commercialized and is designed only to get people to spend money on junk. It's artificial and there will be nothing to eat."

"Oh, Madeline," Laura said, "you've been listening to your father too long. How do you know it won't be fun? You've never been."

"You can go if you like," she said. "but I'm staying here with a friend."

"If she doesn't come," said Nick, "can I bring a friend?"

"She's coming," said Laura.

"No, I'm not," she said. "I don't have to."

"I'd like to bring Ned," Nick said. "You both like Ned."

"I'm sorry, Madeline, your mother is right," I said. "We are forcing you to come with us to Disney World. And once there we're going on all the rides. And you are, too. And then we're going to

Universal Studios where we will go on more rides. So too bad. Get used to it."

She stormed out and went upstairs to her room.

"What's with her?" asked Nick. "Most kids would be happy to go to Disney World."

"There is nothing wrong with her," said Laura.

She followed Madeline in order to try and soothe her.

"I'll make a list of rides my friends recommend," said Nick.

"Good idea," I said. "We will need to get up early each morning to go on all of them."

"How early?"

"Not too early," I said. "First, we'll have a huge buffet breakfast. I've read about them. You eat so much you can hardly move."

"Wow," Nick said.

"Doesn't that sound great?" I said.

"This *is* great, Dad," he said. He hugged me. "Finally. What made you change your mind?"

"I want to have fun," I said. "I'm tired of not having fun. Think about it: For five days all we'll have to do is have fun. That will be our job. No cultural sites, no cultural experiences, no foreign languages, no churches or museums or hikes or beaches, nothing but fun. I've been stressed out since September and I think going to Disney World will be the cure."

"Disney World!" Nick said. "Finally. You know, I'm the only one in my grade who hasn't been."

"Well, not any more," I said. "Disney World. Boy, oh, boy. I can't wait."

Laura left a few days earlier for the start of the conference. I was not keen on flying, but figured if Laura had enough faith in air travel to feel it would be safe for the three of us to fly without her, nothing terrible was going to happen.

Unfortunately, through my job as a psychologist I had interviewed a fair number of men and women over the years who had been employed in airport security. I had met them through state agencies that work with the mentally ill, the mentally retarded, and those once addicted to drugs and alcohol and then quite recently sober. I knew that a massive overhaul of the security system had taken place, but sensed that the infrastructure which had been in place up until September 11th had not as yet been completely eradicated.

"Pardon my French," the security officer said to me as she waved a wand over me, "but the last guy in here was a real asshole. 'Get your fuckin' hands off me,' he says. I'm just doin' my job. Trying to make the skies safer. No reason for him to go off like that."

"I can't understand it either," I said. I was being completely sincere. "I'm thrilled you're here. Honestly. I've wished we had security like this for years. And take your time. I don't care how long it takes. Anything to make things safer."

I met up with the kids after I'd been frisked and we trundled our stuff to the gate.

"Did they think you were a terrorist?" asked Nick.

"They weren't sure," I said.

"Daddy's not a terrorist," said Madeline.

"That sounds like a Courtney Love song," I said. "Kurt Cobain's wife."

"I know who Courtney Love is," she said. "I'm not stupid."

"What a thing to say," I said. "Kurt Cobain's wife. We shouldn't think of her as his wife. We shouldn't think of anyone as someone's wife. Don't you think that's demeaning? Not being a wife, of course, but being referred to as someone's wife as if that person has no other identity outside of being a wife."

"You're pretty nervous about flying, aren't you?" said Madeline.

"I am not," I said. "What makes you say that?"

"Because you're talking very fast," she said.

"Can I get some candy for the flight?" asked Nick.

"No," I said.

"What if I buy it with my own money?" he said.

"It's not a question of money," I said. "I just don't want you to buy candy. I bought bagels from Iggy's, Daniel Boulud salmon, and a bar of Côte d'Or chocolate."

"It's dark chocolate, isn't it?" he said.

"Yeah, so?" I said.

"I don't like dark chocolate," he said. "You know that."

"Live with it," I said.

"I wish Mommy was here," he said. "She would let me buy candy."

"Fine," I said. I gave him money. "Go ahead. Buy cheap, poisonous products without any flavor other than sugar if you must. See if I care."

He grabbed the money.

"You could say 'thank you,' " I said.

At the gate I had to take my shoes off and be searched again. Only three months before, a homicidal Islamic maniac now known as "the shoe bomber" had tried to murder hundreds of strangers on a flight from Paris to Miami in order to demonstrate that the Muslim religion has cornered the ethics market. As a result, thousands of ordinary people were walking around in socks before boarding planes.

"Did *that* person think you were a terrorist?" Nick asked.

"He wasn't sure either," I said. We waited our turn to board. We were no longer among the "families with small children" who got on first. As I had been doing more often since September than should be necessary, I was softly whistling, "Let's Face the Music and Dance," an Irving Berlin song I knew from a recording by Ella Fitzgerald we listened to almost daily at home:

> *There may be trouble ahead*
>
> . . .
>
> *Let's face the music and dance*

"But what if a terrorist fools them?" Nick asked as we walked down an all-white tube to the plane. The passage had few identifiable features or angles and was antiseptic. I thought of hospitals where I'd been. "And he gets on the plane?"

"Lower your voice, please," I said.

"I was whispering, Dad," he said.

"No, you weren't," said Madeline. "You were practically shouting."

"That won't happen," I said.

"But what if it does?" he said.

"I will stop him from doing anything horrible," I said.

"How?" he asked.

"I will crush him like a twig," I said.

"Cool," said Nick.

Nothing was extraordinary about the take-off, but it was our first time in the air since September 11th and every sound or movement seemed portentous until we reached cruising altitude. Then the sky and coastline acquired the jewel-like beauty only obvious when seen from great heights.

"I remember now why I love to fly so much," I told the children. "It's soothing to race above the earth and to see it from such an extraordinary perspective."

"You're scared to fly," said Madeline. "What are you talking about?"

"I know it seems like I'm scared to fly," I said, "but I'm not. I love to fly. OK, since you-know-what-happened I'm not as crazy about flying as I used to be, but I decided to try and remember what I used to love about it."

"You're trying to talk yourself into not being scared," Madeline said.

"I am not," I said. "You know, Churchill flew a lot during the war. He wasn't scared. He's inspiring."

"You've been talking a lot about Churchill since September," she said.

"Well, he was a great man," I said.

"I know," she said. "You've told me hundreds of times."

"It bears repeating," I said.

"Every day?" she said.

Then Nick suggested we play Crazy Eights while Madeline read a book. The plane reached Florida and veered west and when we landed everyone applauded and cheered more wildly than I'd ever witnessed after a flight.

Laura met us at the airport. The Orlando airport looks like a shopping mall where travel is incidental to its true purpose. Adults dressed like children were in states of forced gaiety. Even the porters and cashiers and desk workers were bursting with happiness.

We got in the rental and drove to Animal Kingdom Lodge. To reach the hotel, we went past manicured shrubs and beneath or beside purple and turquoise signs indicating attractions. When we crossed the perimeter of Walt Disney World, I suddenly felt sad and happy at the same time. I recalled sitting before a black-and-white TV at a neighbor's house to watch *The Walt Disney Show* on Sunday night. The program had been banned in the home I grew up in as my parents held Walt's anti-Semitism against him. It was the sort of thing they took personally.

"This is so beautiful," I said. And then I began to sing that classic Disney tune, "When You Wish Upon a Star."

Laura started to sing, too, as she drove, which Nick and Madeline took as provocation to kick her seat and scream at both of us. We stopped singing then in order to yell at them, which was invigorating after the tension brought on by flying.

"Welcome to Animal Kingdom Lodge!" said a young man in a khaki outfit who stood at the entrance to the hotel. Several other employees, dressed in identical clothing, joined him to assist in taking our bags. All of them were perfectly groomed, like prize cattle, and the way they expressed themselves made it appear as if they were thrilled to see us. I liked them at once.

"But they don't mean it, Dad," said Madeline.

"I know that," I said. "But it's nice. Who cares if they mean it or not? Why is that important? What matters is how they treat us."

"You never used to talk this way," she said.

"I've changed since September," I said.

The entrance hall was set up like a hunting lodge in Africa. The walls went up three stories, a fake fire was roaring in a hearth, and beautiful African percussive music had been piped in to create the effect that we were near a real village whose inhabitants were celebrating our arrival. Clusters of numb-looking children were gathered in circles around TV screens where Disney cartoons showed continuously. The whole effect was remarkably therapeutic, as if we'd all been dipped into a vat of liquid Prozac, and at once the outside world mattered less than before. From the windows, we saw a facsimile of an African savannah on which roamed actual giraffes and antelopes.

"This is better than being in Africa," I said. "You'd never guess that a third of the continent is dying of AIDS or that starvation occurs routinely or that the colonial legacy has destroyed the integrity of traditional economic and cultural life. I led a press trip to Mali for Oxfam America in 1984 and I saw an entire village camped out in front of a pharmacy begging for food. And then on the same trip, I saw in Ethiopia how a police state operates—undercover agents followed me around whenever I left the hotel. Many children in Addis Ababa wore burlap sacks instead of clothing. But this? This is wonderful! I love it here! I want to stay here forever! Forever and ever!"

"I told you, Dad," Nick said. "See? I knew you'd like it."

"How can you mean that?" asked Madeline. "Doesn't it bother you that this is a fantasy of Africa? This isn't really the way Africa is. I studied Africa in school. We're not really learning anything about Africa by being here."

"Maddy," Nick said. "Please try to have fun. Why do you have to be serious all the time?"

"I'm not being serious," she said. "I have nothing against this place. We just got here. It *is* beautiful. But why do they say it's African? It's not. We're in Florida."

"It's a fantasy, Madeline," I said. "It's someone's fantasy of Africa."

"Yeah," she said, "but not mine."

"Let's eat," said Nick.

"We don't have time," I said. "We have to go to the Magic Kingdom right now."

"We're here for five days," said Laura. "I'm not going to run around like a lunatic."

"But it's getting late. There's a lot to do. Nick and I made a list and I've read a book on Disney World that rates all the rides and attractions. We're not going to waste time eating when we could be on a jungle cruise."

"I don't want to go on a jungle cruise," said Madeline.

"That was just an example," I said. "But it was given four stars out of a possible five."

"I want to relax by the pool," she said.

"It will be fun to go to the Magic Kingdom," I said.

"No," she said, "it will not be fun."

"You'll feel better if you eat something," said Laura.

"I have an idea," I said. "Nick and I will take the shuttle to the Magic Kingdom and you can both stay here."

After Laura and the children ate lunch and went swimming, we got on the bus for the Magic Kingdom. Then we joined a crowd that turned into a stampede toward the front gates. We all started talking incredibly fast and our eyes dilated and our hearts raced and we became rather silly. It was love at first sight: I enjoyed what I saw and heard, but wanted more. We all did. That was unavoidable. That was the point. I know for certain that the Disney Corporation did not release chemicals into the air that turned us all into insatiable,

happy idiots, but the feeling of giddy desire swept over us so rapidly and so pervasively that I'd swear mind-altering drugs had been
sprayed on us as we waited to get in. And we weren't even inside, I
reminded myself, hallucinating joyfully, conjuring up images of
what lay in store.

"Main Street U.S.A.," I said to the children after we entered.
"Isn't it beautiful? Isn't it wonderful? Look at the care that went
into these buildings and streets! Everything's so clean and perfect!
And the costumes—they're spectacular!"

"It isn't real, Dad," Madeline said.

"We're escaping, Madeline," Laura said. "It's a nice escape from
reality."

And it was. Only that morning we'd seen pictures in the paper
of the recent suicide bombing at the Moment café in Jerusalem in
which nearly a dozen people had been murdered by yet another
terrorist who wanted to make a point. But there, in front of me, was
cotton candy pinker than any I'd seen before and perfectly popped
popcorn and sweet, nonsensical music played on a computer meant
to sound like an old-fashioned organ grinder.

"Oh, let's just take off all our clothes and run naked through
these streets!" I said. "Is this place something else? Is this place the
best?"

"I told you," Nick said. "I've been trying to get you here for
years."

"I wasn't ready," I said. "But I am now."

I started to unbutton my shirt.

"No," said Madeline. "Please. Don't. What is it with Daddy?"

"Your father is having a manic episode," said Laura. "He'll be
fine in a minute. Just don't say anything that might upset him."

" 'I saw the best minds of my generation destroyed by madness,
starving hysterical naked,' and so on and so on and so on," I said.

We were rushing by the shops on the main street heading toward
Cinderella's castle. Life-sized cartoon characters entertained small

children in the Crystal Palace, a restaurant, while their parents made videos. The food they ate was inedible, but so what? The kids had dazed expressions on their faces as if they were possessed by good spirits whose mission it was to fill them with bliss. It was like seeing a happy version of *The Exorcist*. Then when we reached the circular plaza in front of the castle, ecstasy flooded *my* veins—the sheer beauty of the invention, the recollection of having seen the black-and-white version Sunday nights as a child, the disabled men and women being wheeled to view the castle, the people with Down's Syndrome being led closer, the old and the infirm, even the grotesquely obese folks who hardly managed to say no to their desires—all of us were welcome, all of us had a place in Disney World—this was a pilgrimage in the truest sense.

While I was in throes of religious passion, deepened perhaps by kismet or decades of self-imposed exile from actual faith, I was led by Laura and Nick to Frontierland. Madeline continued to gripe, sputtering like a boiling kettle, due to what she observed to be hypocrisy and betrayal. All this time she had adopted the Eurocentric—historical, literary, gastronomical, cultural—values of her father and now, in just hours, his core was revealed to her and she knew he was a simp.

Madeline's mood improved somewhat after going on rides, but Laura and I could tell she would have preferred to be elsewhere. She screamed dutifully as we hit curves, but in the watery darkness of certain attractions, surrounded on both sides by singing robots shaped like people or animals the size of toddlers, her doubts about the purpose of our visit trumped any little excitement she might have felt. Everything she observed was dampened by a need to strike out on her own.

"We missed the opportunity," Laura said later that night over drinks and dinner. We were in a room meant to look like an African club of some sort. Many flavors had been blended together so it was impossible to tell what it was we were eating, but it was all quite good. "We should have come when the children were smaller."

"They are burned out," I said. "Cynical."

"No, we're not," Madeline said. "I'm having a good time. I just don't see why we have to spend every minute going on rides. And you have to admit the place is totally phony. I don't see why we had to come here for a week. Two or three days would have been enough."

"Five days is not a week," I said.

"Whatever," she said. "I can't talk to you."

"All I meant was it's not a lot of time."

"It's not a week," said Nick. "It's five days, Maddy."

"I'm not talking to you either," she said.

"Is it OK if she talks to me like that?" he asked.

"No, it's not," I said. "Madeline, say you're sorry."

"You're all impossible," she said.

"I'm not impossible," said Laura.

"I told you I didn't want to come," she said.

"Well, too bad," I said. "You're stuck here. That's right, you're stuck in Disney World for five days and there's absolutely nothing you can do about it."

"I don't have to go on rides," she said. "I can stay at the hotel all day tomorrow and swim, if I like."

"Oh, that sounds like fun," I said. "Sitting all day by yourself by the Uzima Springs pool while obese tourists the color of worms eat and drink so much they can't move while their horrible children run around like hyperactive spaniels yapping and peeing in the water. Oh, that sounds like much more fun than going on rides."

"You're not helping," said Laura.

"Well, I'm sorry," I said, "but I think it's ridiculous to suggest that sitting by a swimming pool is more fun than going on rides."

"I'm not against rides," Madeline said. "I just don't want to go on them all day."

"Have you ever gone on rides all day? You should try it. Think of it as a cultural experience. How do you know you won't like it if you've never done it?"

"Fine," she said.

"Is that a 'yes'?" I asked.

"Leave her alone," Laura said.

"Fine," I said.

Then Laura and Madeline walked out on us.

The next day, to mix things up a bit, I arranged to visit Universal Studios and Islands of Adventure. The change would do us good, I thought. Perhaps Madeline's disagreeable state had been brought on by the childlike quality of the Magic Kingdom. The helplessness inculcated in her by observing colorful mice, for example, might not be a problem in theme parks where many rides and attractions, I'd read, centered upon avoiding disasters like being eaten by a shark, killed by a tornado, crushed to a pulp in the paws of a giant gorilla, buried alive in an earthquake, murdered by psychotic cartoon villains, or ripped apart by chunks of metal while speeding along on a metal track suspended upside-down on a roller-coaster.

Immediately, the four of us went on a ride having to do with Spiderman, which proved satisfactory. At times it appeared as if we were falling tens of stories from a New York skyscraper. Then holograms tried to kill us with guns. We enjoyed ourselves so thoroughly that when the ride ended, we got back in line at once for seconds.

That seemed the point. Nothing we did at Universal filled us up like good sex or a full meal. We were reduced, either like a kid or succubus, to the point of desire. We were not filled with longing, we *were* longing. And the longing was based on terror. At least the best rides were. And when we were terrified, of course we howled.

How many times since September had we wanted to howl? And to howl, surrounded by strangers, in a public place devoted to our happiness, was liberating in ways impossible to anticipate. We howled out of grief, longing, fear, and rage. We howled like dogs.

Howling could be heard all over Universal. The air was thick with screams. Apparently, the designers of the park have tapped into some base human instinct.

It became clear that many of the rides and attractions were based on things gone dreadfully wrong. A beast breaking out of its cage was a dominant theme, but natural disasters, such as tornadoes and earthquakes, also were used to galvanize us. I found it all hugely entertaining, as did Nick and Laura, but Madeline appeared again to be a curmudgeon, passing judgment on what I knew to be the efforts of technicians, writers, and the marketing department.

"I don't see what's fun about an earthquake," she said after we'd emerged from the fiery and wholly realistic ruins of a subway stop beneath the streets of San Francisco. "People die in earthquakes. It's horrible."

"No, it's not," I said. "It's made up."

"Oh, really?" she said. "Why is it fun to pretend to be part of a disaster where people have died?"

"That's a good question," I said. "Nick, what do you think?"

"What?" he said. "I wasn't paying attention."

"Madeline wants to know why it's fun to pretend to be in an earthquake."

"It's not fun," she said. "That's not what I said. I said it's not fun."

"You're the only one who didn't have fun," I said. "Have you thought about that?"

"What if they made a ride based on being in a concentration camp?" she said. "Would that be fun?"

"No," I said.

"So why is this any different?"

"I suppose the random quality of dying in an earthquake as opposed to being tortured and then murdered, singled out as it were, due to your supposed race or religion has something to do with it."

"That's ridiculous," she said.

"I didn't say it made sense," I said.

"What if someone you knew had died in an earthquake? Do you think you would have enjoyed pretending to be in one?"

"You're trying to trick me," I said.

"You see my point," she said.

"Yes," I said. "But people do enjoy being frightened knowing that when the ride is over, everything will return to normal. Whatever *that* is."

"Oh, I see that," she said. "I just don't understand why the rides have to be based on real events that actually kill people."

"They don't," I said.

I had gathered from a guidebook that the most frightening rides at Universal were Dueling Dragons and the Incredible Hulk Coaster. During a recent periodontal surgery, I had been able to imagine and then sustain for the duration of the procedure a vision of what it might be like to be buried alive. The two roller coasters noted had obviously been designed by people whose sadistic fervor mirrored that of oral surgeons.

"Let's go on those," I said.

"That's not happening," said Madeline.

"Oh, really?" I said. "So maybe it's not all this nonsense about commercializing death that bothers you. Maybe you're just scared."

"I have an idea," said Laura. "Why don't you and Nicky go? It will be a father-son bonding experience."

"Yeah, Dad," said Nick. "Let's bond."

He gave me a hug.

"Hands off," I said.

"Dad! You're hurting my feelings! You're damaging my self-esteem!"

"Good," I said. "This way you'll have something to talk about in therapy when you're an adult."

"Oh, you're scared," he said. "You're a girly man. Oh, Daddy's a girly man. He's scared of going on the roller-coasters. Boo hoo."

I insisted we leave at once. Within the hour we were back inside Disney World, this time at MGM Studios. I was certainly not going to discuss my emotional needs with a child on the lot of an amusement park. The marvel of Disney was the way fantasy had replaced any thought of conversation.

"Now then," I said, "let's see who's scared."

We joined the line for Rock 'n' Roller Coaster.

"I bet this will be like Space Mountain," said Nick.

"Space Mountain? That's just a kiddie ride," said the man in front of us. "This here's a *ride*."

"I take it you've been before," I said.

"Me and my wife come four, five times a year," he said. "I bet we been on it more than a hundred times."

"I bet we have," said his wife.

"It's our personal favorite," he said.

"Oh? Why's that?"

" 'Cause it's so darn scary and fun," he said. "It's thrilling, believe you me."

I determined rather quickly that he was exaggerating his speech in an effort to entertain us. I admired the effort. In fact, we couldn't help but admire everyone's efforts. Employees whose job it was to see to it that we had a nice day were especially deserving of our praise, but veterans of the establishment sought us out periodically and seemed to think it was their duty to provide us with the information necessary for us to enjoy our stay. The gentleman before us was no exception.

In short order, we joined him and his wife in a metal wagon resembling a convertible automobile. Then we were shot into darkness at sixty miles per hour within a few seconds, turned upside-down, and blasted by music and bright lights. The effect was sudden, of course, and soon after we stopped, the family agreed we should devote ourselves to going on every roller-coaster in all the parks. Ironically, our brains were being washed of doubts, fears, and misery through these shared acts of technologically induced terror and replaced with desire for more of the same. We reveled in the sameness, we embraced it like a cloak.

Nick and I ran to the Tower of Terror, which was said by my guidebook to demonstrate what it would be like to be trapped in an elevator and dropped multiple stories at an extraordinarily rapid pace. The fear experienced by us in anticipation of the ride was invigorating. It was as if raw, grated horseradish had been put under our noses. Two boys of Nick's age, abandoned by their petrified fathers, asked to join us. Overwhelmed and made utterly senseless by their worries, they could not stop talking. It was like meeting a fellow American abroad.

When the ride ended, we began to tell Laura and Madeline about the terror we had brought into our lives and to discuss, more specifically, the relationship between the fantasy of terror and the real terror of real terrorism, but they were hungry and wanted something to eat. I insisted there was nothing to eat within miles of where we stood, but Laura bought the children ice cream which proved to be inedible.

" 'Have a nice day,' " said Nick. He spoke of the vendor. "Can you believe that? She said, 'Have a nice day.' "

"What if I don't want to have a nice day?" I asked.

"Exactly," he said.

Then I suggested we go on more rides.

"Is that all you care about?" asked Madeline.

Laura and Madeline had decided instead that we had to see "Beauty and the Beast—Live on Stage." We ran to the auditorium and joined hundreds of little children on long benches. The parents of these children appeared to be in a state of arrested development and looked no older than their offspring. Obesity, new clothing, and a very high standard of personal hygiene were also common features of the crowd.

Before the show started, we had imagined ourselves to be capable of observing critically, but as soon as the actors took to the stage we were helplessly moved. Almost nothing is left to chance in Disney World. Within minutes, Madeline was telling us how she remembered the video from when she was five years old, how she had wanted to know, "Why does he keep going into the woods when he knows the wolves are there?" And I was recalling the earliest occasions of love for her and how the feeling was caught up in anger. I was angry at the wolves. I wanted to devote my life to protecting her from the wolves. And now that she was fourteen years old and preparing to live in ways fundamentally separate from Laura and me, my ability to protect her had, I'd come to believe, been diminished by chance and necessity. I looked at her beside me and thought: I've lost my little girl, I've lost my daughter. And what about those wolves?

I could see, too, from the way Laura dabbed her eyes and Nicholas appeared transfixed that I was not the only member of the family hoodwinked and riled up. By the time the performance ended, the four of us were emotionally exhausted.

"They control everything," I said. We were on our way out. "It's fantastic. Nothing that goes on here escapes them. They tell us what to feel and when to feel it. All those baby-sized robots everywhere? Little baby robots. We're just like them. Maybe they were once people, too. Maybe Disney has found a way to snatch bodies and put electrical implants into brains and force them to sing and dance the same things day after day. Laura, did you ever go to the World's Fair in 1964?"

"Yes," she said.

"Remember seeing all the little robot kids dressed up in costumes from all the different countries?"

"It's a small world after all, it's a small world after all," she sang.

"What's wrong with that?" I asked.

"Nothing is wrong with that," said Laura. "It's a lot better than saying you hate everybody."

"Exactly," I said. "And if total control is necessary to bring about harmony, so be it."

"I am never coming back here," said Madeline.

"You don't have to decide that now, honey," said Laura.

"Aren't you amazed?" I asked. "One man's vision created this park. He must have been a genius. We are who he wants us to be. We have become the Disney version of ourselves."

"That's exactly what I hate about it," she said, "I don't know who I am and he's trying to tell me who I'm supposed to be."

"That's very philosophical," I said.

"Heavy, man," said Laura.

Madeline stopped dead in her tracks.

"Are you doing what I think you're doing?" she asked. "Are you making fun of me?"

"Yes," I said.

"Mom?" she said. "You are, too?"

That night the children opted to eat on their own at the hotel. Laura and I reserved a table at California Grill with a view of the Magic Kingdom. Our waiter, who, we learned, was originally from the kingdom of Morocco, served us with deference and respect. Most of the dishes were by now familiar to us. There was a run on tuna at all the upscale restaurants in Disney World. Things also came in trios: trios of beef, duck, and pork were the most popular. Nothing tasted as if it had been prepared by human beings, but it all tasted good. I could readily imagine we were inside a space shuttle being served food cooked and packaged on Earth by Disney robots and then brought to the table by subjects of planets where conquest had proven successful.

"Isn't this great?" I said after Ahmed had cleared away the first course. "Why can't the whole world be just like this place?"

"This restaurant?" asked Laura.

"Sure," I said, "this restaurant. But more than that I mean Disney World. Why can't the world be more like Disney World? It's clean, quiet, safe, and civilized. Best of all, people are devoted here to having fun. There's no hatred between races or ethnicities or religions. No one's fighting over land or access to water or oil. No one's fighting over anything."

Ahmed returned to pour the wine. It was a good wine, from California, a Chardonnay: lean and balanced rather than unctuous like many Chardonnays from that state.

"This is very good wine," Laura said to Ahmed.

"Oh, thank you, madam," he said. From the way he said it, I thought he was going to say he'd picked the grapes himself. "I am so glad you enjoy it."

Then he left for the kitchen.

"See?" I said. "There's Ahmed. Nice enough fellow. No *jihad* for him. He's not on any sort of holy crusade against the West. And do you know why? Because he's happy."

"He does seem content," Laura said.

"Exactly," I said. "He's content to have a job waiting tables at Disney World. Can you blame him?"

"But how would we know?" asked Laura. "We don't know a thing about Ahmed. Maybe it's all a façade and he's harboring resentment toward us."

"That's the beauty of it," I said. "How he feels doesn't matter, does it? There's something greater than Ahmed and that thing is Disney World. He's down, he's angry, he's upset about something. Doesn't matter. He's a professional. And his professionalism comes from recognition that he's here at Disney World. This isn't Six Flags, Laura. This place has a vision."

"This place is make-believe," she said.

"Says who?" I said. "Who says that turning the Middle East over to the Disney Corporation wouldn't be an improvement?"

The silence that precedes the eating of flesh disrupted the flow of our thoughts. Then music played through the restaurant's loudspeakers drowned out the last sounds of private talk. Ahmed returned with our main courses and suggested, rather affably, I thought, that we direct our attention to the dark skies and well-lit architecture of the Magic Kingdom. Then bursts of light which we knew to be fireworks rather than well-placed bombs distracted us. When it was over, most diners conveyed their appreciation for the night's events through applause and whoops.

"Fireworks, every night," Ahmed said. And then the customary bonhomie of "enjoy your meal" or words to that effect.

THE GRAND TOUR

Holidays are an undertaking which require massive logistical efforts. I must spend half the year planning to get away. And for what? The children are no longer children. Madeline and Nicholas are no longer sweet and cuddly. That was a long time ago. No, as they near adulthood, they've become like everyone else I know: unpleasant and difficult. No, worse. They criticize what I say and how I dress, the ways Laura and I speak to one another, our tastes and interests, oh, they miss absolutely nothing about us and feel it's their duty to report back. It's like going on holiday with our parents.

But frankly, who can blame them? Laura and I have gotten old. We like doing the same things, day after day, having the same conversations, wearing the same clothing, going on about how much better the music of our youth had been compared to what they listen to, telling them with blatant hypocrisy about the evils of sex and drugs and alcohol, enjoying nothing more than sitting for hours in restaurants and then spending most of the next day talking about what we've eaten, laying in bed late at night, just the two of us, and going on about saving for college and our work rather than making love, taking one another utterly for granted after sixteen years of marriage, fighting about the smallest details of our lives and not even acknowledging the possibility that our frustration and rage is the result of the unavoidably depressing fact that we're old and tired and limited in our passion for everything. In sum, we've become like our parents.

At this point, some families I've known might drum up activities that could bring us together. Something along the lines of skiing, skating, biking, or singing, who knows? Who cares? Why not dress in identical sweat suits and caps emblazoned with logos and emblems saying "Haas Family: We're #1!"? As Nirvana put it in a song title: "Smells like teen spirit." Families like that look like the horse guards in front of Buckingham Palace.

I suppose we could cancel the holidays and put the kids in camp for the summer. Then they might learn something useful like how to build fires. But Laura and I can't bear the thought of sending them away.

While it is more difficult than ever before to find things we all want to do at the same time, we want to be together more than apart. No one else outside of our little group comes close to being as irritating, which we mistake for intimacy. And we need intimacy like an addict needs heroin. The alternative is withdrawal.

We don't have much time left. Oh, sure, we'll always *stay in touch*, but less than three years from now Madeline's off to college and Nick isn't far behind. Soon we'll be back where we started twenty years ago, before the children, filled with longing, reminiscing about holidays, more individuals than a family, waiting for the phone to ring, hoping for a little visit over Thanksgiving or Christmas, knowing we never managed to enjoy our time when we were together, knowing now it's too late. That will be the final step. Then we'll have become our parents in *every* way possible.

Pathetic, isn't it? But these were my thoughts the winter before Madeline would turn fifteen and Nick would become twelve. Why bother to go anywhere?

"Why don't we just stay home?" I said to Laura one night. "You garden. I'll read books, write, and walk the dog. It will be very nice. It will be quiet."

"I'm sorry," she said. "What did you say? I wasn't listening."

We were in bed and Laura was reading the morning paper. She

left each day for work so early that the only time she had to catch up on the day's events was a half hour before falling asleep.

"That's fine for you," she said after I'd repeated what I'd said and we'd argued awhile about whether or not we ever listened to one another properly. "You don't have a job. I need to get away. I like these trips we take as a family."

"Well, I don't," I said. "I hate them. And what do you mean I haven't got a job?"

"You haven't got a boss," she said. "You don't have a schedule. You only do what you want to do."

"You say that like it's a bad thing," I said.

"Fine, you work hard, congratulations," she said. "Never mind. Sorry I said anything." She went back to the paper and then remembered something else I'd said. "You don't really hate the holidays, do you? You can't possibly mean that."

"Well, I do," I said. "No one appreciates the effort it takes to organize the trips. And then when we get there everyone complains."

"That's not true," she said. "We all love and appreciate you."

"Oh, sure," I said. "Sure."

"You have the strangest way of asking for sex," she said.

Then the next morning, which was a Sunday, I insisted we talk about plans for the summer. We had left our old, decrepit neighborhood a few years ago and now had a home in West Cambridge worth spending time in.

"Oh, cool," said Madeline. The irony in her voice was barely detectable. "We're going to have a family meeting."

"Charlie's family does this every Sunday night," said Nick. "He hates it."

"It is a little contrived, Dad," said Maddy. "You have to admit."

"I don't have to admit anything," I said. "I want to have a discussion about what we're going to do next summer. Why is that contrived?"

"I don't know," she said. "It just is."

Then she went back to reading the *New York Times* magazine. She was turning into a complete snoot.

"Put that down," said Laura. "Your father and I want to have a serious discussion."

"Thank you," I said to Laura. "I could do with a little support from you every now and then."

"I always support you," said Laura. "If you're going to take that tone with me, I'll leave the room."

"No, you won't," I said. "You haven't eaten yet."

"That's it," said Laura. "I'm not going to be insulted."

Then she walked into the living room with the Styles section. Nicholas went upstairs to begin what was certain to be a full day of playing *Warcraft II* on the computer. I sulked and then followed Laura.

"OK, I'm sorry," I said.

"Sorry for what?" she said.

"Whatever it is you want me to be sorry for," I said.

"That is not an apology," she said.

"I meant I'm sorry for insulting you," I said.

Madeline came in the room.

"I don't want to have a family discussion," she said. "It's just going to deteriorate into a fight."

"It won't," I said. I kissed Laura. "See? We made up."

"We haven't made up," said Laura.

"Oh, come on," I said. "I said, 'I'm sorry.' "

"You talk to me the way your father talks to your mother."

"Honey," I said. "Sweetheart? Don't we have a rule? We don't talk about how we are just like our parents. It will only make me angry."

"Too bad," she said. She was reading wedding announcements. The people in the photos appeared to be about eleven years old.

"Please," I said. "I'm sorry."

"Fine," she said. "But I want you to think about what I've said."

"OK," I said.

"OK, you will think about what I've said?"

"OK, I will think about what you've said."

"Are you being sarcastic?" she said. "You better not be sarcastic."

"I'm not," I said. "I think what you've said is very thoughtful and helpful."

"You guys!" said Madeline.

"What?" I said.

"I can't stand it here," she said. "I'm going to move to Marianna's house."

"Fine," I said. "I'll help you pack."

Then Nick came downstairs.

"What?" I said. "Did the computer break?"

"See, Mom?" he said. "He's always putting me down."

"I am not," I said. "It's just that I'd like you to do something more useful with your time than sitting in front of a computer and playing video games all day."

"Like what?" he said.

"Anything," I said. "Oh, I know. I have a crazy idea. How about a book? Why not read a book? That would be nice for a change."

"You don't think I read?" he said.

"No," I said.

"Well, I do," he said. "For a half hour every night before going to sleep."

"And that's it?" I said. "That's your idea of reading enough? No, you'd rather play mindless video games than read. That's obvious."

"Would you please leave him alone?" said Laura.

"I'm just getting warmed up," I said.

"I mean it," she said. "He's an eleven-year-old boy. All his friends play video games. That's what they do."

"Did I ask whether or not his friends play video games? No, I did not. I'll tell you something. When I was Nick's age I was reading Kafka!"

"I wouldn't brag about it, Dad," said Nick. "You were a nerd. You had no life. Why would you want me to be a nerd like you?"

"OK," I said. "Fine. I'll drop it. OK. Look, let's talk about the summer, OK?"

"We're not going to have to talk about feelings?" asked Nick. "Because if we are, I'm going back upstairs."

"No," I said. "Feelings will not be part of the discussion."

"I don't care much where we go," said Laura. "As long as it's beautiful and fun."

"But did you have any place in mind?" I asked.

"Provence," she said. "Let's go to Provence."

"It would be nice to go to France," said Madeline. "It would help me improve my French."

"It's not school," said Nick. "It's vacation."

"I know that," she said. "But why else am I learning French? I'm good at French. I like French. So it would be nice to use it. You'll see when you take a language in school next year."

"I don't want to go to France," Nick said.

"Where do you want to go?" I asked.

"You don't want to hear what I have to say," he said. "So there's no point in telling you."

"Oh, come on," I said. "That's not true."

"I want to go some place where people speak English," he said. "I want to go some place where there's stuff to do. Let's go back to Hawaii. Let's go to San Fran'."

"I'd go back to Hawaii," said Laura.

"What kind of stuff do you want to do?" I asked.

"Swimming, horseback riding, surfing," he said. "I'd like to go skydiving."

"We can do all those things in France, Nick," said Laura.

"But they speak French," he said.

"That's the point," said Madeline.

"I loved San Fran'," he said. "We could go back to Zuni—

I loved their Kumamoto oysters and French fries! And we could go back to The French Laundry, too."

Nick had gotten a lot of caché from the parents of his friends when he'd spoken with them about The French Laundry. He spent evenings in their households regaling them with tales of the table. Nick had become a raconteur.

"Or New York," he said. "Let's spend a month in Manhattan. I'm not trying to be mean, Dad, and I like going to Europe, I'm not saying that, but last year when you took me on the subway to see the Yankees play the Mets was the most fun thing I did all year. Especially when Piazza hit that grand slam on a pitch from Clemens and the Yankees lost."

"I don't want to spend a month in New York," said Laura.

"I could finally go to restaurant Daniel," said Nick. "Dad? Do you think it's better than The French Laundry?"

"It's different," I said. "I think it's more classically French. And there's a certain formality about the room and service."

"It's just a restaurant, Nick," said Laura.

"I have to object," I said. "It's not just a restaurant. It's a temple, isn't it? A temple of gastronomy!"

"There's more to life than restaurants, Scott," she said.

"That would depend on the restaurant," I said.

"Then what's wrong with going to France?" Laura asked. "France has some of the world's best restaurants. You'll be very happy there."

"No, I won't," I said. "It will be work. If we go to France, all I'll do is eat, go to markets, and interview farmers, chefs, and shopkeepers."

"Does this mean you never want to go to France?" she asked.

"No," I said. "It's just that writing about food has become work. Besides, what will we do there? Sit in a garden, cook, and eat?"

"What's wrong with that?" she asked.

"I agree with Nick," I said. "I want a more active holiday. I don't want to sit around eating and getting fat. I can do that here."

"You have put on weight," she said.

"Not that you'd notice," I said. "Anyway, I want to go someplace where food is not that important. I don't want to work on vacation."

"So Italy's out, too," Laura said.

"Right," I said.

"You want to go someplace where the food is bad so you don't have to work?" she asked. "Do I have that right?"

"Right," I said.

"OK," she said. "Fine. I can live with that. If we have to eat bad food to get you out of the house this summer, I'll do it. Where did you have in mind?"

"How about the western islands of Scotland?" I asked.

"I'm not going to Germany," she said.

"No one said anything about Germany."

"Not yet," she said.

"You're not being fair, Dad," said Madeline. "Just because you don't want to eat good food doesn't mean we all have to suffer."

"It kind of does," I said.

"I can't believe you're doing this to me," said Nick.

"Ohio," I said. "We could see the Civil War battlefields of Ohio."

"I think you're being rather selfish," said Laura. "You should be able to control yourself around food. It's just food."

"But I know what will happen," I said. "We'll go to a restaurant in Aix, let's say, and the food will be good and I'll want to sit there for hours and then I'll go into the kitchen and interview the chef. Then he'll introduce me to the man who sells him ducks and I'll interview him, too. Then we'll have to visit cheesemakers, bakers, and butchers. It won't be a vacation at all. Do you remember what happened last summer?"

The summer before we had spent a week in the Valais region of Switzerland and instead of hiking I had toured vineyards. Then we'd gone to Piedmont where instead of reading or swimming I had spoken with dozens of food and wine producers.

"That doesn't have to happen again," Laura said.

"Fine," I said. "I'll compromise. I won't put a ban on France or Italy, but I don't want to spend the entire month in either country. And I don't want to spend a lot of time near food. I want us to do something we all enjoy as a family."

"Like what?" asked Nick.

What we needed to do, I finally realized, was come up with holidays that would keep us so busy we couldn't think straight. I decided to arrange for a grand tour. If we kept moving, no one would have time to complain. Laura and I would choose our favorite places in Europe. It would be a good, old-fashioned holiday much like the ones taken by families who go sightseeing rather than the way we normally traveled. We would start in Venice and go to St. Moritz and end up in Paris. It'd be half the Orient Express, in reverse, with nonstop cultural experiences, hiking in the mountains, lots of high-end shopping, and, what the hell, plenty of time spent in Europe's best restaurants. Why not surrender to what I lusted after? To hell with the consequences.

Over the years, we had tended to go to one place and remain there in order to get to know it well. Now that the children were older, their restlessness was beginning to define more of our choices.

This might be good, I reckoned, as we would discover new things about ourselves through visiting *many* places. For example, the children would understand by touring what I had known for some time: America had become an empire.

Each year Europeans regarded us more and more in the same way the Romans and then the English had been seen by provincials whose territories they toured. Few things are as entertaining. We were thought to be imperialists intruding upon what I took to be quaint, impractical ways of doing things.

What the Europeans may not have realized is that we were

escaping the heart of the empire. Back home there had been a steady, annual growth of jingoism and flag-waving, an effortless homogenization of varied cultures, a dulling of the senses, a tendency to replace observation with emotion. Everyone wanted to tell others how they felt a good part of each day. And a lot of what people felt was that America is number one. But who's counting?

The children would finally grasp through touring what it means to be an American. The quirks we would see might restore to us our originality. That originality was disappearing under an onslaught of brutal sameness back home.

In order to secure rooms, apartments, restaurant reservations, car rentals, train tickets, and schedules, it was necessary to spend an extraordinary amount of time communicating with dozens of men and women in the service and hospitality industries of six sovereign nations. Hundreds of hours were devoted to surfing the Internet where I learned all sorts of details such as the price of bus tickets, store hours, and the location of our car rental agencies. Each communiqué was then laid neatly in a folder that by the time we were prepared to leave was about an inch thick. I organized the papers on the basis of a timetable: data on Venice preceded Switzerland and so on. Planning the holiday had become a military exercise, but the organizational requirements helped keep me sufficiently distracted from what Freud called the psychopathology of everyday life. I complained about all the work, but it was certainly better than doing anything challenging or productive.

The one objection in advance of the trip was raised by Madeline, who wondered why we were spending nearly three weeks in a remote Swiss village on the Austrian border. We had been before.

"Oh, you loved it," I said.

"They have a spa," said Laura. "After hiking, we can go to the spa and relax."

"The most economical method of using the spa is to buy a fam-

ily pass that costs approximately two hundred and fifty dollars a
week for the four of us. Otherwise, you have to pay about fifteen
dollars per person for each visit. The spa is located three hundred
meters from the flat we're renting. You have to bring your own
towels."

"Are you getting work done on anything other than planning
this trip?" asked Laura.

"Not that I'm aware of," I said.

"I don't see why we have to go to Scuol for almost three
weeks," said Madeline. "How am I supposed to practice my
French?"

"You can speak French there," I said. "Everyone will understand
you."

"But they don't speak French," she said. "They speak Romansch."

"What's Romansch?" asked Nicholas.

"Romansch is a modern variant of Latin with a grammatical
structure similar to Italian. Many Romansch words sound Por-
tuguese. Some believe that Romansch speakers are the descendants
of Roman soldiers who settled in Swiss valleys centuries ago."

"But I'm not studying Romansch, Dad," said Madeline. "I'm
studying French."

"Right," I said. "But since Romansch-speakers comprise only
one percent of the population of Switzerland, it's reasonable to assume they have facility for other languages, such as French or German. Did you know that twenty percent of Switzerland is
French-speaking?"

"Are you going to be like this the whole time?" she asked. "Because if you are I'd rather stay home."

"Madeline, the research I do is invaluable for these trips. Why do
you think everything goes so smoothly when we travel? It's no accident. I put a ton of work into the planning so that once we get
there, we fit right in. Why not show a little appreciation?"

"I just want to have a good time," she said.

"You will," I said. "I promise. We always do, don't we?"

"Yes," she said.

"So why would this time be any different?"

She rolled her eyes and made a face meant to convey that what others found confusing, she found obvious. It was a face people her age made often and one I had made quite a lot when I had been fifteen, too. I wasn't so far gone to have forgotten what it had been like to be on her side. This time, however, it saddened me to see the chasm between us widening. The wonder of it all was nearly gone and the world as she saw it had been reduced to the obvious. But I loved her all the more, rather suddenly, for taking the time to show me how much she had changed since childhood. And through that look insisting I show her my love.

We had asked to stay at a friend's flat in Venice. Marco and his wife Claudia live in Udine, two hours away, with their daughters, Camilla and Susanna, but they kept the dwelling for sentimental purposes and rental income. We had exchanged properties a few years back. Then they had been kind enough to give us the flat every June for a week seeing how much we loved the city. After we returned from the current holidays, their oldest daughter, who turned seventeen in the fall, would be staying with us for a couple of months.

To get from the airport to the flat, we could have hired a water taxi, but that mode of transportation is regarded as a luxury in Venice and priced accordingly. Instead we took a public bus that dropped us off at Piazzale Roma where we took a *vaporetto* or water bus.

Vaporetti are always filled with humorless Venetians and tourists from all over the world. We saw fewer Americans than usual since we were now at war. As usual, we looked like buffoons with our entire luggage. The Venetians gave us condescending looks that made us feel we had no right to be in their city. Dressed as if they had stepped out the pages of *Vogue*, the locals demonstrated a sartorial confidence bordering on arrogance. It was as if centuries of art and historical dominance of the Mediterranean had been reduced to a pair of absolutely killer plastic eyeglass frames, shirts of Egyptian cotton, and color coordinated outfits. What was marvelous, too, was the way in which Italians celebrate human form and not just youth. The old men wore suits tailored to accentuate their shoulders and what remained of their hips and the old women had on scarves that made me think of what they had looked like when they'd been girls. It wasn't a question of romance. Rather, here is a culture or society that prizes memory and the recognition of power. Power does not reside in youth, the clothing suggests, it is found instead in those who've got the money.

We went down the Grand Canal. Laura looked weary, but tired in the way she appears after a long trip that brought her home. It was a sexy kind of tired: languorous and slinky. Laura's movements change when we're in Venice. Never in a hurry, here she slows down more than ever in order to take in the sights. Indoors looking at paintings or in view of the architecture, she sashays in order not to miss anything. We waltz through the city rather than move with intent toward a goal as is my practice. And the ways water changes the way we look at things—simplifying, provoking recall, calming, cleansing—add to her pleasure.

We disembarked at Accademia, just below the bridge and beside the museum. A vendor selling slices of coconut in a fountain got Nick's attention. Then we walked past men and women dressed in what was meant to suggest Renaissance attire. They had on funny hats and stockings and turquoise or burgundy colored vests. The women wore dresses that ballooned out and seemed to contain the world. These performers sold tickets to a concert of Vivaldi's *Four Seasons* taking place that night at the Scuola Grande di San Rocco. When we'd gone before, our family's reactions ranged from boredom to torpor. The children got revenge the next day.

The way to the flat brought up memories. I saw the children shrink in size and heard their voices get higher in pitch. But now they knew the way and led us over footbridges and down alleys. They didn't take a false step.

Claudia and Camilla met us with kisses and a bottle of sweet, late harvest wine. "You are at home here," she said. Claudia has a musical, tremulous voice I find soothing and her pale blue eyes look sad. She speaks often of affection for Americans, and for the Jews, and although our conversations over the years have been brief, her regard for vulnerability has always made her deeply appealing.

The rooms are dark in the flat. Italian homes do not have window screens or air conditioning. Claudia kept the tall, wooden shutters closed to keep out the heat and *zanzara*—Italian for mosquito, a word I prefer as it mimics the insect's buzzing. The place is furnished like a set from a 1950s neo-Realist Italian movie with clunky furniture and Formica tables and bed mattresses in big frames. Seated in the darkness with Claudia added to our disorientation, which was quite pleasant. We knew we had left home and though we might feel at home, the flat wasn't ours. We became a bit like actors in an Italian drama speaking emphatically and using English words that resemble Italian: In fact, absolutely, certainly, no problem.

We made final arrangements for Camilla's visit and then they left. Laura undressed to nap and I took the children on what is our daily routine in Venice.

We go each morning to the Rialto market. It was past noon so the fishmongers were cleaning up, but shops and produce stands stay open longer. Over the years, I've written about a few vendors and when we return they greet us like regulars. There's a show of affection in which every gesture and statement is exaggerated. We all know it's a comedy, quite ridiculous, but also what cements the contact. We're in a play together. We play like children hopeful and keen rather than adults waiting for something to happen.

The owners of Casa del Parmigiano, dressed like surgeons, sliced prosciutto as if life depended on the width of the cuts. Facing the shop, Georgio Santini handled forest berries as if caring for infants. The market teems with entrepreneurial spirit, but none of it matters much in terms of money. I think they do it to keep from going mad.

"I'd like a lot of berries," said Nicholas.

I gave him some Euro and he stepped up to the stand.

"*Lamponi*," he said. "*Fragole. Per favore.*"

At the cheese shop, Madeline helped negotiate a sale of buffalo-milk mozzarella and ricotta so fresh it wiggled when cut. The owner once told me his father had started the business in 1936. The purchase we made was a way to establish contact between our families. Or so it seemed when buying small bundles of cheese.

We ate in a café I like beside the open area where fish is sold. The fishmongers were hosing the area down. I saw snails trying to get out of a few wooden crates and then eels writhing in flat trays. A light rain fell and looking at the children I trusted for a few minutes in fortune.

We returned to the flat to cook Laura a meal of fried zucchini blossoms. She refused to get out of bed and sounded delirious, but we insisted she wake up. Otherwise, she'd be up all night. She ate what was served with cold white wine that cost a few dollars.

She got dressed. Then we strolled through the city, proud to know our way around.

The children took the lead. They'd first been eight years earlier on a house exchange we had made with a woman who owned half a villa on the island of Lido. But it isn't just the recollection of who we'd been as a family that delights them each time we return. We have tended to let them loose in Venice and its islands in the lagoon and have more confidence and certainty.

The children had not memorized the dates of paintings or the names of painters, nor could they identify what they found attractive about the palaces, but who better to react to the ephemeral, the passage of time implicit in art and architecture, than children? Each day is an eternity for them.

Venice is as devoted to tourism as it had once been to domination of the Mediterranean by naval power and control of the world's most profitable trade routes. You cannot go five feet before bumping into someone selling an insignificant object which commands your attention. We rather enjoy walking its alleys and bridges in an effort to discover what lies beneath the futility. It's not quite ruined. No matter what they keep doing to commercialize the remains of its glory, the city's paradoxical integrity is still visible. Corruption has always been a part of its success and the legacy is evident in the way the city operates like a huge carnival, year-round, at its apex in the formal pageantry of Mardi Gras. The shopkeepers, restaurant owners, waiters, and of course the gondoliers are always on the lookout for an easy mark. But as Henry James wrote in *Italian Hours*: "Half the enjoyment of Venice is a question of dodging the tourists."

We had intended on our first day back to walk to the Scuola Grande di San Rocco, which is Laura's favorite museum in Venice. She has stood there for hours, neck stiffened, looking up, or down at a hand-held mirror, in order to see the passionate interpretation of loss and struggle and redemption as depicted in Tintoretto's biblical cycle of paintings on the ceiling. She loves to watch and can absorb extraordinary pain by looking and not saying a word.

The rain got heavier. We brushed against buildings in narrow passageways and entered shops in order to keep dry. One place was selling first-rate goblets and bowls which cost more than the book value of my car. Then we reached San Rocco just as the real downpour began. A storm was sweeping through the city. We'd only once before seen lightning and thunder in Venice. Storms are always dramatic, only more so in Venice. The old buildings are illuminated and then cast into darkness; it's like watching someone undress and then throw on a robe, and the crashing is so loud you feel as if you're in a car accident.

Laura had promised us she would only spend forty-five minutes inside San Rocco, and that we would return the next day, but with the storm she had an excuse to stay longer. Madeline accompanied her and the two of them moved beneath the art with mirrors. As usual, the place was empty. I took Nick into the next room where we looked at *The Crucifixion*, which is my favorite painting by Tintoretto. I find it difficult to look at art without trying to figure out a narrative and here was the climactic scene of *The Greatest Story Ever Told*.

"I thought you weren't religious," Nick said.

"I'm not," I said.

"So how can you like this painting?"

"I think it's easier if you're not religious," I said. "Then you can see it as a story."

"Pretty depressing, huh?" he said. "I mean, look at the faces. Everyone's unhappy."

"Death of hope," I said.

"So why are we sitting here looking at it?" he asked.

"Because it's beautiful," I said. "Don't you find it amazing to see how realistic and different everyone's expression is in the painting?"

"Sure," he said, "but it's depressing." He shifted on the uncomfortable seat next to mine. "Let's get out of here."

"Right," I said. "Let's blow this joint."

We walked over to Laura who by now was enraptured.

"Ready to go?" I asked.

"Aren't you into this?" she said. "Just look up."

She handed me a mirror.

"Moses, right?" I said.

The four of us craned our necks to look at more paintings and then I agreed to wait in the foyer downstairs with Nick. An Austrian family asked me for directions to the train station and then a couple from France wanted to know how to get to the Rialto Bridge.

"You see?" I told Nick. "I am practically Venetian. I look like a local."

"I know, Dad. You're cool. You are super-cool. Giving out directions to wet tourists. Oh, that is my idea of cool."

Then Laura and Madeline joined us and we waited for an end to the storm.

"Why is it better to wait here?" asked Laura. "We could be looking at paintings."

"Well, then go back upstairs," I said.

They returned to the upper hall and then the rain stopped and soon we left for the flat. Even the sound of the children's footsteps filled me with joy as we climbed up and down footbridges. They walked ahead of us and led us through Campo San Barnaba. The flat was just up ahead, beside a quiet canal, facing a nunnery. We got out of wet clothes and prepared to doze off before departing that night for a friend's restaurant. I say "friend" the way Italians use the word. I had once written a story about his place and now he refused to let me pay for dinner.

The children went upstairs to watch a preview of the World Cup final that was going to be played on Sunday. Laura and I made love while a young woman sang opera from a flat across the canal. A boat puttered by. Then an old woman shouted in response to the singer: "*Basta! Basta! Basta!*"

The days began, as always, by walking with the children to the market while Laura slept in. We tried to move like Venetians who, whether hasty or on a stroll, have a proprietary look like cats. It all belongs to them. They seem to derive confidence from the buildings. On our way, we took in the smells of freshly baked bread. A few bakeries still exist in the city and early in the morning it's as if you can taste crust before putting any in your mouth.

After we'd shopped, we got a table at our café by the market.

"Do you mind if I have a *cappuccino*?" asked Madeline.

"No, of course not," I said. I remembered the days when she had hot chocolate in the same café, accompanied by some *dolce*, but now she was older and more aware of looking like a girl. It was the second summer I'd seen men look at her the way men can look at women. She had at first been too young to know what was behind that look. Now she understood.

"If that guy looks at you again," I said, "I will get up and kill him."

"Don't be an idiot," she said.

"Well, he's rude," I said.

"He hasn't said anything," she said.

"He doesn't have to," I said.

"Oh, Daddy's a macho man," said Nick.

"You're both idiots," she said. "And if you don't stop, I'll meet you back at the flat."

"I meant no harm," I said.

"Can we talk about something else, please?" she said.

"Red Sox are in first place," said Nick.

"It's June, Nick," I said. "The Red Sox own June."

After discussing whether or not the superior record of the Yankees was due to merit or not, we left for the flat. Nick woke Laura up and we served her the bounty of our purchases on a terrace that faces a hidden garden.

Laura organizes the time in Venice around viewing artistic masterpieces while I make certain we shop for food and eat at the restaurants of friends. The arrangement satisfied all of us. The children had once found going to art museums one step above shopping for furniture, but they were older now and had acquired levels of serotonin necessary for standing in front of dry paint that depicts the Virgin Mary, the infant Jesus, the crucifixion of Jesus, the martyrdom of worshipers, and the miraculous acts of saints. We bargain with the children, providing them with a variety of trinkets and sweets in order to prolong viewing times.

After the art and bribes, we return to the flat to hear the opera singer and her enemy. Then we nap for a few hours. I am often struck by how well suited we are to indolence despite efforts throughout the year which suggest the opposite.

Before dining, Nick and I wait for Laura and Madeline at a friend's bar called Al Cantinone già Schiavi. We are not good friends, however, and have to pay for drinks and bar snacks known as *cichetti*. Nick points to the snacks he wants, which are on display in a glass case: *baccala*, pickled *cippolini* wrapped in anchovies, fried olives, each day it varies. Then he takes his iced tea and I lift my flute of *prosecco* and we stand beside the canal and talk. No moments are more pleasant than these.

Laura and Madeline arrive, all dressed up, looking more than elegant, looking as if they belong, and then we go to a friend's restaurant or have pizza at La Perla, an out of the way pizzeria so hard to find there are more Venetians than tourists drinking beer and eating.

On the walks, in the darkness, the children don't stop talking and observing and even brightly colored, worthless glass shown in well-lit shop windows acquire value. Venetians are a sad bunch and so much that's on display is designed to amuse them. I'd be dolorous, too, surrounded by structures to remind me that where I live everything of importance took place centuries ago. It's a city with no future.

Before going to bed, we stroll on the Zattera, a wide walkway near the flat on the island of Dorsoduro. I forget that I've told the family about Ezra Pound's walks here. I repeat myself. Then further up there's this hand-holding that goes on between the four of us when we reach the tip of the Zattera, within view of both San Marco and the island of Giudecca. We decide not to fuss about it.

Aren't we all too old for this sort of nonsense? But instead we stop to allow an embrace from the breeze.

Three days later, we're on the road. We've picked up a rental and are headed for the Dolomites, a region of the Italian Alps on the Swiss and Austrian borders. We had intended to drive straight through to Scuol, but a friend in Venice had a friend in San Cassiano who insisted I visit his hotel and spa for a couple of nights with my family.

"He don't expect nothing," said my friend in Venice. "Just check the place out. It's really quite beautiful."

I did a bit of research and discovered that the hotelier and his family also owned spas in Monaco and St. Moritz, a ski mountain, and the region's hydroelectric plant. After moments of soul-searching, I decided if I had to accept everything for free, I would make the sacrifice. We were, after all, at war.

The trickiest part of the venture was deciding when to leave Venice for the mountains. If we stayed to watch the World Cup final, we would wind up driving on alpine roads that had no lights. But if we left too late, we would miss the game. And we had to arrange to eat at the right time. Restaurants in Italy serve lunch strictly between twelve and two. We got to a village that appeared to be about an hour south of San Cassiano, had lunch in a trattoria, and were just in time to see Brazil beat Germany. Nicholas was thrilled and the *mozzarella e pomodori*, *penne arrabiata*, and *linguine con gamberini* were first-rate. Then we got back in the car and continued our drive, which took a lot longer than an hour due to curving, two-lane alpine roads.

I had expected the hotel to be in a pasture surrounded on all sides by pine forests, but it was not. Rather, it was dead center on a long street of ski shops and empty chalet rental apartments. People in costumes greeted us at the curb and then at reception. All over the world, at tourist haunts and hotels, there is lately a trend to have staff dress up in outfits of their forebears. They do this in order to create the impression among guests that the individual servant represents generations of servitude. In this instance, the clothing was Tyrolean. The men wore breeches, ruffled shirts, vests, knee-high stockings, and buckled shoes. The women had on huge dresses leaving only their hands and necks exposed.

When we arrived, the woman at the front desk, who turned out to be the owner's wife, was speaking on the phone in a language I did not recognize. She explained it was Ladino, which apparently is a variant of Latin like Romansch. From what I was able to determine during our stay, locals use Ladino to talk about foreigners in front of them and to compose folk songs which require the use of accordions and acoustic guitars. The hotel owner later told me many of these melodies are romantic stories about hiking, skiing, and the pursuit of maidens who want no part of those singing about them.

After being shown to our rooms, which had exposed pine and enormous beds with thick eiderdowns, the children insisted we take them swimming below ground at the pool in the hotel's grotto. I had brought with me a copy of *Koba the Dread*, a book by Martin Amis, which is about the twenty million people murdered under Stalin's orders. The children swam laps and Laura and I read while lounging in extraordinarily comfortable chairs.

"Can you imagine?" I asked her. "Stalin murdered all the old Bolsheviks! Not just his enemies, but his friends and allies. I had no idea."

"You didn't know?" she said. She sipped from her bottle of spring water.

"I must have been blind to it," I said. I, too, took a sip. I don't understand how people can differentiate between most types of bottled water. They taste the same to me and I have come to believe the relative success of certain companies is due more to marketing than to superiority of the product. "Too busy reading about

Hitler, I suppose. And being on the Left so many years, I always sort of forgave Stalin. I wouldn't say I was an apologist for the communists, but I believed their help in defeating the Germans compensated for the excesses of the regime."

"Hey, Mom, Dad!" yelled Nick. "Look at me dive!"

He leaped into the water and then came up for air.

"Fantastic!" we shouted.

"But he tortured and murdered millions," I said. "It's a wonder anyone survived. You know, as I read this book I feel ashamed of not having spoken out against Stalin. Or against Lenin or Trotsky for that matter. They were all horrible human beings. Murderers."

"Don't you find reading this sort of stuff depressing?" she asked.

"Of course I do," I said. "But it's our responsibility to know what happened, isn't it?"

Nick and Madeline cavorted in the shallow end of the pool and then Nick got out and went to the self-service bar. We heard the wet slap of his feet on the tiles and then the whirring of a blender.

"Can we talk about Stalin later?" said Laura. "I would like to relax. Do you mind?"

"I made a fruit shake," said Nick. He had appeared by Laura's side.

"Oooh," said Laura, "what kind? I want a taste."

"Banana," said Nick.

"Laura, I'm trying to talk to you about Stalin. Nick, you're interrupting a private conversation. Your mother and I were talking."

"Was it about me?" he asked.

"No, it was not about you," I said. "Now please let us continue."

"This is good, Nick," said Laura. "Go make me one."

"No, don't," I said. "They might cost money."

"We're on vacation," she said, "and I want a fruit shake."

"You know," I said, "we never have serious conversations any more. We're constantly being interrupted by the children. We were in the middle of talking. Can we please continue?"

So we talked some more about Stalin and his imprisonment and torture of millions of Russians. Then after Laura drank her fruit shake, we showered, went back to the rooms, and dressed for dinner. The hotel had a one-star Michelin restaurant and a well-known chef who was eager to cook for us. The food was excellent.

The next day we hiked the Alps beside the hotel. To reach the trail we were after, it was necessary to walk through the property of farmers. It is the same way in Switzerland: You unlock and lock gates, say hello to families working in the fields, and continue on your way. The ascent was steep at first and then leveled out. We walked through a forest and then got above the tree line. At an inn below a cliff, beside a church no longer in use, we had lunch with other hikers. Then we walked back down the mountain, got lost, and returned to the hotel.

The owner of the hotel, dressed in a Tyrolean outfit, was in the lobby serving white wine and a sort of local snack. He was fit, rather affable, likeable in every way possible and seemed fully conscious of the benefits of leisure activity. After changing out of the clothing we had hiked in and while the children went swimming, we joined him. Then he invited us to dine in the restaurant's private room in view of the kitchen. The meal was even better than our first as it was made up of a tasting menu devised by the chef to highlight local ingredients used in traditional recipes. Over the main dish, a remarkably juicy beef slowly roasted in fresh hay, it became easier for me than ever before to imagine a life of being wealthy.

"What was I thinking all those years?" I asked Laura. "All those years I spent endorsing Marxism and socialism. What a waste. This food. This place. It's . . . it's wonderful. I love it. I just love it!"

"Are we paying for the meal?" asked Nick. "Because if we're not, I'd like dessert."

"I'm talking to your mother," I said. "Do you mind?"

"I just want to know whether or not I can have dessert. Is that OK?"

"You can have dessert," I said.

To reach Switzerland the next day we drove through Italy and then Austria. We crossed the Swiss border by making a steep descent on a road that zigzagged into a valley. At the bottom, two Austrian guards stamped our passports. Then we went over a little bridge and had our documents inspected by an official in Switzerland. The Swiss government has not applied to join the European Union. The nation stands apart, not quite neutral, but certainly practical. Entering and exiting its boundaries is a formal, old-fashioned procedure quite like the way it once was in the rest of Europe. One can only imagine what it was like during the war. A half hour later, we were in Scuol.

The rental agency was in the center of town. After handing over payment to a realtor, we were given keys, a booklet of instructions, a timetable for the trains and buses, and a dried sausage. The local people use German to speak to foreigners, one of the few languages other than English in which I can think and communicate with any confidence. We were directed to our flat and when we arrived there minutes later began the process of riding with our luggage up a coffin-sized elevator manufactured by a firm called Schindler. I called it Schindler's lift, a reference Laura had to explain to the children.

Rather small and clean like Switzerland, the flat's economy suggested we had been provided with no more than what was necessary for a few weeks hiking. The only strictly decorative object was an enormous, algae-colored glass bowl suspended on a macramé rope from the ceiling and filled with Christmas tree ornaments. I removed it at once.

Then we shopped for groceries in one of the village's three supermarkets. Making an appeal for hygiene, purity, and freshness, food was arranged on shelves in a bland, orderly fashion. Nothing looked too good, but nothing looked too bad either. Shoppers did all they could to avoid eye contact and loaded up baskets and carts, guiltily admitting in the process to hunger. It was obvious that most of them saw eating as a chore akin to sex. They would rather be doing paid work or engaged in activity that led to a final product. No one spoke above a whisper. The well-lit room had a medicinal smell.

The children wanted to know why we had left Italy to come to a country where there was nothing to eat. It is difficult to find food you want in Switzerland, I explained, but not impossible. The raw-milk cheeses, butter, yogurt, cured and dried meats, and breads are the best in the world. Besides we were not here to eat, we had come to hike in the mountains.

"I'm not hiking every day," said Nick.

"We just got here," I said. "We don't have to decide now. Maybe we will hike every day, maybe we won't."

Then we bought stuff and went back to the flat. Enough time remained in the day for a walk of about two miles to Pradella, a settlement east of Scuol made up of nearly a half dozen stone houses.

On the way, we passed by an elderly couple who looked thrilled to be alive, to say nothing of walking on a wide, dirt path beside woods and in view of the mountains. She was stout and had an uneven gait suggesting recent hip surgery and her husband had on thick glasses and a formal suit that gave him an air of ridiculous dignity. She spoke to me in Swiss-German to explain that while it had taken the two of them over an hour to reach Pradella, we were younger and could probably get there and back in half the time.

The walk took us along open pastures, beside chestnut trees, and so close to the En River we heard it roar over the sound of tractors going by. The air was clean and fragrant. It wasn't even a hike and already everyone's mood had improved.

When we returned to the flat from Pradella, Laura and Madeline wanted to have cups of herbal tea and read, but I insisted we all go to the spa, which is called the Bogn Engiadina. Scuol is in the Lower Engadin and "bogn" means "bath" in Romansch. The spa is a communal affair of spring-fed hot or cold pools, saunas, and showers, not a health resort or posh setting. We got towels and walked over. The spa's glass dome, paneled in yellow and blue, was visible from our balcony.

The most popular section at the Bogn Engiadina is a circular, outdoor heated pool with a current that flows counter-clockwise. As you ride the current, pulsing jets of water massage your body and at the end you are doused by showers cascading from large, flat metal spouts. Other than a need to cleanse themselves, the Swiss require quiet. I would say they are most at home walking in the mountains. The people floating by us, whether old or young, had pinched looks that conveyed unspeakable thoughts. As time passed in the water, these faces became more relaxed and then they sagged a little as if lifted of a burden, which I found curious since few of them spoke and no one appeared to be enjoying anything.

When I was not with Laura, the children, and the floating Swiss, I went alone to "the naked zone," an area of the spa restricted to persons over the age of sixteen who found it preferable to be naked among strangers rather than clothed. Talk was in whispers. I did not see anyone give offending looks. The mix of men and women, young and old, attractive and plain, appeared to be devoted to a type of satisfaction often associated with religious experience. I mean to say the silence was respectful and our souls were bared. I often expressed these thoughts to Laura and she would say I was lying in order to see naked women, but the subject is not the only one about which we disagree.

After showering and dressing, we left the spa and returned to the flat to cook dinner. Most of the restaurants in Scuol serve large portions of the local cuisine made up mainly of sausages, potatoes, and cheese. In my opinion, the Swiss prefer a diet of so-called comfort food because they are a very uncomfortable people who worry a lot and often suffer from the weight of sadness. They consider it impolite to burden others with their concerns and instead choose to hike and ski. I rather like Swiss food.

"I love Scuol," I said to the family that night after dinner and over a game of cards.

"It's beautiful, Daddy," said Madeline. "The spa was very nice. And I'm looking forward to hiking tomorrow."

Nick suggested he be exempted from the hike and we came close to ignoring him.

"You used to love to hike when you were little," Laura said. "What happened?"

"I still like hiking," he said. "It's not that. But we just got here. I want to relax. Hiking should be special. Not something we do every day."

Laura enjoyed being in charge of deciding which hikes we would select from *Walking Switzerland the Swiss Way*, which is a first-rate book. Five years back, our favorite hike had been from the tiny village of S-Charl to Süsom Give. The distance is about eight miles and on the walk we entered wide valleys formed by glaciers where cows grazed. This would be our hike the next day.

Scuol is a typical Swiss community after nightfall. People tend to abandon the streets for their homes where after an early supper they go to bed. Shops open early.

"*Aufstehen!*" I shout each morning in Scuol to wake the children up. "*Aufstehen! Jemand muss aufstehen! Hallo! Aus dem Bett! Aufstehen!*"

Then we eat, lace on our boots, and head for the postal bus that will take us to the mountains. On the way, we fill up water bottles at one of the village's several fountains. Two spouts are available: One provides water from a well and the other has naturally effervescent spring water. I insist we race to the station.

"It's not pleasant when you get militaristic," says Laura.

"Look, if we don't hurry, we'll miss the bus."

"Fine," she says, "so we'll miss the bus. Big deal."

"I think it's a big deal. I think it's a very big deal. How can you say that? How can you say it isn't?"

"You're ranting," she says. "I'll meet you at the station. What time does the bus leave?"

"I am not ranting," I say. "I just don't want to miss the bus. OK? If I don't speed the group along, we *will* miss the bus. And I cannot believe you don't even know what time the bus leaves! How can you be on time if you don't know when you're supposed to be someplace? You are never on time! We are always waiting for you! Always! The bus leaves at 8:35. How can you not know that?"

"Bye," she says. "Bye, bye, honey. See you. See you at the station."

Then I take one of the children and we rush to catch the bus. Moments after we arrive, Laura shows up with the other child. The bus pulls in ten minutes later. We line up to board with other hikers, many of whom are in their sixties and seventies, but robust and limber. Now the Swiss, notoriously silent, are talking: about the weather prediction for the afternoon, condition of boots, maps, which trails are best for seeing animals like marmots and ibex, whether or not the bus will leave on time. There's a first date flush to their faces, a rose color like blood that's been diluted with milk, they are so excited to be going into the mountains it's as if the rest of the year and history and their families count a lot less. We show our transportation passes to the driver, pay a supplement, find seats.

Then we climb through a dense pine forest, pass by a horse farm, and along the way little groups of hikers get out at stops in the middle of nowhere. Our stop is the last one, S-Charl, once a prosperous center of smelting in the region and now a collection of stone houses, two inns, and three restaurants.

The trail winds past an inn and then you have to open and close

a gate its width. The last time we were here the children were as
small as mice, I think, and now each one is gangly, towering, and
awkward like an octopus. The thought that Laura and I are losing
them and soon will be back where we began depresses me enormously so I tell everyone that we are walking too slowly and must
keep a decent pace.

We see cows. We see clouds. Our boots are muddied when we
have to cross a brook. Nicholas asks to have a freshly baked pretzel
I bought in Scuol. Madeline tells us how relieved she is to be in a
new school where no one has yet formed an impression of her. The
children walk far ahead of us holding hands. Laura and I talk about
the impossibility of saving for college. We stop for a picnic inside a
stone courtyard next to stables where cows are kept each summer.
Then we ask a hiker to snap a photo of us seated on a long gray
bench beside milk cans three feet high and a sign above us to indicate place: Astras-Tamangur-Sesvenna.

The way back requires an ascent to a hill atop which there's
a plaque in memory of a man who appears to have died while
hiking. Swiss friends have informed me that certain walks became a tradition in their families and I suggest to Laura and the
children that this hike, years from now, might become important
to us and a way to gauge time. I expect no one to take the idea to
heart, but each one of them embraces the sentiment in a way that
disgusts me and by the time they're done talking about sweetness, I
am sorry I said anything.

The trail at the bottom of the hill goes through pine scrub and
then wetlands where five years earlier we'd seen goats splashing
about. Only this time, it was just us beneath low clouds. The children, fifteen and twelve, grasped hands like friends, rather than sib-
lings. Why didn't they hate each other? But no point looking back.

The hike ends on a crest nearby where the Swiss have built an
inn and a restaurant which has an outdoor garden. A postal bus to
Zernez will arrive soon. From Zernez, there's a regional train that

takes thirty-seven minutes to reach Scuol. We have time to drink in the garden.

All around us Swiss-German hikers are talking about the day in the mountains. I enjoy hearing about the animals the hikers spotted and their plans for the next day.

"See?" Laura says to Nicholas. "You had a good time, didn't you? You enjoyed hiking more than you thought you would."

"*Ja, sicher,*" he says.

"What does '*sicher*' mean?" she asks.

" 'Sure,' " he says. His pronunciation of the word is Swiss, lilting rather than guttural like German. In an environment where no one speaks English, both children have picked up a good number of Swiss-German words or expressions. Laura has resisted learning the language as she associates German with the war.

The bus arrives precisely at 3:02. On the way down the mountain, we drive through Switzerland's only national park, an enormous tract of land riddled with perfectly groomed trails where, if you're lucky, you can sometimes see marmots, eagles, and herds of chamois, elk, and ibex. In days to come, we will hike throughout the park.

The bus stops beside the station where we must wait only a few minutes before boarding a train. We will go past the same villages almost daily: Susch, Lavin, Guarda, Ardez, and Ftan. The Romansch names are musical, almost whimsical, to our ears and suggest old melodies. The houses we see on walks we will take through some of these places also place a kind of spell on us. The homes are often colorful and several have *sgraffito,* a folk art of primitive design depicting lions, serpents, warriors, and shepherds, often accompanied by instructive sayings to greet passersby.

Each time the train approaches a station, a recording of a woman's voice announces the name of the place and requests passengers who want the train to stop to press a circular red button: "*Lavin, halt auf verlangen.*" I find the repetition every day comforting and the woman's voice as soothing as a psychiatrist's. The train routes of the Swiss take the landscape and architecture into account and before long this trip between Zernez and Scuol, and back, has achieved for us all the makings of a play. We see the same painted houses, the same waterfall, the same castle, the same hills, the same mountains, and the same cows and horses at almost the same time each day. It's like being small again, practically a child, when the world seemed safe because our parents were in it.

Back in Scuol we buy cheese and bread for dinner, get rid of our gear at the flat, and spend a couple of hours in the spa.

"This is the most relaxed I've been all year," says Laura several nights later over raclette. "I love spending time in the mountains with my family. The spa is perfect. We have everything we need."

"I admit that I like swimming every day," says Nick. "And today was great."

We had gone on a nine-mile hike that started in S-Charl and took us past an alpine farm that sold fresh, raw milk and then into a remote and rock-strewn valley leading up to a cliff on the border of Italy. On the way, Madeline and I had heard the shrieking, high-pitched whistles of marmots warning others in their colony that intruders were near. Nick had spotted a young ibex cooling off on a patch of melting snow.

"Things work here," I said. "Switzerland is functional. I love Italy. Who doesn't? You'd have to be crazy not to love Italy. But what is there to do in Italy other than eat, shop for food, and look at art?"

"Oh, come on," says Laura. "Let's face it: If it wasn't for the hiking, I wouldn't be here. The Swiss are not like Italians. They're tense and rigid."

"Daddy's best friends are Swiss," says Madeline.

"They are not typical," says Laura. "But even Ursli and his family are not what I'd call mellow."

"It's not just the hiking," I say. "It's being in a place where things work—there's an infrastructure here, an attention to detail, an appreciation for efficiency that I find very reassuring."

"Right," says Laura, "it's very Germanic."

"It's not," I say. "We're in the Romansch region and things still work. Besides what is wrong with being Germanic?"

"If you don't know what is wrong with being Germanic," Laura says, "I am not going to be the one to tell you."

"The Swiss are not Germanic," I say. "But I will say that certain of their characteristics appear to resemble things we associate with Germany: efficiency, for one thing."

"I'd like to see Germany," says Nick. "That's where Grandpa Walter's from."

"It is," I say.

"Why don't you tell Nicholas why Grandpa Walter left Germany?" says Laura. "And while you're at it, tell him what happened to his family that couldn't get out."

"I know what happened," says Nick.

"So what's so great about Germany?" asks Laura.

"I wasn't defending Germany," I say. "I was talking about Switzerland."

"I must have confused the two," she says. "Besides you always defend Germany."

"I do not," I say.

"Children, you tell me. Does your father defend Germany or not?"

"I'm not getting involved," says Madeline. "Thank you very much."

"I think he defends Germany," says Nick.

"Thank you, Nicholas," I say.

"And you defend Switzerland, too," says Laura. "That Swiss efficiency you love so much enabled their banks to take the money in accounts deposited by victims of the Holocaust who died during the War."

"But you can't blame the Swiss for that," I say. "Banks are banks. No one should be put in the position of having to defend a bank. And to suggest that Switzerland and Germany have anything in common when it comes to the War . . ."

"Is shocking," said Laura. "You must be shocked."

"But Switzerland *is* different and that's why I love it here," I say. "I can't see going on holiday to Bavaria. I was brought up by my father to appreciate German culture—I happen to love the literature, the language, the food, and the wine. Like it or not, German culture is part of my legacy. So the Swiss are somewhat Germanic. So what?"

"The Swiss," says Laura, "are lucky to have the mountains."

A few days before we are set to depart, Ursli arrives with Rolf, his lover, who has AIDS. We propose a walk to Ramosch, a village close to the border of Austria. The trail is flat and no more than ten miles distance. I rarely see Ursli outside of holidays. Over the years he's become part of our family. We think of holidays, we think of Ursli.

So it's especially jarring to see how much he's aged in a year. He's unhappy, preoccupied with Rolf's health, and even though we walk through farmlands, over a wooden bridge suspended above the River En, and then into a stone village that seems ancient in its integrity, in the way the buildings appear to be hewn out of the earth, his mood does not lift. He talks instead about the bombings in New York, war, and being lonely. He and Rolf now live apart.

"I'd love to go to the mountains and walk," he says. "But look at Rolf. This is all he can manage. He walks like an old man."

And then I wondered if Rolf would be around next summer when we returned.

Alsace is not on the way to Paris from Scuol, but after several weeks hiking I thought a pilgrimage to a temple of gastronomy was in order. For ten years, I had read and heard about Auberge de l'Ill, a three-star Michelin establishment in the Alsatian village of Ill-haeusern run by the Haeberlin brothers and the son of one of the two men. I booked a table one month before leaving for Europe.

To get to Alsace from Scuol, it is necessary to drive through Austria and Germany. To entertain the family while in Austrian territory, I mimicked the voice of Arnold Schwarzenegger, an actor whose work I much admire while fully recognizing his limited range. Then we entered Germany. We drove along Lake Constance. Only two weeks earlier, a Russian plane carrying dozens of children on their way to holidays in Spain had collided with a DHL transport plane thirty-six thousand feet above us. There had been a huge explosion and everyone had died.

The mountains no longer visible, we continued north until reaching Freiburg where we stopped to eat in a beer garden beside a brook in the center of the old town. Laura tends to speak about Germany and the Jews whenever we are on German soil and the conversation we had over lunch was no exception. The Holocaust is an obsession of mine and so I tend to keep quiet about it. Laura has several other concerns in her life and can talk about the war without inhibition. I envy her calm and certitude. Once I start talking about the Jews and Germany, it is hard to stop. The children did not know what to make of our agitation and talked a great deal more about sunlight, shade provided by a chestnut tree, an old English busker doing Beatles songs near our table, and the taste of food that arrived on wooden planks.

A bridge over the Rhine is the way into France. The first thing we saw after crossing over were long stretches of fields in which potatoes seemed to be growing. Green tufts were visible above rows of tilled, dark earth. Everywhere we looked the land was very flat. It may have been pounded flat or it has always been flat. I am not familiar with the geological history of Alsace.

The hotel was a posh affair in Sélestat called Abbaye La Pommeraie. A booklet in the lobby noted that it was once part of a real

abbey belonging to the Cistercian order. I explained to the children
that the order was founded in 1098 by Saint Robert of Molesme
who established its first abbey in Cistercium, near Dijon. The order
had seventy-three rules, I said, one of which (number twenty-three)
started off by noting: "Let the brethren sleep singly each in a single
bed." I supposed the monks in this former abbey had been prosperous until the French Revolution when no doubt the property
was taken over by the state and they were expelled.

We had little time before dinner. Laura took her customary nap,
Madeline read a book, and Nicholas asked me to walk with him
into town to buy an *International Herald Tribune*. He wanted to check
box scores.

It was late in the day and the Saturday market was ending. The
bricked pedestrian streets, which were quite narrow, were filled
with vendors who had placed cheap, colorful clothing on long
boards positioned atop gray, metal frames or poles. The customers
had roots in other continents mostly: Arabs and Africans, from the
north and west of Africa or the Middle East where the French once
had colonies. It appeared that locals had gotten used to having them
around to do work they no longer had any interest in doing. For
their part, the foreigners seemed pleased to be in a country where
civil order prevailed. It was a good arrangement for now.

We could not find a newspaper. But it is always pleasant to hold
hands and look at buildings. No sight had the kind of significance
that draws crowds. We entered squares and saw a church and went
by a canal. In front of a butcher shop, a big, unleashed dog, hobbled
by age, came toward us with an inquisitive look before circling and
settling down in front of the plate glass window behind which cuts
of bloody meat were displayed.

I knew Sélestat had suffered during the war. I supposed its Jews
had been exterminated. In 1944, the Germans tried to recapture
the town, but failed to do so. In the process, thousands of soldiers
and civilians had lost their lives. It is impossible to tell nowadays that

any of these horrible events took place. The town bills itself as a gateway to the wine region of the Alsace. I did not mention the war to Nicholas.

Then we returned to the hotel and dressed for dinner. The drive to the restaurant took longer than anticipated. We got lost and asked directions in a village. Laura and Madeline worked on the fellow in French, but then gave up and handed him over to me. My French is useful only in shops, restaurants, and hotels so we communicated in German.

The restaurant was memorable. The French knack for creativity, tradition, and restraint in the kitchen is well known. Before dining, we were led to a garden beside a canal where the children had fruit drinks and Laura and I had glasses of champagne. The water beside us flowed rapidly, but branches got stuck in long reeds and ducks managed to stay in place along the banks. Madeline remarked that it seemed as if we had landed in a fairy tale, an agreeable thought, and then a kind of pleasure took hold of us. When it was time to dine, we were shown to a good table in a well-lit room. An old man in a suit, whom I believed to be Jean-Pierre Haeberlin, strolled from table to table greeting people in a manner suggesting all of us were friends rather than customers. But his service, and that of the others working, was not puppylike as it so often is in the States, but dignified. He bestowed dignity.

The room was filled with all sorts. Among them were a pair of German businessmen, a man having an affair, a family with two young girls in matching sequined dresses, one ruby colored and the other turquoise, two men in love, and an old married couple. The couple having an affair spoke little, but everyone else could not stop talking.

At last we ordered food and wine. The details of the meal were as one might expect. Who can fault the French when it comes to gastronomy and viniculture? The goose foie gras, river fish, Trimbach Clos St. Hune Riesling and so on had flavors so stimulating that our sense of everything else other than what we tasted seemed irrelevant. As we ate, it was as if the four of us were on a journey, etc., etc., etc.

Then we finished up and were taken back to the garden. The idea was to have cognac or scotch and by doing so to fix the place into our memories, like a final blow, but Nick was tired so I asked for the check.

When the check was brought over, Nick tried to take it from me, but did not succeed.

"I just want to see what it cost," he said.

"Are you paying?" I asked. "Unless you're paying, you don't need to know."

I looked at the check.

"What a steal," I said.

"How much was it?" asked Laura. "More than The French Laundry or less? You are insane when it comes to spending money in restaurants. I don't know why I go along with it."

"Are you paying?" I said. "Because if you're not . . ."

"Oh, give me a break," she said. "It's my money, too."

I showed her the check: 419.85 Euros, which was about $440.

"*That* is not a steal," she said.

"I think it is," I said. "First of all, it includes tax and tip. And we've been here over four hours. So divide the sum by four. You get about $110 an hour. Divide that sum by four—we're four people. That makes about $28 per person an hour. Do you have any idea what it would cost to be in family or individual psychotherapy? A lot more than what we're paying tonight, let me tell you. And therapy—why, you can go to a shrink for 50 minutes and have nothing to say and you still wind up having to pay $150 for the session."

"Thank you, Daddy," said Madeline. "The meal was delicious."

The next day we left for Paris. We took the A4 and on the way saw signs for Euro Disney. Having spent the morning in the picturesque village of Ribeauvillé and then, driven by wheat fields beneath an open sky, we understood the appeal of Disney to the French. The countryside and villages of France are charming, but nothing about them is cartoonish. No wonder the French devour comic books. Little else gives them relief from their formality which I believe drives them crazy.

We felt no comparable desire to acquaint ourselves with America's most obvious contribution to their well-being. The French need Euro Disney, we don't.

A short while later, we arrived in Paris for six nights. Booking two rooms at the Prince de Galles, in the eighth *arrondissement*, had been a matter of cashing in points from a sort of hotel program linked to one of our credit cards. We would remain half the time before transferring to the Plaza Athenee, an even more posh hotel nearby. There an enormous two bedroom suite was ours due to efforts made on our behalf by individuals employed in the property's marketing department.

Those who speak French well find France amusing, but I cannot and so view the capital as a place to eat. That the city is beautiful adds to my appreciation. Laura and Madeline were able to communicate and understood there is more to Paris than markets, charcuterie, and restaurants. But within days, we had eaten at temples like Guy Savoy, L'Arpege, and Taillevent.

Before the current trip, I had read a new biography of Baron Haussman, the architect of modern Paris, and knew my way around. No place I've been is more enjoyable for loafing and walking. Parisians devote themselves to pleasure specific to the observation of strangers. Whether you are strutting on a boulevard, strolling in a park, or seated at a café, voyeurism is the activity most everyone is engaged in. The men and women worry so much about how they look they have little time for anything else.

We managed during our stay to succumb to the intoxication of posh digs. Nicholas suggested, as we had at the hotel in Santorini, that we remain at the Plaza Athenee the rest of our lives, which we discussed with more reason that I would have thought possible. Everything about this hotel was flawless. Parisians worship luxury and will do whatever is necessary to have some of it in their lives. While this willingness to please has led outsiders to their culture to view them periodically, such as during the war, as available at a price, I think it would very much depend on the price.

Our last morning in Paris, before returning home, we spied Chevy Chase with his wife and children at a nearby table in the hotel dining room. He had on a baseball cap and new, informal clothing. I had seen *European Vacation* and for a few moments wondered why the people with him didn't look at all like his family in the movie.

Over the long winter after these events took place, Laura, Madeline, Nicholas, and I spend weekend evenings in front of a fire eating good food and talking about our lives. Sooner than any of us can imagine, everything that's important to us as a family, all that love, will be what we have when we're apart. All that's left. But for now Laura and I are content being at home with the children knowing we have not fucked them up. Then again . . .

ACKNOWLEDGMENTS

Thanks to Trena Keating for her editing skills and willingness to laugh; Jeffrey Posternak of the Wylie Agency for his wisdom and loyalty; Bruce Gellerman, Jon Marston, Mark Navin, Andrew Caffrey, Ken Bader, and Robin Young for teaching me how to talk on *Here and Now*, the noon show on WBUR, the National Public Radio affiliate; Sally Swift and Lynne Rossetto Kasper for their camaraderie and for running my work on Minnesota Public Radio's *The Splendid Table*; Gordon Hamersley of Hamersley's Bistro and Silvano Marchetto of Da Silvano for teaching me how to cook; Karen Bilezerian, Hugo Pizzinini (of Hotel Rosa Alpina), Emily Haynes, Mike Nolan, and Ryan Harbage, for their kind support and help; Erika Leiben for her thoughtful observations and good heart; Fred Horton and Katherine Ryan for their sweetness; Susanna Kaysen for being a friend; Kitty Kiefer, Jonathan Starr, and Hazel Kiefer for lots of reasons; Larry Bean at Robb Report for editing my work; "Ursli" for being part of our family; Ludovica and George Barrow and Harley, Claudia, Camilla, and Susanna Checchini— *persone molto gentile*; my parents and sister for showing me the meaning of travel and love; and of course Laura, Madeline, and Nicholas for being themselves.

ABOUT THE AUTHOR

Scott Haas is a producer and on-air talent for "Here and Now," a nationally syndicated show broadcast from WBUR, an NPR affiliate. He also reports monthly for "The Splendid Table," syndicated nationally on Public Radio International. Haas received a James Beard nomination for Best Short Radio Piece in the United States in 2003 and won First Place awards from the Associated Press in 2000 and 2001. He has written for *Gourmet,* is a contributing editor at *The Robb Report,* the author of *Hearing Voices,* and cowriter of *The Da Silvano Cookbook.* In addition to being a writer, Dr. Haas is chief psychologist at a teaching hospital associated with Boston University Medical School. He lives in Cambridge, Massachusetts, with his wife and two children.